ROUTLEDGE LIBRARY EDITIONS:
LANGUAGE AND LITERATURE OF THE
MIDDLE EAST

Volume 9

MODERN LITERATURE IN THE
NEAR AND MIDDLE EAST,
1850–1970

MODERN LITERATURE IN THE NEAR AND MIDDLE EAST, 1850–1970

Edited by
ROBIN OSTLE

LONDON AND NEW YORK

First published in 1991 by Routledge

This edition first published in 2017
by Routledge
2 Park Square, Milton Park, Abingdon, Oxon OX14 4RN

and by Routledge
711 Third Avenue, New York, NY 10017

Routledge is an imprint of the Taylor & Francis Group, an informa business

© 1991 Centre for Near and Middle Eastern Studies (now the London Middle East Institute, SOAS, University of London)

All rights reserved. No part of this book may be reprinted or reproduced or utilised in any form or by any electronic, mechanical, or other means, now known or hereafter invented, including photocopying and recording, or in any information storage or retrieval system, without permission in writing from the publishers.

Trademark notice: Product or corporate names may be trademarks or registered trademarks, and are used only for identification and explanation without intent to infringe.

British Library Cataloguing in Publication Data
A catalogue record for this book is available from the British Library

ISBN: 978-1-138-68297-9 (Set)
ISBN: 978-1-315-45973-8 (Set) (ebk)
ISBN: 978-1-138-69907-6 (Volume 9) (hbk)
ISBN: 978-1-138-69909-0 (Volume 9) (pbk)
ISBN: 978-1-315-51269-3 (Volume 9) (ebk)

Publisher's Note
The publisher has gone to great lengths to ensure the quality of this reprint but points out that some imperfections in the original copies may be apparent.

Disclaimer
The publisher has made every effort to trace copyright holders and would welcome correspondence from those they have been unable to trace.

MODERN LITERATURE IN THE NEAR AND MIDDLE EAST 1850–1970

Edited by Robin Ostle

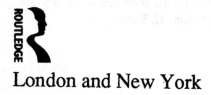

London and New York

First published 1991
by Routledge
11 New Fetter Lane, London EC4P 4EE

Simultaneously published in the USA and Canada
by Routledge
a division of Routledge, Chapman and Hall, Inc.
29 West 35th Street, New York, NY 10001

© 1991 Centre for Near and Middle Eastern Studies
Typeset by Laserscript
Printed and bound in Great Britain by
Biddles Ltd, Guildford and King's Lynn

All rights reserved. No part of this book may be reprinted or reproduced or utilized
in any form or by any electronic, mechanical, or other means, now known or
hereafter invented, including photocopying and recording, or in any information
storage or retrieval system, without permission in writing from the publishers.

British Library Cataloguing in Publication Data
Modern Literature in the Near and Middle East, 1850–1970.
– (Routledge/SOAS Contemporary politics and culture in the Middle East series)
1. Arabic literature – critical studies
I. Ostle, Robin
892. 709
ISBN 0-415-05822-8

Library of Congress Cataloging-in-Publication Data
Modern Literature in the Near and Middle East 1850–1970 / edited by Robin Ostle.
(Routledge/SOAS Contemporary politics and culture in the Middle East series)
Includes bibliographical references and index.
ISBN 0-415-05822-8
1. Middle East – Literatures – History and criticism. 2. Arabic literature – Africa,
North – History and criticism. 3. Hebrew literature – History and criticism. 4.
Persian literature – History and criticism. 5. Turkish literature – History and
criticism. 6. Literature, Comparative. I. Ostle, Robin. II. Series.
PN849.M5M6 1991
809'.8956–dc20

90-44715
CIP

Contents

Foreword   ix

PART I THE AGE OF TRANSLATION AND ADAPTATION, 1850–1914

1 Modernization and literature in the Near
   and Middle East 1850–1914   3
   Malcolm Yapp

2 Turkey   17
   Saliha Paker

3 The Arab world   33
   Pierre Cachia

4 Iran   45
   Julie Meisami

5 Modern Hebrew   63
   Tudor Parfitt

PART II FROM ROMANTIC NATIONALISM TO SOCIAL CRITICISM, 1914–1950

6 The political setting 1914–1950   79
   Charles Tripp

7 Turkey   90
   Geoffrey Lewis

8 The Arab world   104
   Robin Ostle

vi *Contents*

9   Modern Hebrew   116
    David Patterson

10 Iran   130
    Homa Katouzian

**PART III THE AGE OF IDEOLOGY
AND POLARIZATION SINCE 1950**

11 The age of ideology and polarization   161
    David Pool

12 Turkey   170
    Cevat Çapan

13 The Mashriq   180
    Edwar al-Kharrat

14 The Maghrib   193
    Ahmed al-Madini

15 Israel   213
    Leon I. Yudkin

Bibliography   226
Index   236

Foreword

This volume represents the first attempt that has been made to conduct a detailed comparative survey of the principal modern literatures of the Near and Middle East since 1850, namely Arabic, Hebrew, Persian and Turkish. In spite of the fact that there is much common ground between the historical and cultural developments of the different linguistic areas of the Near and Middle East in the modern period, nevertheless much teaching and research remains restricted to the individual language areas, and there is relatively little awareness of what takes place across these linguistic boundaries. The book is designed to make students and teachers more aware of what they share with their counterparts working in other languages, without losing sight of those features which are peculiar to the creative writing of their own areas.

There is always an arbitrary process involved in imposing chronological divisions on literary evolution, and this is even more so when a single chronological scheme is devised for no fewer than four literatures. However, the three divisions proposed seemed to have enough common elements of historical experience to justify the following thematic approach to all four literatures: the age of translation and adaptation from 1850–1914; the decades of enthusiastic romantic nationalism which characterized the period between the two world wars; and the variety and conflicts of ideology that have marked the Near and Middle East since 1950. Inevitably these themes have been more relevant to some literatures than to others, from period to period, and the authors have not been slow to indicate this whenever they felt it necessary. One common assumption that underlies the volume as a whole is that all four of the literatures here surveyed have been profoundly affected by wider processes of political and social change. Virtually all the chapters in the book tend to support this assumption, and indeed each part of the book has an historical and political introduction which sets the context for the literary chapters.

x *Foreword*

On the whole the three parts of the book conform to a common pattern, with the following exceptions: the abundance of Arabic material since 1950 seemed to call for two separate chapters devoted to the *Mashriq* and the *Maghrib*; sadly, it was not found possible to include a chapter on modern Iranian literature since 1950. In mitigation, one can point out that the chapter on Iran which concludes Part II is one of the most comprehensive in the book, and refers to material which extends well beyond 1950. Taken as a whole, the various chapters provide striking evidence that the Near and Middle East has remained very much a common cultural area since 1850, in spite of the political and linguistic differences between its regions and countries.

The thanks of the editor are due in the first place to the School of Oriental and African Studies whose financial support led to the original symposia from which this volume evolved. The authors of the individual chapters are all international specialists in their own fields who gave most generously of their time and expertise. The greatest debt of gratitude is owed to the staff of the Publications Office of the Centre of Near and Middle Eastern Studies in SOAS who coped cheerfully with the problems of a difficult manuscript. I should like to mention in particular the editors at SOAS Tony Allan and Diana Gur, April Heywood and Dinah Manisty. They were all unreasonably patient with an editor who was more than usually dilatory.

Robin Ostle

PART I

THE AGE OF TRANSLATION AND ADAPTATION 1850–1914

1 Modernization and literature in the Near and Middle East 1850–1914

Malcolm Yapp

An invitation to an historian to write a chapter on the historical background to a period of literary development implies a belief in the truth of the proposition that there is some relationship between social, economic and political changes, in literary form and content. This truth, of course, except to Marxist writers, is not self-evident; in particular, those who would endeavour to extend the proposition to embrace the quality of literary work stand on treacherous ground indeed. It is not my purpose, however, to debate this interesting proposition here; instead it will be assumed that some relationship does exist, and suggested that in the Near and Middle East during the period under review the relationship may be described in terms of three theses. These are, first, that the most notable characteristic of the Near and Middle East during the period with which we are concerned was that it was passing through a phase of modernization; second, that the form and content of Near and Middle Eastern literature during these years was related to the process of modernization; and third, and more speculatively, that differences in the literary development of the various regions of the Near and Middle East are linked to variations in the extent and character of modernization.

It will be useful to begin with a definition of modernization. The term is used to denote the new process of transition from a traditional to a modern society. To forestall protest, it should be said at once that of course there is no such thing as either a traditional or a modern society: the first term embraces a variety of societies which are not static, and the second merely describes the forms of societies in the second half of the twentieth century, with no suggestion that the process of change has come to a stop. Traditional and modern societies are ideal types compounded of a mix of attributes. These attributes are as follows. Politically, traditional societies are distinguished by what Michael Oakshott termed minimal government, that is to say governments have few functions, being mainly concerned with defence, the administration of some criminal justice, and

4 Modern literature in the Near and Middle East

the construction and maintenance of a few public works; for these purposes they take only a small proportion of national income in the form of national revenue. State institutions in traditional societies are correspondingly elementary. By contrast, in modern societies the state has many functions, takes a large proportion of national income and develops elaborate institutions with many employees. The concentration of so much decision-making within the state is a powerful factor inducing its citizens to define or redefine their political loyalties. Economically, traditional societies are largely subsistent or revolve around innumerable local markets. Exchanges of goods are limited by poor communications, the largest proportion of the national income is derived from agriculture, and industry consists principally of handicrafts. Modern societies tend to have good communications, a single market for most goods, derive the larger part of their national income from non-agricultural sources, and employ most of their citizens outside the agricultural sector. Industrial production tends to be organized on a large scale. Socially, traditional societies are commonly composed of many compartments, arranged in no particular fashion, and are responsible for regulating many aspects of the lives of their members including their personal law, education and, often, their economic organization. In a traditional society the great majority of citizens live in rural areas and are illiterate. Modern societies are usually divided into great horizontal bands known as classes, which are arranged hierarchically. A large proportion of their citizens live in cities and are literate. Their law and their education are shared, and usually under the control of the state.[1]

Used in this fashion the concepts of traditional and modern societies are surprisingly useful in discussions of change in the Near and Middle East during the nineteenth and twentieth centuries, because in 1800 Near and Middle Eastern societies conformed closely to the traditional model, whereas in the last years of the twentieth century they approach the modern model. This is not to say that they conform in every respect: politically and socially they have most of the attributes of modern societies but economically they present some different features, most notably the failure to develop any substantial manufacturing industry.

During the period 1850–1914, impelled partly by external but more by internal factors, the Near and Middle East travelled some way along the road of modernization. The pace and pattern of modernization, however, differed from one state to another and from one region to another. Broadly speaking we can identify three different models of state development. These are, first, the Ottoman model in which the leading element was the drive for political modernization inspired by the wish to develop European-style military forces. In this model the political sector led, and economic and social modernization lagged behind and were subordinated

Modernization and literature 5

to the needs of political modernization. Second is the Egyptian model in which, as a consequence of the development of the cotton economy, the leading sector was the economic. By contrast, the political sector slipped behind after the collapse of the military modernization programme of Muhammad 'Ali in 1841 and the end of the ambitions of Isma'il in 1879. During most of our period Egypt was under British occupation: this fostered a conservative view of the role of the state, greatly reduced the military forces of Egypt, and held back from support for public educational provision. The third model is provided by Iran where there was neither a political nor an economic nor a social impetus for modernization, or at least any impetus sufficient to overcome the forces which withstood change. In consequence there was very little modernization in Iran during this period; in 1914 as in 1850, Iran had a system of minimal government, a largely subsistence economy and was divided into mainly illiterate social compartments.[2]

This is not to say that all regions in all states moved at the same pace. Everywhere the changes were most marked in the cities and large parts of the countryside were almost untouched by modernization. Within the Ottoman Empire, Western Anatolia changed much more rapidly than did the east and Syria faster than Iraq, while Arabia hardly changed at all. Lower Egypt altered more quickly than did Upper Egypt, in line with the advance of the cotton economy, and, in Iran, Azerbaijan and Khurasan experienced more modernization than did areas in the south. Some communities were more responsive to the pressures for modernization than were others: government servants more than those outside government, Christians more than Muslims. A link with a community in Europe was often a potent factor influencing the rate of change, a circumstance which applied not only to Christians but also to Turks in the Ottoman Empire, Azerbaijan, and Central Asia, who drew on the experiences of Turks in Russia.

It will at once be observed that there are some very broad correspondences between the process of modernization and the literary development of different parts of the Near and Middle East. Judged simply by the crude measures of the timing and volume of publication, it is noticeable that Iran lags behind the Ottoman Empire and Egypt. It is possible to trace a more precise relationship between modernization and literary change but first it is necessary to establish some systematic basis on which to rest the inquiry.

Our inquiry may be summarized as follows: who wrote (read, performed, watched) what, and when, and why? Of this gaggle of questions the only ones which can be answered with any pretensions to confidence are: who wrote or performed what and when. To the others,

6 *Modern literature in the Near and Middle East*

only the most tentative and incomplete answers can be offered. Before those answers can be elaborated it is necessary to collect more information under a variety of categories, including those of literacy levels, outlets, patronage, and motivation. No systematic effort has been made to collect such information for this paper; rather the aim has been to set up the categories and make a crude test of their value.

LITERACY LEVELS

Writers write for markets and what and how they write is influenced by those markets. The market is broadly shaped by the size of the literate population, although it is not determined by that factor as illiterate people may be reached by oral literature; hence the enduring importance of poetry, stories, and sermons. In this context one may express surprise that the theatre was relatively slow to develop in the region. More complex literary forms and more sophisticated concepts may readily be communicated only in written form. Although one must not underestimate the extent to which illiterates gained access to written work by having it read to them by others – a factor of particular importance in relation to the readership of newspapers – there is some rough relationship between the production of literary works and the number of literates. There are some estimates of indifferent quality available for the number of literates in the Ottoman Empire, Egypt and Iran. In the Ottoman Empire literacy grew from 2 per cent in 1868 to around 15 per cent in 1900, although this latter figure should be regarded with much suspicion. Also, it undoubtedly disguises a much lower rate of literacy among the Muslim population generally and the Turkish population in particular because literacy among the Christian groups was more widespread than literacy among Muslims. In 1927 literacy in the Turkish republic was estimated at 10.6 per cent and it is reasonable to suppose that it was lower than this amongst the Turkish population of the same region in 1900. Literacy in Egypt in 1900 was around 10 per cent and in Iran well below 5 per cent. Literacy figures alone are a crude measure, for many of those classified as literate were certainly either incapable of reading a serious work or were unwilling to attempt the enterprise. Also these figures combine the outputs of both the traditional and the modern educational systems, and for our purpose the output of the modern system is more relevant because of the focus of the following chapters upon change and the influence of Europe.

Another way of approaching the matter is to look at the output of institutions of modern higher education. Such institutions were founded in the Ottoman Empire in the late eighteenth century and then refounded or revived in the 1820s and 1830s and further developed thereafter: the

Harbiye was founded in 1846, the Teachers' Training College in 1848, the famous civil service college, the *Mülkiye* in 1859, *Galatasaray* in 1868, eighteen additional specialized institutions of higher education under 'Abd ül-Hamid and the Ottoman university in 1900. In Egypt similar institutions date from the 1820s, falter in their development between 1841 and 1860, and then expand rapidly until 1882. From 1882, however, the low level of expenditure on public sector education meant that the private sector became relatively more significant in the output of graduates. In Iran institutions of modern higher education are founded from the 1850s: a language training school, the equivalent of similar institutions founded in the Ottoman Empire and Egypt in the 1830s, was set up only in 1873, and a college of political science (which may be compared with the 1859 Ottoman *Mülkiye*) as late as 1901. No statistics are readily available for Egypt, but it has been calculated that the Ottomans had produced about 5000 graduates from public institutions of higher education by the early twentieth century, to which total should be added an unknown number representing the total of graduates from foreign schools, from schools run by religious communities, from private schools and those who were educated abroad. In the same period Iran produced about 1100 graduates from the *Dar al-Funun*, founded in 1852, to which total some additions should be made on a much smaller scale.

Little can be deduced from these statistics and observations but three general points may be made. First, the number of what may be called 'modern literates' was increasing rapidly in the later nineteenth century; second, the numbers were still small and should be thought of in thousands rather than any larger figure; and third, the output of Iran was decidedly lower than that of either the Ottoman Empire or Egypt, reflecting the smaller and later effort put into education by Iran and the slower rate of modernization. Finally, one general word of caution about the use of the concept of 'modern literates' as an index of readership in Near and Middle Eastern languages should be inserted. The acquisition of a foreign language may actually hinder the process of translation and adaptation because if one can read the works that one wishes to read in a foreign language it is unnecessary to reproduce them in one's own language. This factor may help to explain why certain categories of literature feature less in the development of Arabic, Persian and Turkish writing during this period than might otherwise have been expected to be the case.[3]

OUTLETS

The second category mentioned above is that of outlets, by which is meant institutions or mechanisms which intervene between the writer and his

8 *Modern literature in the Near and Middle East*

readers, facilitate or hinder his contacts with them, and shape the character of his writing both in form and content. One of these items must be printing. One would not wish to underestimate the capacity of the old manuscript copying system to feed the market; Marsigli (1732:I, 40) estimated in the late seventeenth century that 90,000 men were engaged in copying books in either Istanbul or the Ottoman Empire (the text leaves the matter unclear). Nevertheless, in speed and price the copying system could not compete with the printing press which itself was the beneficiary of major technical advances during the nineteenth century: the replacement of the wooden hand press with the iron press around 1800; the introduction of the cylinder and of steam power at the same time; the advent of the rotary press (of such importance for newspapers) in the middle of the nineteenth century, and then, during the 1880s, the coming of the linotype and monotype systems for casting hot metal type.[4] Little is known of the extent to which these technical innovations penetrated the Near and Middle East as most writers have been content to date the introduction of the printing press without asking the question: what type of press? It is clear that printing in certain languages was established at an early period: there was a Jewish press in Istanbul from the fifteenth century, an Armenian press from the sixteenth century, and a Greek press from the early seventeenth century, at which period there is reported to have been an effort to establish a press to print Arabic and Turkish material in Istanbul.[5] The first Ottoman press of which we have good evidence, however, is that which operated in the eighteenth century and which encountered resistance from religious groups.[6] At times the press was closed but its activities revived at the end of the eighteenth century and by 1842 about 200 works were said to have been produced on it (Emin 1914). By that date the US missionary press in Beirut was also in operation (Tibawi 1966). In Cairo, the Bulaq press was established in 1821 and during the first twenty years of its existence produced 243 works in Turkish, Arabic and Persian (Bianchi 1843). By the time our period commences, therefore, facilities were well established for the printing of books in Arabic, Persian and Turkish within the Ottoman Empire and Egypt as well as in Europe and India. The situation was different in Iran, where printing was slower to develop and where lithography remained the principal method of book production until the end of the nineteenth century. Although lithography offered some advantages for the production of work in Arabic scripts as well as for the reproduction of illustrations, and although there were significant technical advances in litho techniques in Europe during the nineteenth century, the process remained a slower and more expensive mode of production, especially for periodical production, throughout the period. Jellygraph offered a cheap alternative method of newspaper production but was unsuitable for long print runs.

Modernization and literature 9

The output of books in the Near and Middle East during the years with which this chapter is concerned is difficult to estimate; those estimates which exist are all dependent upon inadequate information and either underestimate, through counting only works which have survived, or overestimate, through counting works which are mentioned as being contemplated but which were never actually published. It is estimated that between 1835 and 1885 some 3000 works were printed in the Ottoman Empire and a listing for 1890 gives a total of 303 works produced in that year (Shaw 1977: II, 128). A careful examination of the *salnames* would give a more precise figure but the total production during the period under investigation is likely to be of the order of 10,000 to 20,000 works, which would be about the annual output of a major European country at the end of our period. Egyptian publication probably approached that of the Ottomans but the number of publications in Iran was much smaller; Browne's list of works is admittedly incomplete but it amounts to only 162, and even with the most generous additions indicates once more the gap which separates Iran from the other two states during this period (Browne 1914: 157–64; for Egypt see van Dyck 1896).

The output of newspapers and periodicals, another important outlet for literary publication, is also difficult to estimate with any accuracy. In the Ottoman Empire and in Egypt, the first newspapers date from around 1830 but in both states the great age of expansion occurs in the 1860s and 1870s. The newspapers were sold in single copies at around 1 or 2 cents a paper or by subscription at about 10 to 15 dollars a year. Periodicals, which were the more usual outlets for work of a literary character, sold at 5 to 20 cents a copy with subscription rates in proportion. It is interesting to note that these prices did not cover all the production and distribution costs, indicating that periodicals were dependent either upon advertising or upon patronage or both for survival. In particular, the device of subscription enabled wealthy supporters of periodicals to provide a subsidy and also to use the periodicals as a means of distributing views or information which were congenial to themselves. Most newspapers and periodicals were printed on their own small presses. By the beginning of the twentieth century the circulation of some Ottoman newspapers had reached 20,000 copies an issue; Egyptian papers had rather smaller circulations. In Iran, newspapers and periodicals were much slower to become established – the first newspaper dates from the 1850s and the principal journals in Persian were produced outside Iran in Istanbul, Cairo and Calcutta. The major outburst of publication occurred only after the 1906 Revolution. Before that date the largest circulation was less than 1000 and even after 1906 the circulations of individual titles did not rise much above 2000, although *Majlis*, which featured parliamentary debates,

10 *Modern literature in the Near and Middle East*

is said to have had a circulation of 10,000.[7] According to Emin (1914: II), there were 389 newspapers and periodicals in the Ottoman Empire in 1913, of which 161 were Turkish, and 118 Arabic (Emin 1914: pt II). The total may be compared with India which produced nearly 1200 newspapers and periodicals in 1900 (Vambery 1906: 195). A further difference between the periodicals of the Ottoman Empire and Egypt on the one hand and those of Iran on the other is that by 1914 the two former states had developed a range of specialized periodicals to accommodate different interests whereas the Persian periodicals remained primarily political in character. It is noteworthy, however, that no country was able to make a purely literary publication viable.

Lastly, it is necessary to look at the question of outlets from the point of view of publishers, bookshops and libraries. In Europe publishing developed in the following order: monasteries, universities, corporations and guilds, printers, booksellers and independent publishers.[8] The nineteenth century was the age of the booksellers who turned themselves into independent publishers. No similar type of sequence has been elaborated for the Near and Middle East but one obvious difference from the European model concerns the much greater part assumed by the state in publishing in the Near and Middle East during the nineteenth century. During the first half of the nineteenth century the state and state institutions play a dominant role and, although subsequently other sources of publication assume greater importance, the state retains a central position, particularly in the Ottoman Empire. This circumstance derives in part from the historic situation of the state in the region but more particularly from the leading role played by the state in the process of modernization. In the Ottoman Empire and in Egypt it was the state controlled translation bureaux which produced translations of European publications which were seen as useful in the search for models of development. In Iran, 'Abbas Mirza embarrassed the British Envoy with a request for a translation into Persian of the *Encyclopaedia Britannica*; significantly he contented himself for the time being with translations of articles on gunnery and fortifications (Jones-Brydges 1834: 340). In Turkestan General Kaufmann ordered a history of Russia to be translated into Kazakh in the hope of promoting an affection towards Russia.[9] For the most part the institutions of higher education set up by the states published text books and manuals for use in their tasks but they extended their range to provide works covering a wider field. In this way the fact that modernization in the Ottoman Empire was military-led came to have a significant effect upon the development of writing, because the largest single group of such publications comprised those books which were appropriate to a military education. The same observation is true of Egypt before 1841 and of Iran: many of the publications of the *Dar al-Funun* reflected the importance attached to military training in that institution. The state was also dominant in Egypt and in the Ottoman Empire during the early years of the publications of newspapers and periodicals in Arabic and Turkish.

While states were so dominant it was unnecessary to develop a variety of outlets: text books were used in the state schools and colleges and the early periodicals were distributed free to government servants and foreign embassies. It was only with the development of private publishing from the 1860s that it was necessary also to develop a system of retail outlets. In general, it does not seem that booksellers took the leading role in the Near and Middle East which they assumed in Europe. Most periodicals relied on subscriptions; many newspapers were sold directly by the publishers (often the same individuals who were also the writers and printers) on the streets. With the exception of the state sector, publishing remained a very small-scale operation, employing few people and tiny amounts of capital. Booksellers did, however, begin to play a part similar in character, although not in scale, to that of the great circulating libraries which developed in parts of Europe, operating as private libraries lending books on the basis of an annual subscription. There was, of course, a great and old tradition in the Near and Middle East of establishing public libraries as a charitable act but such libraries had served the traditional and especially the religious sector. Public libraries serving the modern sector were slow to develop, but the movement gathered force during the latter part of the nineteenth century and in Iran modern-minded people grouped themselves around the project for the establishment of a national library.

PATRONAGE

The remarks made in the previous paragraph have implications for the matter of patronage. As few books and fewer periodicals could hope to pay for themselves through sales alone, authors were necessarily dependent upon patronage unless they were sufficiently affluent to pay for their own literary ambitions. In fact, most journalists were poorly paid. It follows that many books and articles were written because someone else (and not only the reader) wanted them, and their subjects and forms reflect this circumstance. The state was the principal patron and the state's needs played a major role in determining the character of literary output, not least through the simple device of censorship. In this context it should be noted that it is difficult or impossible to distinguish between the personal interests or predilections of the sovereign and the actions of the state. In the Ottoman Empire under 'Abd ül-Hamid II there was strict censorship of

12 *Modern literature in the Near and Middle East*

political expression which had the effect of diverting writers towards non-political subjects. Patronage of religious phenomena led to a growth of publication in that area. In Egypt the Khedive Isma'il sought during the late 1870s to enlist the press as his ally in his struggle to resist the encroachments of Europeans upon his government (Sabry 1924: 2). Similarly, 'Abbas Hilmi II was a promoter of the Egyptian press which he used to use for support against British and Ottoman pressure; his relations with Shaykh 'Ali Yusuf both as financier and as protector against the consequences of scandal are well known; at various times he also subsidized Mustafa Kamil, al-Kawakibi and probably Murad Bey (Mayer 1978 and Schölch 1981: 87). The British authorities behaved differently. Partly from liberal conviction and partly from contempt, Lord Cromer ignored the Arabic press but veiled British influence was a factor in determining press attitudes. In 1909 Sir Eldon Gorst revived the 1881 censorship, although his action was reversed by his successor, Kitchener.[10] It was not only in their own territories that states intervened to buy the pens of writers; the Ottoman authorities sought literary assistance in support of their claims in Egypt.

The state was, however, not the only patron. In the Ottoman Empire religious communities were able to support publications as did foreign missionaries. After 1908 political parties became important patrons of literary production. In Egypt the smaller role of the state left more room for wealthy groups and individuals, particularly those with a large stake in the cotton economy, to influence publication. Prince 'Abd al-Halim, a claimant to the Khedivate, patronized James Sanu'a; Mahmud Riyad sought and paid for the help of Jamal al-Din al-Afghani and Adib Ishaq; and *al-Jarida* was supported by the group of wealthy landowners who eventually came together in the *Umma* party (Keddie 1972: 96–7; Jerrold 1979: 216–31). Coptic factions also paid for their own publications. The small role of the state in Iran's modernization left relatively more room for other elements including landowners, enlightened members of the *'ulema*, merchants (Hajji Zayn al-'Abdin Taqiov was said to have bought 500 copies a year of the Calcutta publication *Habl al-Matin* and distributed copies to those whom he wished to influence), and other groups, such as the Armenians (the Armenian financier Basil financed *Iran-i Naw* from 1909) (Browne 1914: 25, 52). The strong political element in patronage had two effects: first, it diverted literary energies towards political subjects and, second, it obliged writers to adopt a sensational style which would better attract patrons. Those writers who spurned patronage and relied on their readers were also driven to adopt particular forms: the translation or adaptation of the French novel was a major Grub Street activity, and even a promising soldier like Mahmud Shevket undertook such translations, in addition to his translations of military works from German, probably in order to supplement his income (Swanson 1975: 371).

MOTIVATIONS

The age of translation and adaptation was deeply influenced by the progress of political events. That the Near and Middle Eastern model for imitation was France, and French the European language which was first studied and in which books, ideas and models were sought are political facts which derive from the following circumstances. During the late eighteenth and early nineteenth centuries, when the Near and Middle East first sought enlightenment from Europe, France was the intellectual and political leader of the continent and, above all, the greatest military power as the Revolutionary and Napoleonic Wars made plain. Not until 1870 did France surrender her claims to pre-eminence in Europe, and Germany and Britain appear to be alternative models. And by then the mould was set and French too well established to be easily dethroned. Even when Near and Middle Eastern readers wished to be informed about the evident superiority of the Anglo-Saxon powers, they did not go to writers in English or German but to a Frenchman, Edmond Demolins. The influence of Russian was felt only in limited areas, mainly through the Turks of the Tsarist Empire and through their contacts in the Turkish speaking areas of the region, and also through the Greek Orthodox population, particularly in consequence of the Russian educational efforts in Syria which followed the Crimean War. The predominance of French in this context makes an interesting contrast with the development of modern Hebrew literature, when the model or inspiration was German, or the development of Indian literatures, so heavily influenced by English. Political change in the Near and Middle East was also a significant factor in shaping the development of Arabic, Persian and Turkish writing. In the Ottoman Empire the whole nature of the reform movement influenced the formation of literature: political groups, such as the Young Ottomans and the Young Turks, played a large part in developing the language. In Egypt, the roles of Isma‘il and ‘Abbas II have already been mentioned but in a broader sense politics was an important foundation stone of the journalistic revolution. And in Iran, the Constitutional Revolution had the most powerful effect in unleashing a torrent of publication.

Economic and social change had a much smaller effect on the development of literature. With the exception of Egypt, where cotton was the engine for the manufacture of a significant new landed class, no important economic group appeared which could become, in the region, the factor in literary development which such groups became, as patrons,

14 *Modern literature in the Near and Middle East*

subjects or writers, in Europe. The circumstance that so large a part of the new modern élite was part of the state system, either as civil or military functionaries, or even as contractors to the state, influenced the development of literature in several ways, some of which have been suggested above. The most significant social change was experienced in urban areas, especially those, like Beirut, Alexandria, Istanbul, Izmir and Salonika, which experienced the largest growth. Although, in general, the Near and Middle East did not experience any significant shift of population from rural to urban areas during this period, as the advance of port cities was matched by the retreat or stagnation of cities in the interior, the urban population did grow at least in line with the general increase of population at the rate of something like 1 per cent per annum. City life saw considerable changes, for example in the position of women, and the development of a women's literature was a new phenomenon which began to appear in Egypt and the Ottoman lands. Social problems, such as those experienced in the modern cities, did become a noticeable subject of Near and Middle Eastern literature. A second feature of social change (and one which also had economic and political aspects) was the rise in the relative standing of the non-Muslim minorities *vis à vis* the Muslim population. The influence of this fact on Arabic literature through the part played by Syrian Christian writers needs no emphasis. The absence of any significant non-Muslim group in Iran may be an important factor in explaining why that country moved more slowly than did the Ottoman Empire or Egypt.

The pace and character of the modernization experience of the Near and Middle East left their marks on the literature of the period. But when all is said and done, modernization was limited and its impact weak in many areas. As a consequence much room was left to fashion. If one left out of account the printing of older texts and the continued exploitation of earlier traditions of literary endeavour, one could sum up the literary development of the Near and Middle East during the period under consideration in terms of entertainment, utilitarianism, narcissism and serendipity. Indeed, serendipity appears to be the only explanation for some of the books which were chosen for translation, because they appear to have nothing to recommend them from any point of view and were presumably simply the books with which the translator came into contact. By contrast, many of the most important books of nineteenth-century Europe, for example *The Origin of Species*, were not translated during the period with which we are concerned. It is not the purpose of this chapter to offer judgements on the quality of Middle Eastern writing during this period, and it is certainly not intended to offer any comments on the purely literary merits of the work accomplished, a task for which the author is

Modernization and literature 15

singularly ill-fitted. It may, however, be appropriate to comment on the intellectual quality of the writings of the period. On the whole the verdict must be that, with a few exceptions, the writing is characterized by second-hand ideas, imperfectly understood and poorly adapted or elaborated. In literature, as in other matters, the Near and Middle East was in only the adolescent stage of modernization.

Modernization may also have influenced the choice of forms of literary expression. Poetry, the connection of which with the modernizing experience is not immediately obvious, was the least affected. The development of history (as opposed to chronicle), with its effort both to convey and analyse information, is an obvious response to the demand for an understanding of the process of change. The essay is an excellent device for conveying either information or argument, and the newspaper for broadcasting the news which a changing society found of practical value. And the novel was a suitable vehicle (before television) for the entertainment of a new, secular, educated class. Modernization certainly influenced themes, even in poetry with the growth of the patriotic ballad, a phenomenon matched on the stage by the patriotic play. On this note it may be appropriate to conclude with Browne's provocative comparison of Ottoman patriotic writing with that of Egypt and Iran. The former, he remarked, was like that of Britain with its emphasis on the equivalent of 'Rule Britannia' and on the theme of victory or death on the battlefield: the latter resembled the patriotism of Ireland with its harping on the glories of martyrdom (Browne 1914: xxxvii). Perhaps that distinction may also in some ways reflect the different ways in which the countries approached the task of modernization, as well as their different historical and religious experience.

NOTES

1 There is a large literature on the subject of modernization. The following books provide a useful introduction to the subject. Black (1967); Levy, (1966); Eisenstadt, (1966) and (1973): UNESCO (1966) provides much useful comparative material and ideas; and Rudolph, (1967), is an interesting criticism of some of the assumptions of modernizing theory, drawing on a study of India.
2 Most books dealing with the history of the Near and Middle East during the nineteenth and twentieth centuries in some way touch on the question of modernization. As this book is primarily addressed to students of literature it may be useful to supply a guide to some of the more significant and easily accessible publications. Gibb and Bowen, (1950–7), for all the many criticisms made of it in recent years, remains a valuable starting point. Two general accounts of the process of modernization in the region are contained in the essays in Polk and Chambers (1968) and Ward and Rustow (1964). On social change see Coon (1952) and van Nieuwenhuijze (1965). Intellectual history is

16 *Modern literature in the Near and Middle East*

the subject of Hourani (1962). A good outline of economic developments may be obtained from Issawi (1982), and Owen (1981). On changes in the Ottoman Empire see Lewis (1961), Berkes (1964), Davison (1963), Findley (1980), Mardin (1962), Ramsaur (1969) and Shaw (1971). On the Arab lands Holt (1966) provides a good outline which may be filled out with Tibawi (1969), Salibi (1955), Vatikiotis (1969) and Batatu (1979). For Iran, Avery (1965), is a useful outline which may be supplemented by Nashat (1982), Bakhash (1978), and Abrahamian (1982). This chapter does not embrace Afghanistan and Turkestan but in connection with literature and modernizing movements the following works may be noted: Gregorian (1969), Schinasi (1979), and Bennigsen and Lemercier-Quelquejay (1964). A longer critical bibliography of the subject is to be found in Yapp (1987).

3 On educational developments see Szyliowicz (1973).

4 For the development of printing see Hoe (1902), Isaacs (1931), and McMurtrie (1943).

5 Ubicini (1853: i, 248–50). On the early history of printing in the Near and Middle East see Cheikho (1900).

6 On the early history of printing in the Ottoman Empire see Babinger (1919).

7 Kamshad (1966: 36–7), provides a short bibliography for the Persian press. For the Egyptian press see 'Abduh (1949) and (1942) and Hartmann (1899).

8 Mumby (1949), provides an outline based upon English experience.

9 Vambery (1906: 41). Vambery writes 'Kirghiz' but I have judged that he was adopting the usual practice of using this term to signify 'Kazakh'.

10 For British activities see, Marshall (1928), Mellini (1977: 180–5) and Tignor (1966: 162, 298–300).

2 Turkey[1]

Saliha Paker

The general title of Part I assumes the dominance of translations over the original literatures of the given period, thereby raising a number of questions. First of all, to what extent is it valid to describe a period of more than fifty years in a given literature as an 'age of translation and adaptation' in which the original literature is assumed to have remained subordinate? How is the notion of the 'dominance' of translated and adapted literature to be defined? And how are the translations and adaptations of this period to be related to the original literature into which they were introduced? The survey that follows will attempt to look into these questions in the context of a functional evaluation of translations in the Ottoman–Turkish literature of the *Tanzimat* from 1859, the *Servet-i Fünûn* from 1896 and up to the years immediately following the Constitutional Revolution of 1908, concentrating in particular on the *Tanzimat* period in which literary translations played a decidedly formative role.

In the light of major developments in translation studies in the last fifteen years it is now possible to analyse literary translations not only in relation to source literatures/literary systems, but more importantly, in relation to target literatures/literary systems.[2] Target-orientated analyses, of a descriptive rather than prescriptive kind, are necessarily linked to the recognition of the importance of historical and functional studies of translations. It has been seen that the systems theory, originating from the works of Tynianov and Jakobson in the 1920s, then re-worked and formulated in terms of a 'polysystem' theory by Even-Zohar in the 1970s (Even-Zohar 1978a: 1979) can serve as the basic framework for such studies. To put it briefly, the polysystem theory conceives of literature as a dynamic structure, a system of multiple systems, of which the various strata are in a state of permanent opposition and conflict (as may be seen in the tensions between literary types and models of canonized/official/high status and those of non-canonized/unofficial/popular status) and are consequently subject to shifts in position. In the context of this theory,

18 *Modern literature in the Near and Middle East*

translated literature too is seen as a system involved in the dynamics of the larger polysystemic framework, occupying either a central or peripheral position in it, but 'fully participating in the history of the literary polysystem, as an integral part of it, related with all other co-systems' (Even-Zohar 1978a: 119).[3] This conception of translations provides a convincing explanation for the dominance of translated literature and its function in the *Tanzimat* period.

TRANSLATION IN THE *TANZİMAT* PERIOD

It is generally accepted by historians of Turkish literature that the birth of modern or 'New' Turkish literature in the second half of the nineteenth century was intimately related to European influence, French in particular, and that translations as the crucial means of influence played an enormously significant role in introducing new poetic models and such new literary *genres* as the drama and the novel.[4] There is no doubt that it was the 'principle of innovation' embodied in the translated texts that secured for them a 'central' position in the literature of that period. For in the mid-nineteenth century Ottoman literary polysystem, which before the *Tanzimat* had been closed to contact with literatures other than Persian and Arabic, canonized literature (the *Divan* poetry and prose) had reached the point of stagnation, while the lower strata (popular/folk literature) remained equally incapable of generating innovation (cf. Even-Zohar 1978a: 120).[5] That the leading literary figures of the *Tanzimat* were deeply aware of this general state of inertia was clearly reflected in their efforts to seek out re-generating forces in the literature of the West that was just beginning to be available to them.

The *Tanzimat*, meaning 'Re-organization', consisted of a number of administrative, legal and educational reforms, the first and the most important of which was adopted in 1839 – a date which is generally recognized as the beginning of a new era in Turkish history (Lewis 1962: 105–25). The reforms were inspired by European scientific and technological progress since the late eighteenth century, and stood as an irrevocable, though controversial, statement of formal and conscious Westernization. Consequently, it was in the context of a gradual process of cultural transformation that changes in the literary system began to be observed after 1859. However, the reception of European literature was far from being a simple process. Such *genres* as the novel and the drama were indeed looked upon as new models very much to be experimented with, but even in the works of the exponents of innovation, the established literary models of poetry and the linguistic and stylistic models of prose literature continued their struggle for dominance. Within this context, it

Turkey 19

was mainly through the medium of prose, especially journalistic prose and works for the theatre, that translated literature succeeded in making its way from the periphery towards the centre of the polysystem.

What is generally regarded as a 'first step' towards the literary innovations of the *Tanzimat* is the body of translations mainly from French literature into Turkish, the first three of which appeared in 1859, each representing a new literary *genre*: Western poetry, philosophical dialogue, and the novel (Kudret 1979; Özön 1985; Tanpınar 1982). Significantly, a year later in 1860, one of the translators of these works, İbrahim Şinasi, wrote the first Turkish domestic comedy *(Şair Evlenmesi)* in the Western tradition. These works and others that followed were concrete manifestations of a growing interest in and reception of European culture and should be correlated with the aims and functions of some institutions of the period, established in the capital:

(i) The government 'Translation Chamber' *(Babıâlî Tercüme Odası)* founded in 1833 for the purpose of teaching European languages, especially French, to Muslims and of training them as translators of official documents. After the first *Tanzimat* edict, this office began to function like a school for aspiring young Ottoman writers and statesmen, gradually assuming the nature of a progressive society with a new world view and a new political ideal inspired by the West (Tanpınar 1982: 143).

(ii) The 'Academy' *(Encümen-i Daniş)* established by the government in 1851 to organize the selection, translation and production of teaching materials in science, history and literature for a prospective university *(Darülfünûn)*. Composed of statesmen, Muslim and non-Muslim teachers and scientists, young historians and European orientalists of the time, the 'Academy' was intended to maintain continuous cultural contact with the West. Despite its brief life-span till 1862, it succeeded in having a considerable number of historical works, among others, written and translated, though most of these were left unpublished (Tanpınar 1982: 144–5).

(iii) The 'Ottoman Scientific Society' *(Cemiyet-i İlmiye-i Osmaniye)* founded principally by Münif Paşa in 1860 to encourage Turkish scientific studies by introducing modern Western scholarship in the sciences. Apart from sponsoring public classes in natural sciences, geology, history and economics, it brought out the first Turkish *Journal of Sciences*, the monthly *Mecmua-i Fünûn*, which ran intermittently from 1862 to 1882, covering translations and original writings in philosophy and history as well as geography and the sciences, thus helping to create a medium for new scientific and scholarly prose (Sevük 1944: 116).

(iv) Newspapers such as *Ceride-i Havadis* (1840) the first unofficial newspaper in Turkish founded by William Churchill, an Englishman,

20 Modern literature in the Near and Middle East

which was of great importance in making abundant use of translated material (literary as well as non-literary) from the West and in acquainting the public with foreign news and viewpoints; *Tercüman-i Ahvâl* (1860), *Tasvir-i Efkâr* (1862), *Tercüman-i Hakikat* (1878) and many others which assumed the function of the principal and most lively medium of the intelligentsia striving not only to inform but also to educate the public.

Almost all of the pioneers of innovative change and the foremost translators of European literature worked at one time or another in or for such establishments. Münif Paşa, for instance, who was responsible for one of the first translations in 1859, learnt French in the Translation Chamber, worked for the *Ceride-i Havadis*, learning English at the same time, and was the principal founder of the Ottoman Scientific Society and its journal (Sevük 1944: 116); Ahmed Vefik Paşa, best known for his translations of Molière, was a member of the 'Academy' and taught history for the Ottoman Scientific Society (ibid.); Şinasi, in many ways the founder of modern Turkish literature and the first translator of European poetry, was the founder and chief editor of *Tasvir-i Efkâr*, one of the most literary and consciously instructive of the newspapers; Namık Kemal, the most eminent of the *Tanzimat* writers and the first translator of Montesquieu into Turkish (op. cit.: 121), was trained in the Translation Chamber and was initiated into the new literary movement while writing for *Tasvir-i Efkâr*, which he later took over from Şinasi (Tanpınar 1982: 344) and finally Ahmed Midhat, perhaps the most prolific writer and translator of the period, founded and ran *Tercüman-i Hakikat* which served as a major medium for his literary output and for the polemical views of the poet and translator Muallim Naci, his son-in-law. It must also be pointed out that all those mentioned above were instrumental in setting down the norms of literary translation that were to affect original writing as much as translations in the *Tanzimat*.

The three translations from French literature that appeared in the year 1859 were important not only because they were the first of their kind, but also because they represented a range of translational norms and strategies that were adopted or rejected by later translators for reasons that will be explained further on.

Tercüme-i Manzume (Translations of Verse) by İbrahim Şinasi, were the first translations of Western poetry in Turkish, in the form of a collection of selected verse from La Fontaine, Lamartine, Gilbert and Racine, published with the originals, and all lexical additions and changes in the order of verse lines indicated on the translated texts (Özön 1946: 451; Tansel 1946: 467). Şinasi, as mentioned above, was a conscious innovator and his use of the *Aruz* verse for the translations was evidently intended to make his selection 'acceptable' in poetic form as well as in content according to the norms of the home system;[6] his attempts at 'adequacy' in translation, insofar as textual (literary and linguistic) norms were concerned, served to promote his use of a new and relatively simple lexis and style.[7] These verse translations are known to have had more influence on Şinasi's own poetry and on later generations than on his contemporaries (Tanpınar 1982: 195), a point which can partly be accounted for by the dominance of established forms of *Divan* poetry.

Münif Paşa's *Muhaverat-ı Hikemiye (Philosophical Dialogues)* was also a selection, consisting of conversational pieces from Voltaire, Fénelon and Fontenelle. Münif Paşa was an educator as well as an innovator, and his translations carrying philosophical and moral concepts new for Ottoman readers, showed his fundamental interest in the dissemination of philosophical thought in clear and intelligible prose, as did his writings in the scientific journal, *Mecmua-i Fünûn* mentioned above (Özön 1941: 390, 393). His choice of a conversational context for his translations was no doubt made with a view to 'acceptability' which was not diminished but enhanced by his attempt to give a fairly 'adequate' rendering of the original in a prose of simple syntax. Tanpınar, who describes Münif Paşa's prose in his translations as the 'most advanced' of its time, also notes that it was the same translations that 'started the debate on the moral principles underlying the *Tanzimat* movement'. (Tanpınar 1982: 180–1).

Terceme-i Telemak (The Translation of Telemak), known as Grand Vizier Yusuf Kâmil Paşa's version of Fénelon's novel *Les Aventures de Télémaque* (1699), was written in the ornate poetic prose style, *İnşa*, which was the dominant model of the canonized system.[8] Furthermore, the preface to the translation indicated that the translation had been undertaken with a view to rendering it not as fiction, which, it was implied, would have been beneath the dignity of a grand vizier, but as an account of wise statesmanship, or a 'mirror for princes', of which there were abundant examples in the literature of the East (Özön 1985: 115–16). Clearly it was this view on the translator's part which led to his summarizing some features of the original that he deemed irrelevant to his purpose, and which was the underlying reason for his preference for the dominant norms of the Ottoman literary system over those of 'adequacy'. Its 'acceptability' is confirmed by the fact that although it was initially circulated in manuscript, it achieved great success, was finally printed in 1862, reprinted in 1863, 1867 and 1870, and was used in high schools for prose composition (Kudret 1979: 12; Özön 1980: 117). It was in reaction to this translation that twenty years later in 1881, Ahmed Vefik Paşa, one of the chief figures of the *Tanzimat*, produced his own version of *Télémaque*, which he claimed to be not only 'a literal and accurate' translation but one in which 'every word would produce pleasure' (Özön,

22 Modern literature in the Near and Middle East

1980: 117). Evidently, this translation was meant to be both 'adequate' and readable and the translator's choice of syntactic and lexical simplicity, as opposed to the ornateness of the previous translation, was intended to serve his purpose. It must be noted, however, that Ahmed Vefik Paşa's version did not enjoy the popularity of the older translation, a point which is interesting in showing not only the continuation of linguistic struggle (in the 1880s) for dominance between canonized Ottoman and relatively simple Turkish prose, but also the functions of literary translation in relation to the opposite poles: i.e. how some translations serve to preserve the canonized established forms, hence assuming a conservative function, while others serve as means of introducing innovations (cf. Even-Zohar 1978a: 123).

Within the system of translated literature itself, the struggle mentioned above may be seen in terms of a competition between 'acceptable' and 'adequate' translations or between the norms of the target (Ottoman) and the source systems – a point leading us to observe a phenomenon in the context of journalism which had significant implications. In 1862, the same year as the publication of the first translation of *Télémaque*, the newspaper *Ruznâme-i Ceride-i Havadis* (the daily version of the first unofficial weekly newspaper *Ceride-i Havadis* as of 1860) first published a brief summary of Hugo's *Les Misérables*, then a few months later serialized a highly abridged translation of the same novel, under the title *Mağdurîn Hikâyesi* (Kerman 1978: 351; Kut 1985: 197).⁹ It has been said that the narrative style of this version was the same as that of the standard police report of the time and that the source text was abridged to the point of reducing the novel to a crime story (Özön 1985: 122). That this version is attributed to Münif Paşa (Kerman 1978: 351; Akünal 1980: 110–11) who was responsible for an 'adequate' translation of the *Philosophical Dialogues*, raises a question: was this 'vulgarized' translation prompted by the expectations of the readers or were there also other factors involved? The answer seems to be related to the fact that the reading public at large were not familiar with the full-length European novel and its characteristic delineation of plot and character, while some translators, like that of *Les Misérables*, were at pains to introduce the *genre* as a major vehicle of ideas (Akünal 1980: 110). It would, therefore, appear that the translators' attempts in mediating texts to make them 'acceptable', set down the norms that were reflected by the newspapers which, by the 1870s, had assumed the function of a medium for the dissemination of translated literature.

The serialized translation of *Les Misérables* was followed seven years later in 1869 by Pellico's *Mes Prisons* in *Terakki* newspaper and Chateaubriand's *Atala* in *Hakayiku'l-Vekayi*; in 1870 by de Saint-Pierre's *Paul et Virginie* in *Mümeyyiz*; in 1871 by Voltaire's *Micromégas* and Dumas *père's Le Comte de Monte Cristo* in *Diyojen*, the first Turkish humorous magazine. According to one account, about thirty translators contributed to the initial serialized parts of *Monte Kristo*, which was eventually completed in book form in 1873 (Özön 1985: 141; Tanpınar 1982: 285). While it cannot be said that the medium of journalism itself fostered 'adequacy ' in translation, it must be granted that these and many other serialized translations that followed, functioned as the main motivating force behind the growth of Turkish vocabulary and the development of simplified prose, in serving to introduce new concepts, terms and styles, and perhaps what is equally important, in bringing to attention the difficulties of having to find linguistic equivalents for the new concepts. Recaizade Ekrem, for instance, who had serialized his translations of *Mes Prisons* and *Atala*, was among the first writers of the *Tanzimat* to complain (in his preface to *Atala* in book form in 1874) of the insufficiency of the present linguistic resources of Turkish in meeting the needs of the original text. Furthermore, among the serialized translations listed above, two were re-translated by other writers keen on improving on the first versions: *Micromégas* by Ahmed Vefik Paşa (in 1871) and *Les Misérables* by Şemsettin Sâmi (in 1879). The latter's translation of *Les Misérables* published under the title *Sefiller* (covering the first eight chapters which were completed by Hasan Bedreddin after 1908), was bitterly attacked because it was allegedly too close to the original in style and too literal (Kerman 1978: 353, 354–5). Five years later in the preface to his translation of *Robinson Crusoe* (1885), Sâmi defended the 'adequacy' of his translations by claiming that it was impossible to convey new ideas in the established Ottoman prose and that in trying to stay close to the original and write in simple prose, he was consciously forcing the possibilities of the Turkish language to its ultimate advantage. That it was possible for this translation to be reprinted in 1934 and read by a republican generation is an indication of the extent of Sâmi's innovation. But such a degree of 'adequacy' in translation appears to have been rare. For, in addition to the linguistic difficulties, the apparently growing demand for translations, the opportunities of serializing them in newspapers and magazines, and the presumed taste of the reading public were factors that encouraged 'acceptable' rather than 'adequate' translations.

The writer who was the leading advocate for an extreme form of 'acceptability' and who, in a sense, institutionalized it was Ahmed Midhat. Founder of the newspaper *Tercüman-i Hakikat*, as mentioned above, and of the first Turkish publishing house in Istanbul, he was a prolific writer, translator and journalist, dedicated to the cause of promoting the pleasure of reading on a popular level in a society which was just beginning to read newspapers. In fact, Ahmed Midhat did more to popularize literature than perhaps any other writer of the *Tanzimat*. His translations ranged from

24 *Modern literature in the Near and Middle East*

Xenophon's *Cyropaedia*, Ann Radcliffe's *The Mysteries of Udolpho*, Hugo's *Les Burgraves*, Dumas *fils' La Dame aux Camélias*, to popular novels of Parisian life by Paul de Kock and detective stories by Xavier de Montepin, later to be translated abundantly by others. He among others in the *Tanzimat* period has generally been criticized by literary historians for his 'random' or indiscriminate selection of translations. Tanpınar, for instance, has remarked with some contempt that 'for his gigantic appetite, Xavier de Montepin and Eugène Sue were of the same stuff as Cervantes and Hugo, and Zola could easily be put aside in favour of Paul de Kock' (Tanpınar 1981: 462). But Ahmed Midhat's translational policy had very much to do with his general intention as a writer. In the preface to his translation of Paul de Kock's *La Fille aux Trois Jupons* (*Üç Yüzlü Bir Karı*) (in 1875) in which he collaborated with Ebuzziya Tevfik, he dismissed both literal and free translation on the grounds that the one would be inelegant in Turkish and the other incapable of rendering the connotations of the original. His preference was for 're-writing in Turkish the general import of the story', i.e. of the original. This, as noted by Özön, meant that Ahmed Midhat's versions resembled the original in basic structure and line of action, while the stylistic features and the moral structure remained his own (Özön1985: 224). It has also been claimed that this policy was in fact a pretext for Ahmed Midhat for proliferating his own literary output and also for diminishing the differences that might exist between his original works and his translations, thereby elevating the status of his original works to that of the European literary models (Sevük 1944: 210; Özön 1985: 223). His collection of short stories, *Letaif-i Rivayat* (1870–95), consisting of translated or 're-written' as well as original pieces, may be taken as a significant indication of such intentions.

Even-Zohar's views on the implications of such phenomena is of particular relevance at this point. His hypothesis is that when translated literature assumes:

> a central position... it actively participates in *modelling the centre* of the polysystem. In such a situation it is by and large an integral part of innovatory forces, and as such likely to be identified with major events in literary history while these are taking place. This implies in fact that no clear-cut distinction is then maintained between original and translated writings, and that often it is the leading writers (or members of the avant-garde who are about to become leading writers) who produce the most important translations. Moreover, in such a state when new literary models are emerging, translation is likely to become one of the means of elaborating these new models.
>
> (Even-Zohar 1978a: 120)

The foregoing brief survey shows that the greater part of this hypothesis holds true for the Ottoman literature of the *Tanzimat*. However, it is also a fact that within the same context there is a vast difference between the translations of Şemsettin Sâmi and those of Ahmed Midhat, in that the extreme 'adequacy' of the former strongly distinguishes them from native writing while the extreme 'non-adequacy' of the latter definitely blurs the distinction between translated and native literary products. The reason for this should probably be attributed to the translators' principle of selection and general purpose. It appears that Şemsettin Sâmi was far more selective in his choice of 'new' or 'innovative' literature to be introduced and translated as close to the original as possible, while for Ahmed Midhat such selectiveness was not a guiding principle: his range covered both the popular and the classical, all of which were to be translated for the purpose of entertaining as well as edifying the readers of his newspaper and his books. In trying to achieve this, Ahmed Midhat did not 'violate the home conventions' (cf. op.cit.: 124) but made use of such popular literary conventions as the *Meddah* story within the framework of the foreign models in simple prose, thereby generating new models for the home literary system (Özön 1985: 226–31; cf. Evin 1983: 54ff). While Şemsettin Sâmi's only novel, *Taaşşuk-i Talat ve Fitnat* (1872), is considered the first Turkish example of the *genre*, Ahmed Midhat is generally accepted as the first short story writer and novelist in modern Turkish literature (Tanpınar, 1981: 463): a point which must be correlated with the latter's position as a major exponent of 'acceptability' in translation.

THE RISE OF THE DRAMA

The 1870s witnessed the publication of Ahmed Midhat's first short stories in *Letaif-i Rivayat* (1870) and novels (*Hasan Mellah*, 1874; *Hüseyin Fellah*, 1875; *Felâtun Bey ile Rakım Efendi*; 1875) as well as the first novels of Şemsettin Sâmi (*Taaşşuk-i Talat ve Fitnat*, 1872) and Namık Kemal (*Intibah*, 1876). But the new literary *genre* that aroused the most interest in this decade was drama. As mentioned above, Şinasi had written the first Turkish play (*Şair Evlenmesi*), a satirical comedy of manners inspired by the comedies of Molière as early as 1860 and had serialized it in the newspaper *Tercüman'i Ahval*. This play, which had initially been snubbed by the *Ruzname-i Ceride-i Havadis* as an old wives' tale (Sevük 1944: 127), did not have much impact because it was not staged until much later. As is known, interest in the Western theatre was initially aroused by the productions of Italian, French and English travelling companies in Istanbul and Izmir in the 1840s, which were intended mainly for the resident Europeans and Levantines. In the late 1850s Armenian

26 *Modern literature in the Near and Middle East*

actors (whose earliest performances for their own community dated back to 1810 in Istanbul (Enginün 1979: 14)) began to produce plays in Turkish, thus laying the foundations of the Ottoman theatre.

So far as translations were concerned, the plays that occupied a prominent place in the repertoire of the Ottoman stage (*Gedikpaşa Tiyatro-yi Osmanî*, set up by Agop Efendi in 1869 (Özön 1966: 656)) were translations and adaptations from Molière. Ahmed Vefik Paşa, previously mentioned for his translations of *Télémaque* and *Micromégas*, is by far the best-known translator/adaptor of the master of French classical comedy, though there were others who also produced successful versions from the same playwright for the stage. Ahmed Vefik Paşa's corpus of sixteen Molière plays falls into four categories (Sevük 1944: 138), showing an interesting range of translational strategies: four translations in prose, of which *İnfial-i Aşk* (*Le Dépit Amoureux*) is abridged; five in decasyllabic verse; two with Jewish (*L'Avare/Azarya*) and Greek (*Georges Dandin/ Yorgaki Dandini*) characters replacing their French counterparts; and five adaptations, which may be described as plays bearing the same plot structure as the original but rewritten entirely in conformity with the domestic linguistic and cultural norms. Of these, the adaptations of *Le Mariage Forcé* (*Zor Nikâhi*) of *Le Médicin Malgré Lui* (*Zoraki Tabip*) and *Georges Dandin* were the first to be published (in 1869) and staged, while the rest were published while Ahmed Vefik Paşa was governor in Bursa (1879–82) where he set up a theatre and personally directed the production of his translations and adaptations with players from Istanbul (Özön 1941: 143). The success of the first two adaptations by Ahmed Vefik Paşa prompted others to follow the same strategy with equal or greater success: Âli Bey's adaptations of *Les Fourberies de Scapin* (*Ayyar Hamza*, 1871) and *Georges Dandin* (*Memiş Ağa*, 1872), Teodor Kasab's version of *L'Avare* (*Pinti Hamid*, 1873) were all highly popular on the stage. *İşkilli Memo* (1873), another adaptation *(Sganarelle)* from Molière by Kasab, is of special significance in that it was subtitled *orta oyunu*, indicating its close affinity with the traditional form of Turkish improvised farce performed in open space. In the midst of a controversy over whether or not a spectacle such as the *orta oyunu* was worthy enough to be shown in the theatre, Kasab's intention was to draw it on to the stage, thus lending it respectability, while at the same time rendering Molière's play 'acceptable' for an audience used to the *orta oyunu* (cf. Sevük 1944: 140). In general, the popularity of adaptations for the theatre was such that they continued to dominate the Ottoman/Turkish stage well into the 1920s. Hence it may be said that in the way of establishing a trend for rendering foreign dramatic literature 'acceptable' for the Turkish audience, Ahmed Vefik Paşa did for the theatre what Ahmed Midhat was doing for fiction.

Turkey 27

However, the 1870s were also busy years for those who produced original plays as well as those in translation. The uproar caused by Namık Kemal's patriotic–romantic play *Vatan-yahut-Silistre* (1873) in the Gedikpaşa theatre and the subsequent censorship on plays before production did not prevent Namık Kemal, Ebuzziya Tevfik and Ahmed Midhat from continuing to write in exile, or others from producing plays. The bulk of the poet Abdülhak Hâmid's dramatic works, which are, significantly, closet plays rather than performable ones, also fall in the period between 1873 and 1883. It may be said that the major function of translated drama in the Ottoman literary system, be it of major or minor plays, was in introducing a *genre* that necessitated for the first time a direct relationship between writers and the public, and one that was based on the use of a simple and intelligible language. It is perhaps on this account that products of dramatic literature, as much as journalism, helped to advance the movement for linguistic simplification.

In this context, it is worth mentioning in particular the collaboration of Manastırli Rıfat and Hasan Bedreddin, who started a series under the general title of Temasa for the purpose of publishing 'original plays representing the ways of the East and translations of select works of the West' (Özön 1941: 139–40). Among the many products of this collaboration was the first translation of a Shakespearean work, *Othello* (1876) but from a French adaptation by Jean François Ducis (1792). Ironically, the note on the title page indicates that the translators knew of it as 'a great Italian opera' and that their reason for translating the play lay in 'its representation of the bravery of the Arabs' (Enginün 1979: 22), a point which reminds us not only of the presence of many factors affecting a translator's choice, but also of the importance of the 'acceptability' factor. The next two plays from Shakespeare (*The Merchant of Venice (Venedik Taciri)* in 1884 and *The Comedy of Errors (Sehv-i Mudhik)* in 1887 by Hasan Sırrı) may be taken as the first and the closest to 'adequate' translations from English literature into Turkish: they were almost fully translated (though in prose) and from the original language, not from the French (op.cit.: 30). The first of these was published with an introduction on Shakespeare, describing him as 'the master of English poetry and prose', but noting at the same time that the 'violence and barbarism in his inclinations and language were no doubt prompted by the times he lived in' and that abusive language was expurgated in the translation. Indeed expressions and some passages that could offend Jewish and Christian sensibilities were omitted from the translation of *The Merchant of Venice* (op.cit.: 33–8) – a strategy which indicates the importance of the socio-cultural norms in the home system.

As for the full translations of Shakespearean tragedies, it is of some

28 *Modern literature in the Near and Middle East*

significance that none appeared before 1908. In 1881 the Italian actor Alessandro Salvini had performed *Hamlet* and *King Lear* in Istanbul, but in 1889 Ernesto Rossi's repeated attempts to stage the same plays and *Macbeth* were prevented by the censors of Abdülhamid II, the actor being allowed to perform *The Merchant of Venice* and *Othello* instead (op.cit.: 16). In the years following, even Verdi's *Othello* was banned. In view of the increasing repression and censorship in the reign of Abdülhamid, it is perhaps not surprising that the first translations to be published after his deposition, and in the same year as the Constitutional Revolution of 1908, were of *Julius Caesar* and *Hamlet* to be followed by those of *Macbeth* (and *Romeo and Juliet*) in 1909, and *King Lear* in 1912 – all by Abdullah Cevdet, a prominent Young Turk who had spent most of his life in exile.

The most productive period in the *Tanzimat* in terms of translations and original writing in fiction and for the theatre were the years between 1873 and 1883. In the subsequent years of the Hamidian depotism, the pressures of censorship and restrictive measures significantly gave rise to a flood of translations of detective stories, thrillers, romances, sentimental novels and melodrama, mostly from contemporary popular French literature (Sevük 1944: 298). The entire Jules Verne corpus and the novels of Michel Zevaco were translated in these years. In other words translated literature had begun to function not as a 'primary' innovative activity, but as a 'secondary activity', sustaining the non-canonized or popular stratum both in fiction and drama (cf. Even-Zohar 1978: 120).

In the domain of poetry, despite a considerable number of verse translations, ranging from Şinasi's major attempt in 1859 to the translation of Shakespeare's sonnets (in prose) by Mehmed Nadir in 1887–8 and by Muallim Naaci in 1886 (Enginün 1979: 101,109), poetry in translation does not appear to have had as much of an immediate innovative impact on original writing as did the translation of plays and fiction, for the understandable reason that the canonicity of native poetry was too well established to be challenged by foreign models. As is evident in the case of Namık Kemal and Ziya Paşa, who initiated major changes in theme and content within the established models of Ottoman poetry, and of Abdülhak Hâmid, who was the first to experiment with verse drama and changes in poetic form, it was poetry read and studied in the original rather than published translations that seem to have brought about the innovations which were to find concrete expression in the words of the *Servet-i Fünûn* poets like Tevfik Fikret and Cenab Sehabeddin. However, it must also be noted that the question of the difficulties of translating verse into *Aruz* or syllabic verse was a much discussed topic, especially in the *Tanzimat*, resulting in something of a consensus that narrative and dramatic verse would best be rendered in prose (Tansel 1946: 465). This explains why the

Turkey 29

translations from Shakespeare mentioned above, a French classical tragedy such as Ahmed Midhat's version of *Le Cid* (*Sid Hülasası*) and the three attempts at translating the *Iliad* (by Naim Fraşeri in 1887, Selanikli Hilmi in 1900 and Ömer Seyfettin in 1912) were all in prose.

THE SERVET-İ FÜNÛN PERIOD

In a study of translated European verse between the years 1839 and 1909, it has been shown that out of about one hundred translations of poetry only ten fall in the *Servet-i Fünûn* period, while the rest belong to the earlier period of *Tanzimat* (op.cit.: 474). In the *Servet-i Fünûn* there is also a similar paucity in translations for the theatre for reasons of censorship, as mentioned above. So the *Servet-i Fünûn* may be described primarily as a period in which the initial innovations of the *Tanzimat*, sparked off by numerous translations, evolved into better structured and more polished works of fiction and poetry. In this context translational activity helped especially to consolidate such *genres* as the novel and the short story. Apart from the translation of popular literature mentioned above and the re-translations of major works that had appeared earlier, translated literature in the 1890s and the 1900s included a wider range of writers (such as Daudet, Zola, Maupassant, Schiller and Tolstoy) and gave prominence to the novel and the short story in particular. Halid Ziya (Uşaklıgil), the most eminent of *Servet-i Fünûn* novelists, was also the first to work on and develop the short story after Ahmed Midhat. Significantly, his interest in this *genre* was reflected in his attempt to produce a collection of short stories translated from about fifty contemporary French authors. In reaction to what he thought was the deplorable practice in his day, the author's intention was to reproduce 'accurately and faithfully' the exact content and the characteristic style of each author, presumably to test and prove the flexibility and resourcefulness of Turkish as a literary medium (Uşaklıgil 1969: 295–6; 298–9). But his achievement was entirely frustrated by the textual changes and deletions of the Inspection and Examination Committee of the time, so that the published end product, *Nâkil* (1892–4) bore no resemblance to the original version (op.cit.: 299–300).[10] This shows that in this period, at least some translations would have functioned as a 'primary' innovative activity in the literary system, had they not been subjected to censorship of one kind or another. It is also evident that development in original writing was still dependent on the foreign model.

What was perhaps less conspicuous but certainly as important was that a similar form of dependency existed in the process of the search for and development of literary critical concepts and terminology in the *Servet-i*

30 *Modern literature in the Near and Middle East*

Fünûn. The problem of finding the correct equivalent for the concept of 'criticism' itself had been the subject of discussion in the *Tanzimat* (Ercilasun 1981: 1–4). In their attempts to make critical assessments of European literatures and to formulate them in literary histories which appeared to be increasingly in demand, the literary men of the *Servet-i Fünûn* were involved in a continuous 'translating' process in trying to find the equivalents of French concepts and terms in Turkish and to define and explain them. They have often been criticized for having chosen terms and compounds from Persian and Arabic, and for having kept some French terms for want of anything better, but it was certainly this process which laid the foundations of modern criticism in Turkish letters.

CONCLUSION

In the light of all the evidence above, it can be said that translated literature assumed a 'central position,' as a 'primary activity representing the principle of innovation' in the literature of the *Tanzimat*, beginning in the 1860s and extending into the 1880s. In bringing the Ottomans into contact with the West in an unprecedented manner, the *Tanzimat* was indeed a historical turning point not only in the literary but also in the broader socio-cultural polysystem in which 'established models' were considered outdated and rejected by those who now looked to the West, especially to France for innovations of all kinds (cf. Even-Zohar 1978: 122). Within this context, translated European literature assumed a twofold 'central' function, or a function that was manifested on two levels in the *Tanzimat* period: while translations of European works of canonized status (such as Şinasi's *Translations of Verse*, Münif Paşa's *Philosophical Dialogues*, Şemsettin Sâmi's translation of *Les Misérables*, Ahmed Vefik Paşa's translations from Molière) functioned as a shaping force on the level of 'high literature', non-canonized/popular translated literature and adaptations for the theatre were active on a lower level. It was the dynamic interaction between these two levels (or strata) that contributed to such linguistic and literary innovations as the simplification of prose style and the introduction of the drama, the novel and the short story as the new *genres* into Ottoman literature. However, as a result of the escalation in censorship in the second half of the 1880s, translated literature was to a large extent confined to minor works of literature and re-translations of novels previously published, thereby assuming the function not of an innovative 'primary' activity but of a 'secondary' activity, intent on maintaining the models and strategies established in the preceding decades. It is significant that in these years there was also a parallel decline in the production of original literature.

Turkey 31

But the later literary revival in the *Servet-i Fünûn* period in the late 1890s and at the turn of the century marked a renewed interest in the translation of major literary works not only from French but also from other literatures such as Russian and German. Once more, though not as predominantly as in the *Tanzimat*, translation activity assumed an innovative function in the home literary system.

NOTES

1 Parts of this chapter have appeared in Paker (1986).
2 See Hermans (1985: 7–15), on the present state of Translation Studies; also Lambert and van Gorp (1985: 42–62), and Toury (1985: 16–41) on descriptive studies in literary translation and the possibilities for broadening the field of research.
3 I am grateful to Professor Even-Zohar for a revised copy of his article 'The Position of Translated Literature within the Literary Polysystem' (1978a).
4 See Evin (1983: 41–78) for illuminating references to literary translations in the cultural context of the *Tanzimat*.
5 For a more detailed discussion on stagnation in pre-*Tanzimat* literature see Paker (1986: 70–71).
6 Evin's (1983: 42) claims that such 'selections' of verse 'reflected very much an Ottoman attitude toward poetry in its disregard of the wholeness of a poem', may be taken as yet another norm of 'acceptability' affecting Şinasi's strategy.
7 'Adequacy' in translation is the concept underlying a strategy which aims for 'a reproduction of the dominant textual relations of the original' (Even-Zohar 1978a: 124–5) while 'acceptability' signifies a strategy which tends to conform to the established literary and/or linguistic norms of the target system, with the intention of securing a place for the translated text in that system. Naturally, the degree of 'adequacy' and 'acceptability' and the 'equivalence' thereby achieved, varies from one translation to another, but the 'ideal' translation, if there were such a construct, would be one that is both 'adequate' and 'acceptable'. (For a full discussion of the concepts of 'norm', 'adequacy' and 'acceptability' see Toury 1980: 35–70.)
8 See Somekh (1981: 195–7 for an analysis of the same stylistic model in the Arabic version of the same work.
9 I am grateful to Mr. Turgut Kut for a revised copy of his paper (1985: 195–214) on literary translations into Turkish in Armenian script, which offers some new evidence regarding the serialized version of *Mağdurîn Hikâyesi*. Kut draws attention to a copy, hitherto unnoticed, of the translation of *Les Misérables* in Armenian letters, published in book form in 1963 in Istanbul, attributed to Kirkor Çilingirian (by H. A. Stefanyan in his bibliography of Turkish books in Armenian letters [*1727–1968 Yılları Arasında Çıkan Ermani Harfli Türkçe Kitaplar Bibliografyası*, Erivan 1985: 69, no. 296]) which is almost identical with the serialized version and bears the same title. Indeed, the opening passage of the translation in Armenian script (Kut 1985: 198), with a few exceptions of phrases in a simpler idiom, is the same as that attributed to Münif Paşa. The evidence at this stage does not necessarily refute Münif Paşa's authorship; but in view of the then current practice of publishing Turkish translations first in

32 *Modern literature in the Near and Middle East*

Ottoman and subsequently in Armenian scripts and vice versa (op.cit.: 196–7, 198) it seems reasonable to assume that the translations in Armenian script, although intended for an Armenian readership, did not exist in isolation from those in Ottoman script and that there must have been considerable interrelation between the practices of Armenian translators of Turkish, some of whom were prominent members of the Ottoman intelligentsia, and of Turkish translators. This type of interrelation, which will no doubt become clearer with further research, brings to mind the need for a systemic analysis of translated literature in Turkish, incorporating not only texts in Ottoman but also those in Armenian and Greek scripts.

10 It has not been possible for me to find access to a copy of *Nâkil*. Özön (1941: 236) claims that this collection of translations also included some original short stories by Halid Ziya, but the author himself makes no mention of this point in his memoirs (Uşaklıgil 1969).

3 The Arab world

Pierre Cachia

Between the time when Arabic-speaking peoples acquainted themselves with Greek thought and the beginning of their modern renaissance, not one of their scholars or men of letters is known to have mastered any European language.[1] The contrast with the period we are considering could scarcely be greater. What happened was that the ascendancy gradually acquired by European powers, and demonstrated in many ways, but perhaps most glaringly on the battlefield, forced the Arab intellectual *élites* out of their illusions of self-sufficiency and re-directed their energies towards far-reaching reforms for which acquaintance with the achievements of 'the West' has been, and to a large extent remains, essential.

It was natural that the need should first have been felt at the heart of the Ottoman Empire, and in the eighteenth century military and administrative reforms were initiated there that were bound to widen in scope and to percolate to the Arab provinces. The stimulation, however, came more directly and dramatically to the Arabs with the Bonaparte expedition to Egypt in 1798, especially as the French came not only with an army disposing of the latest technology then available, but also with teams of translators and scientists who were enormously active during their short stay in the area. How deep and lasting a mark the French left is a matter of some debate (Brigman 1984: 10–11). Certainly their initiatives were meant to benefit them, not their temporary subjects; by these they were resented and at best imperfectly understood. Nevertheless to a leavening of open-minded men they had given a glimpse of a way of thinking and acting that bore the stamp of power and seemed to promise all manner of worldly benefits. It is no accident that the next ruler of Egypt, Muhammad 'Ali, set about creating an army on the French model, and he brought about far-reaching changes which he perceived to be necessary to such an army. Besides, the association of Western ways with power and success, first demonstrated by Bonaparte's forces, was all too soon to be confirmed, as virtually every part of the Arab world fell under the sway of one Western European nation or another.

34 *Modern literature in the Near and Middle East*

Western models have played so prominent a part in almost every aspect of the Arab *nahda* that one needs to guard against the assumption that the relationship was merely one of tutelage. It is worth recalling that 'Westernization' was a direction taken by local élites even before they had to bend to lasting foreign rule; that the driving force behind it was never submission but the desire for emulation as the surest means of self-assertion; that 'the West', adopted as an example, viewed as monolithic and often idealized, was an abstraction tinged by Arab perceptions of their needs and aspirations; that the imitation was intended to be selective, even though accompanied by grave miscalculations about what was jeopardized by the choices; and that the progress achieved was seldom on an even front. This last point bears a little elaboration. The most immediately impressive feature of modern Western civilization is its technological attainments, and men of will and action – like Muhammad 'Ali – were quick to see the benefits they would reap from adopting and imitating them. Appreciation of the intellectual curiosity that informs them came later, and acceptance of the philosophic and aesthetic values that are part of the same package, later still. At the same time, each act of accreditation of a foreign-inspired innovation facilitated the next, and by a process not of careful sifting but of validation by association, the civilization that had produced such clearly beneficial inventions as the steam engine and wireless telegraphy, came to be looked upon as holding the answers to virtually every problem of modern life (see Welch and Cachia 1979: 210–35).

By the end of the nineteenth century a new educated *élite* had come into being in the leading Arab countries that did not so much assert as take for granted the overall superiority of the West in almost every respect other than revealed religion. Here – as one of countless examples – is the way Jurji Zaydan (1861–1914) introduces a comparison between 'European and Oriental writers', specifically in connection with their influence on public affairs.

> It may occur to you on reading this title that there is no comparison between the two groups. You may say, 'What is there to link the outstanding writers of Europe, the tips of whose pens determine the politics of their country, with the writers of the East who cut no thread and knot together no rope?' I do not deny this, for I am not unaware of the immense disparity there is between the two countries in degrees of civilization, nor are we ignorant of the high status enjoyed by European writers who hold the reins of government either directly by occupying high positions, or else indirectly by the views they propagate among the leading parties. They are indeed the leaders of thought, the luminaries of civilization, the advisers of the State.
>
> (Zaydan 1900)

The Arab world 35

What strikes one most forcibly in this is that he speaks not of different civilizations, but of degrees of attainment in what he takes to be one civilization. This bespeaks a momentum of change in which many activities were a part. To pick translation out of these is necessary for purposes of analysis, but it is arbitrary, and would be a distortion if not accompanied by a reminder that it was intimately linked with the spread of printing and of journalism, to say nothing of a radical redirection of the priorities of writers and readers alike.

Thanks largely to the work initiated by Jak Tajir, who as librarian to the King of Egypt had access to first-hand material, we are well informed about who the early translators were and what they translated (Tajir *c*.1945; al-Shayyal 1950, 1951). Rather than reel off names and titles available elsewhere, one can concentrate on the main bursts of energy which seem characteristic of the movement. Even before entering into the period under review, it must be acknowledged that the first impulse was given by the ruler of Egypt, Muhammad 'Ali, whose interest was almost entirely in the technology needed by his army. He took advantage of previous efforts, reprinting twenty of the technical translations made in Turkey from about 1780 onward (Heyworth-Dunne 1940), and attracting to his service at least one of the Syrian Christian translators who had worked for the French, Father Zakhur Rahib (d.1831) (Moosa 1970). But with characteristic energy and single mindedness, he was able to carry the movement a great deal further forward (Heyworth-Dunne 1940: 332–3, 341–2). The lessons taught by foreign experts in his schools were translated on the spot, and after revision some were printed for wider diffusion. He demanded of students sent abroad that they translate the texts they used. Between 1809 and 1816 he had an agent scouring Italy and France for more books. In 1835, he founded a School of Languages that improved the quality of the work produced and ensured its continuity and extension, governmental initiatives never ceasing to play an important part in the movement. His and his immediate successor's right-hand man in the most onerous of these ventures was Rifa'a Rafi' al-Tahtawi (1801–73), who has good claims to be considered not only a translator and administrator of prodigious energy, but also the leading intellectual figure of his age. Needless to say, literary texts had no place in these early efforts but new ideas were being disseminated and Arabic was being forced into new moulds in order to express them; in time the combination was profoundly to affect linguistic habits.

To the stream thus started, a sizeable tributary came from Christian missionary work. Christian Arabs – mainly Syrians – were in fact to make disproportionately large contributions to several aspects of the *nahda* in its early stages, if only because (at a time when group loyalties were formed

36 Modern literature in the Near and Middle East

on religious rather than national or ethnic axes) they found it easier than did the Muslims to accept ideas originating in, or transmitted by, Christian Europe. The Anglican Church Missionary Society established a centre in Malta which began printing Arab texts for diffusion in the Arab world as early as 1825, and it was soon joined by an American Presbyterian Mission which in 1834 transferred its activities to the Lebanon. When this provoked a riposte from the Jesuits, more was done for cultural stimulation than for Christian witness. Of direct relevance here is that rival translations of the Bible were undertaken. An Arabic vision of the Gospels had been produced by the Medici Oriental Press in 1591 (Jones 1986), but it does not appear to have enjoyed a wide circulation among Arabs in the period with which we are concerned, for the only part of the Bible mentioned by Arabic sources as already available was the Psalms, first printed in Rome in 1614 (Abbud 1950: 49–50). In the new translations now commissioned, some of the foremost Arab writers of the period were engaged, alongside Western scholars, namely Faris (later Ahmad Faris) al-Shidyaq (1804–87), Butrus al-Bustani (1819–83) and Nasif al-Yaziji (1800–71). In addition, a number of Protestant hymns came into use in Arabic translations, which are of little distinction in themselves, but which can be seen to have affected the diction and – in secularized form – the notions of some later poets, mainly Syro-Americans (Moreh 1976: 24–32). Evidently these Christian translations were intended for a restricted public, but the training provided by such intensive labours in collaboration with Western Arabists was invaluable. Besides, some cross fertilization between Christian and Muslim communities was inevitable, especially as new bridges were built between them to some extent by freemasonry in the 1860s (op.cit.: 98–101), and later and on a larger scale by common national aspirations.

Probably the most significant surge forward occurred when individuals, no longer waiting for the promptings either of the State or of foreign missionaries, but directly addressing a new kind of readership, turned their hands to the translation or adaptation of texts for their literary or entertainment values alone. The first such effort on record (if we except Zakhur Rahib's *Fables* of La Fontaine, produced in France, and an anonymous *Robinson Crusoe*, printed in Malta (Moosa 1970: 210–11)), is Tahtawi's translation of Fénelon's *Télémaque*, not surprisingly the result of the period of retrenchment in governmental activity under 'Abbas, when Tahtawi was reduced to the headmastership of a primary school in the Sudan. This appears to have been a somewhat isolated pioneering attempt, but it was not long before the movement gathered strength. Muhammad Yusuf Najm (1961: 13–21) mentions some seventy French novels translated in Egypt between 1870 and 1914. Some English and Scottish

The Arab world 37

ones also (notably by Sir Walter Scott) also began to appear after the British had made their presence felt directly. The mushroom growth of non-governmental journalism – beginning with *Hadiqat al-Akhbar* founded in Beirut in 1858, but finding its greatest scope in Egypt thereafter – gave a great fillip to this development.[2] Short stories in particular found a ready outlet in journals and even in newspapers, but many novels also first appeared in serialized form in this ephemeral medium, or as special numbers of a periodical.

Understandably, literary histories make much of the masterpieces that then became known to an Arabic-reading public. The bulk of what was translated, however, was not of such a high calibre. It consisted mostly of sensationalist material – thrillers, spy and later detective stories, and penny dreadfuls. The reason is not far to seek: in a *genre* so new to the Arabs, taste was as yet unformed, and swung to the extreme opposite of the formal, diction-conscious literature in vogue until then. Thus a novel that created enough of a stir in 1880 to attract the attention of even Muhammad 'Abduh (1849–1905) was the now forgotten Pierre Zaccone's *La Vengeance*, translated by Adib Ishaq (1856–85) and Salim al-Naqqash, (d. 1884) (Pérès 1937: 267). The theatre also has some claims to pioneering efforts in this field, for the very first Arabic play produced in European style, Marun al-Naqqash's (1817–85) *al-Bakhil,* staged in Beirut late in 1847, is broadly based on Molière's *l'Avare,* and direct translations were soon to follow. Throughout the period under review, however, the live theatre was mostly in the hands of actor-managers whose interest was overwhelmingly in the performances, so that the translations, adaptations or original works which they wrote themselves or commissioned were hardly ever printed in their time, and therefore reached only their own patrons.

It was someone unconnected with any of the acting companies who was first to contribute substantially to written drama. This was a pupil of Tahtawi, Muhammad 'Uthman Jalal (1829–98) who, in addition to his onerous activities in government service as an official translator, a judge, and at one time a cabinet minister, gave the Arabs versions of at least one novel and (in verse) of the fables of La Fontaine, but whose heart appears to have been in the theatre. It is not clear whether it is to him we owe a volume of plays translated from the Italian under the title of *Al'ab al-Tiyatrat* advertised in *Wadi' l-Nil,* IV, 58 (11 Nov. 1870), the novelty of which is stressed in the notice, which is headed: 'A literary innovation and a work of Arabization, or the introduction of a new form of authorship in the Arabic language.'[3] What is certain is that he gave particular attention to the French classical theatre, translating five plays by Molière, and three by Racine. A remarkable feature of his work is that – even though not concerned with the box office – he went further than most writers for the

38 *Modern literature in the Near and Middle East*

theatre in that he chose colloquial verse for the rendering of even the loftiest tragedies.

Apart from such verse plays, the church hymns mentioned earlier, and the monumental but isolated translation of the *Iliad* by Sulayman al-Bustani (1856–1925) in 1904, poetry did not rouse nearly so much interest among translators as did the other *genres*. There are some notable approaches to European lyric poetry, such as Ahmad Shawqi's (1868–1932) translation (now lost) of Lamartine's *Le Lac* while he was a student in France between 1887 and 1891, but this does not seem to have made a profound mark even on his own poetry. As for the English Romantics, it was not until the appearance of the 'Diwan' school early in the twentieth century that they received much attention, and this mostly in journals. A book on Byron containing seven translations was published by Muhammad al-Siba'i in 1912, but the most ample and authoritative translations of English poems were by 'Abbas Mahmud al-'Aqqad (1889–1964), whose poems were not collected in book form until 1929 ('Abdul-Hai 1976: 120–59). It is tempting to relate this phenomenon to the general observation that the concrete products of the West had more immediate appeal than the abstract, but the simpler explanation is that the narrative and theatrical *genres* were totally new to high Arab literature, so that the only models to be followed were foreign ones, whereas poets had in their own culture a rich treasury to draw on.

That the public's interest in Western perceptions was constantly widening and deepening is indicated when translators on their own initiative went beyond texts that may be held to have entertainment value, to thought-provoking, philosophical ones. An important pioneer in this line was Fathi Zaghlul (d. 1914), who translated several of Jeremy Bentham's books – the earliest in 1888 – as well as sociological works by Gustave Le Bon and one by E. Demolins entitled *À quoi tient la supériorité des Anglo-Saxons?* (Tajir *c*.1945: 127–8). The significance of this last choice in British-occupied territory is self-evident. No less evident is the fact that such initiatives were quick to multiply.

The energy and initiative displayed by Arab translators is all the more impressive as they have had to face peculiar problems in addition to those familiar to any of us who have ventured into this field, perhaps with the comfortable assumption that fluency in two languages is all that is required. Shidyaq, one of the pioneers, expressed himself in verse on the subject:

> He who has missed out on translation knows not what travail is:
> None but the warrior is scorched by the fire of war!
> I find a thousand notions for which there is none akin
> Amongst us, and a thousand with none appropriate;

The Arab world 39

And a thousand terms with none equivalent.
I find disjunction for junction, though junction is needed,
A terseness of style when the text calls for
Elaboration, if the purpose is to be attained.
      (al-Sulh 1980: 144)

Obviously the most basic difficulty was the absence of a technical vocabulary not only in the new sciences but also in the new literary *genres*. In discussing novels in 1881, Muhammad 'Abduh had no word for the new *genre* other than a coinage from the French, *rumaniyyat* (Pérès 1937: 267), and for several decades thereafter *riwaya* often did duty for both a novel and a play.

A revealing example of the pressure under which an Arab intellectual had to function, of the ingenuity he displayed, and of the way that disparate endeavours supported one another is Shidyaq's fumbling for an Arabic rendition of 'socialist'. This was when, as editor of *al-Jawa'ib* and no doubt as rushed for time as most editors are, he had to comment on the activities of various left-wing groups in Europe, such as the French *communards*; he resorted to various circumlocutions such as *al-sushyalist al-qa'ilin bi'l-ishtirak fi'l-amlak* before finally coining *ishtiraki*, to which he was led by his own earlier translation of *The Acts of the Apostles* 4:32.[4] His coinage is now accepted, although Spiro's 1903 *English–Arabic Dictionary of the Colloquial Arabic of Egypt* still gave the transliteration *susyalisti* as an alternative. The challenge was compounded by the Arabs' long-established reverence for their language as both the medium of revelation and the repository of past glories. Because the issue has long been played out, it is easy to lose sight of the fact that there was a substantial body of conservatives to whom it was dogma that Arabic was perfect and complete and who – mainly between 1910 and 1925 – engaged the modernists in heated polemic (see Husayn 1937: 327–9), contending that only ignorance of its treasures made it necessary for them to add loan words or even new coinages to it. Furthermore, Shidyaq's hint in the verse quoted above about the difficulty of deciding what had to be abridged and what was to be elaborated shows that from the start Arab translators viewed their task not as one of slavish transposition, but rather as adaptations to the needs of a new public. When working on the Bible, he did not hide his impatience with his English collaborators over their excursions into etymology to decide the precise meaning of a word and their suspicion of stylistic flourishes suggestive of the Qur'an.

At the very least the choice of the material and the style in which it was rendered were reflections of prevailing standards. Thus in the translations produced in the nineteenth century, even when the story-line was fairly

40 *Modern literature in the Near and Middle East*

faithfully maintained, elaborately rhyming titles bear witness to the persistence of the stylistic preferences of previous centuries. A good illustration is *Paul et Virginie*, the climax of which has the heroine on a ship that is foundering within sight of shore, but refusing the chance of being saved by a sailor because she literally would rather die that take off her voluminous skirts; this was translated three times, and in Muhammad 'Uthman Jalal's (1829–98) version (Gibb 1928–30), becomes *al-Amani wa'l-Minna fi Hadith Qabul wa Ward Janna*. Not only are the protagonists given names that are phonetically close to the originals yet recognizably Arabic (although not without some strain), but the text is in rhymed prose throughout and studded with verses and philosophical reflections. He did the same with the play. A detailed comparison of his *al-Shaykh Matluf* with the first scene of Molière's *Tartuffe* (in Ballas 1985) shows that, having converted the characters to Islam, he then toned down both the criticism of the man of religion and expressions of children's rebellion against their parents, to say nothing of other arbitrary changes, all at some cost to the characterization and the dramatic effect.

At the other end of the spectrum are adaptations so free that a later critic (Zahlawi 1949) was to say that most of the writers of the first quarter of the twentieth century were 'creators when translating and translators when creating'. This is well exemplified by Mustafa Lutfi 'l-Manfaluti (1876–1924), who 'translated' several French novels although he knew no French. It is said that – at least at the height of the Romantic wave in the twenties and thirties in this century – hopeful young writers used to submit to journals effusions of their own labelled 'free translations', in the belief that the prestige of things Western was such that they stood a better chance of having them published than if they presented them as original works. Two of the terms used in this process were *ta'rib* and *tamsir*, literally 'Arabization' and 'Egyptianization'. These are not always used in a precise sense (for example, Muhammad 'Uthman Jalal's use of *ta'rib* for rendering into the colloquial is peculiar to him), but both imply a good deal more than mere translation into standard Arabic or Egyptian colloquial. Especially in the theatre, what was involved was nothing less than the transposition of the plot to an Arab or Egyptian *milieu*, and that entailed making the characters behave in accordance with locally acceptable customs. On the practices that took shape at about the time of the First World War, we have the personal testimony of the main architect of modern Arab drama, Tawfiq al-Hakim (b.1899):

> The 'Egyptianized' foreign play used to be described as *iqtibas* [literally 'lighting a piece of wood from a fire', hence 'acquisition' or 'adoption'], just as a foreign novel freely translated (as was done by

The Arab world 41

al-Manfaluti) was described as 'Arabization' – i.e. 'Arabization' [was the term used] in [fictional] literature, and 'Egyptianization' in the theatre. The word *iqtibas* was not used in the strict linguistic sense. In common usage, it meant that the play was neither pure creation nor pure translation. It consisted rather of transferring the topic from one milieu to another, changing the foreign characters into Egyptians or orientals.... .

Amongst us, theatrical *iqtibas* ... amounted almost to semi-authorship, especially in those long departed days when we used to write before women abandoned the veil. At that time, in our sex-segregated society, we had to alter the social relations that existed among men and women in an integrated one; so if we wanted to adapt a play in which a man met a women, we got into all sorts of complications ... . It was impossible to make the wife of so-and-so 'display herself' in front of the husband of such-and-such. We used to get round this in various ways, making this woman the maternal or paternal cousin of that man, and so on, so that men and women in all the plays of that period were related... . The alteration of social relations in accordance with the demands of our *milieu* in turn necessitated changes in the dialogue, the characterization and some of the situations of the play, adding up to considerable departures from the original... . These activities were tantamount to a school for the training of playwrights giving the opportunity to such of them as wished to spread their wings in the future to fly solo... .

None of us allowed himself to write the word *ta'lif* ['authorship'] unless that was what had actually taken place, or if his inventiveness and effort had reached the point of creative writing. If the play was translated, then the name of the foreign author was mentioned in all advertisements, no matter how valuable the contribution of the translator or 'Arabizer' was.... . But if this was not practicable – because the play had been so changed that it had become something else – then it was enough to say, *'iqtibas* from the pen of so-and-so'. It so happened that 'Abbas 'Allam wanted to get rid of this word *iqtibas* that had become customary, so he adopted – and perhaps he was the first to do so – that obscure, ambiguous formula when used by itself; 'from the pen of...' ... This practice spread among all writers until it came to seem natural.

(al-Hakim 1974: 212–1)

A small factor in the equation, but one usually overlooked, is that inherited Arab notions of plagiarism are not identical with Western ones, or at least

42 Modern literature in the Near and Middle East

more elaborately graded, the concern with choice diction being such that only word for word reproduction is condemned outright. The liberties taken by such as al-Manfaluti did give rise to some debate at the time, but in terms of what they contributed or failed to contribute to Arab readers, rather than of an obligation of faithfulness to the originals. A view closer to that prevailing in the West was bound to develop in time, but it is not entirely irrelevant to say that when I started to teach in Egypt in the 1940s, some of my students used to submit essays that were direct translations of easily traceable encyclopedia articles and the like, and – although an all-too-common human motivation is not far to seek in such deceptions – they were genuinely taken aback at the vehemence of my denunciations: they argued that 'the words were their own'.

Indeed many Arab translators impress us as much with their selfless devotion as with their energy. Those who assume an immediate economic motivation behind every initiative would find it hard to explain Muhammad 'Uthman Jalal's persistence in the use of the colloquial, for he could find no patronage for his first book and had to publish it at his own expense, and even the most celebrated of his plays, the adaptation of *Tartuffe*, was never staged in his lifetime (Ballas 1985: 8,13). Much is owed to the determination or out-and-out idiosyncrasies of some men of learning. A French–Arabic dictionary that deserves to be better known is that of Mohammad El-Naggary Bey (1903, 1905), a judge who – besides giving special attention to legal terms – was so fond of La Fontaine that under such words as *loup* or *renard* he reproduces the whole of the relevant fables with Arabic verse translations, most signed by the same Muhammad 'Uthman Jalal. Mikha'il Nu'ayma's (1889–1988) *cri de coeur* has often been repeated:

> We are in a stage of our literary and social evolution in which many spiritual needs have awakened – needs which we did not feel before our contact with the West. As we have not the pens or the brains that can fulfil those needs, let us then translate! And let us honour the translators because they are the mediators between us and the larger human family.
>
> (Khemiri and Kampffmeyer 1975; see also Badawi 1975: 182.)

In trumpeting his call, he was unnecessarily and unjustly derogatory of his contemporaries' creative powers, but he was also putting into words the broad concern with culture evinced by those already engaged in the task he advocated.

One more aspect of our question deserves consideration. We all know that a shelf laden with books is no guarantee that the owner is a well-read man. How much of the translators' sizeable output was in constant currency, impinging upon young minds and helping in their formation?[5]

The Arab world 43

Once again, we have cause to be grateful to Tawfiq al-Hakim, the city-bred son of a judge, for his candid account of the effect some foreign works had upon him in a period extending roughly from 1910 to 1918, when he was still a schoolboy. After recalling his delight at his mother's recounting of folk tales, he writes:

> There began to appear on the market European narratives translated by the Syrians who were good at languages and had been educated in the missionary schools. My mother became fond of these too, and re-told them to us as she had done with previous ones... .

> My pride at passing the primary school certificate at the first attempt had the effect of making me irresponsible, lax, contemptuous, and neglectful [of my studies] – this to say nothing of the lack of constraint I experienced as my parents were away from time to time, and the existence of the 'American Cosmograph' [showing] episodes of the adventure serials that entranced me: after the Zigomar serial came the episodes of Fantomas! Add to all this the Rocambole novels which were available for hire in bookshops... . I had only to pay five piastres a month to become a member, and I could then hire and read the twenty parts of a long story like Rocambole, or the collected works of Alexandre Dumas *père*.

> I remember that I bought out of my pocket money a book newly translated into Arabic: it was by the English philosopher Spencer, on ethics, and I felt proud to be reading philosophy, although I do not now believe that I understood anything worth mentioning in this book or its likes. Our knowledge of English was not such as to enable us to read English philosophical books, and even if it had been, we would not have found the wherewithal in our pockets. As for the Arab philosophers, such as al-Ghazali, Averroes and Avicenna, no one ever directed us to them... .

> The only [literary] translations that had ever appeared then were the first part of Hugo's *Les Misérables* translated by Hafiz Ibrahim in grand Arabic style which we used actually to intone. Then there appeared a poor translation of Tolstoy's *Anna Karenina* which was incapable of suggesting to us that it was of lasting literary quality. It is true that Fathi Zaghlul had translated something by Montesquieu, perhaps *L'Esprit des Lois*, and my father had many copies of this which he was to distribute, but that book did not attract me at the time...

> What I was really eager to read at that age was the plays which we used to see at the Opera House and other theatres, ...but despite long searches

44 *Modern literature in the Near and Middle East*

I found only a few, poorly printed, such as *Buridan, The Martyrs of Love* i.e. *Romeo and Juliet* with all its poetry, *Othello,* and then *Louis XI* with which I was greatly delighted, memorizing from it the entire part of Louis. But I did not find *Hamlet* although I was eager to read it as it had been staged in Arabic, nor did I find a single one of the Molière plays which 'Uthman Jalal had translated into colloquial verse.

(al-Hakim 1974: 81, 122–3,143–9)

This may be compared with the books that another eminent writer of about the same age, Taha Husayn (1889–1973), remembers as having been on sale in the shops of provincial towns. These were mainly devotional works and hagiographies, books of magic, and some folk tales, with not a single translation among them (Paxton 1981: 50). The contrast is striking. And yet even Tawfiq al-Hakim's list is not particularly impressive, nor did the difference ensure that he become a man of wider culture than his more humbly born contemporary. Even more decisive were their temperaments, their consciously made choices, their mastery of languages giving them direct access to other literatures. Indeed Taha Husayn was to comment on one of his own translations:

The aim of those who transpose poetry from one language to another is not to convey to their readers a true picture of it. The aim must be to give their readers an inkling of it, and to lead those who have the time and the resources to get to know it, and to drink of it at the source

(Husayn 1920: 50)

At a time when elements of two cultures were meeting, vying, clashing or intermingling, translation was a revealing index of new directions and new priorities, as well as an important channel for the diffusion of new information and new perceptions; but it was only one of a complex of interacting forces produced by and producing change.

NOTES

1 On how limited the interest of Muslims in Europe was, see Lewis (1964) and (1973: 92–114).
2 Pérès (1937) lists one journal after another that included translated narratives.
3 'bid‘a adabiyya, wa qit‘a ta‘ribiyya aw idkhal uslub jadid min al-ta’lif fi’l-lugha’l-arabiyya,' quoted in Ramitsh (1980: 153).
4 On Shidyaq's labours as a translator, see al-Sulh (1980: 144–65). The particular example cited is discussed on 160–2, where, however, the Biblical passage is wrongly identified as Acts 4:23–5.
5 For a present-day critic's estimate of the most significant translations, see 'Awad (1972).

4 Iran

Julie Meisami

The early development of modern Persian literature has been discussed in a number of important studies, beginning with E.G. Browne's writings on contemporary literary trends and encompassing several important recent works on both general and specific aspects of the subject.[1] In particular, we have learned much about journalism and the rise of the journalistic essay, early experiments in prose fiction, and efforts to introduce European-style drama into Iranian cultural life. Yet a number of important questions concerning this period remain unanswered: questions which relate to the specific role played by literary translation, and the related phenomenon of literary adaptation, in the evolution of modern Persian literature. To what extent did this movement create new models on which writers might base their own compositions, and to what extent did it encourage new audiences which would be receptive of, nay, come to demand, such compositions? It is to aspects of these questions, rather than to a more general consideration of the literary production of the period, that this chapter is addressed.

The history of literary translation in Iran has yet to be written.[2] No historian of modern Persian literature has, to my knowledge, given it more than cursory mention, although most assume that translation played a vital role in the birth of the literature, providing generic and stylistic models for writers seeking alternatives to traditional forms. Moreover, no systematic attempt has been made to survey and classify the works translated, to assess the quality of these translations, to identify the audiences for whom they were intended and establish the extent and nature of their reception, or to evaluate their effect on contemporary literary development. While it is beyond the scope of the present chapter to seek to remedy this gap in Persian literary history, it will attempt to outline the general dimensions of the topic, and to suggest some directions for future research.

This age of literary translation and adaptation, and of the accompanying literary modernization, is bounded by two significant dates: 1854, the date

46 *Modern literature in the Near and Middle East*

of the death of Qa'ani, last of the great neo-classical poets of the Qajar period, and 1921, the date of the publication of Jamalzadah's *Yaki Bud va Yaki Nabud* and of Nima Yushij's *Afsanah*. Although this demarcation of the period may stretch a point with respect to precise chronology, it is, I think, justified, since the two writers whose careers frame, anticipate and synthesize its development are singularly representative of the change in literary tastes and circumstances which took place during these nearly seventy years – a change motivated largely by increasing contact with the West, a major vehicle for which was, of course, translation.

The two writers themselves illustrate the historical and intellectual development of this contact. Qa'ani, as Jan Rypka notes, was 'the first of his contemporaries to be acquainted with European languages, especially French – from which he translated a text-book on botany – and to a smaller extent English' (Rypka 1968: 330); but this minimal acquaintance with the West, which was essentially practically oriented, had no visible effect on the style of the court poet who is considered perhaps the best representative of the literary tastes of the Qajar era. These tastes were subsequently to fade and be replaced by other, perhaps more 'Westernized', literary preferences – a development reflected not only in the writings, but also in the person, of Jamalzadah, who lived most of his life abroad, whose first book was published in Berlin, and who, though drawing upon his native culture for much of his subject matter, was stylistically inspired by Western models and exemplifies both the impact of the West on Persian authors, and the attempt to return to native soil via Western routes.

The dates in question are significant for other reasons. The *Dar al-Funun*, which produced an abundance of both translations and translators, was founded in 1852, two years before Qa'ani's death; Reza Khan's coup, which was to alter radically the entire fabric of political and social existence, took place in January 1921. Qa'ani's age is characterized, again by Rypka, as a time 'when the old was moribund and the new as yet unborn' (ibid.); the literary renaissance of the Constitutional period is seen (by Vera Kubičkova, for example), as an important aspect of the transformation of Iran from medieval to modern (op. cit.: 362). These dates thus represent contrasting poles of cultural and literary life between which both writers and audiences moved in the course of this period which saw the gradual replacement of court literature, with its ornate, repetitive and highly Arabized styles, by a literature which could speak to a wider audience in a language closer to their own.

The literary translations and adaptations produced during this period may be divided into three general categories: prose (including both non-fiction and fiction, in the form of histories, novels, *novellas* and short

Iran 47

stories); drama (in both verse and prose), and poetry. Each category presents specific problems with respect to questions of audience and reception and of style. The first books translated from European languages into Persian (as the example of Qa'ani illustrates) were textbooks dealing mainly with military and other sciences for students of the *Dar al-Funun* and other colleges. To these were gradually added, first, translations of historical works and, later, of novels, beginning with historical novels such as those of Alexandre Dumas *père* (a number of which were translated by Muhammad Tahir Mirza (d. 1897), who also translated Lesage's *Gil Blas*), pedagogical novels such as Fénelon's *Télémaque* and, Defoe's *Robinson Crusoe*, Swift's *Gulliver's Travels* and eventually, more entertaining works such as the science fiction novels of Jules Verne and Conan Doyle's stories of Sherlock Holmes. Especially popular was the translation of Sir John Morier's *Hajji Baba* – which Browne numbered 'amongst the books which had an effect in bringing about the National Awakening' (Browne 1983: 22) – by Mirza Habib Isfahani (d. 1897); he also translated Molière's *Le Misanthrope*. Among the translators produced by the *Dar al-Funun* was the prolific Muhammad Hasan Khan Sani' al-Dawla I'timad al-Saltana (d. 1896), author of numerous historical works, whose translations included *The Memoirs of Mademoiselle de Montpensier*, *The Life of Christopher Columbus*, *The Swiss Family Robinson*, and Molière's *Le Médecin Malgré Lui*. As is clear from their appellations, these early translators were, if not of aristocratic descent, attached to the court or from the upper echelon of the religious classes; thus though they were progressively inclined, their literary style still reflected the influence of courtly tastes, and their translations were in general not intended for a broad popular audience.

Concerning these early translations, Yahya Aryanpur observes:

> Unfortunately, the translators of these works did not pay sufficient attention to observing the literary characteristics of the original texts, and sometimes adorned them with Persian verses, in the manner of Iranian story-writers. Further, along with translations of masterpieces and outstanding examples of classical literature they translated into Persian banal works such as The Memoirs of Madame [sic] de Montpensier... by the French novelist Ponson de Terrail. Even more amazingly, they wrote prefaces and introductions to trivial, commercial crime novels, in which they discussed the necessity of spreading knowledge and acquiring education and skill, and praised the generosity and assistance of the sacred royal personage who was inclined towards such high and lofty goals. But despite these shortcomings, the translators... were obliged to follow the style of

48 Modern literature in the Near and Middle East

writing of the original texts, and, as far as they could, write simple and natural passages, and refrain from introducing the rhymed and ornamented phrases formerly considered necessary features of literary prose. Thus, had these translations not existed, today's literary style, which is close to the language of common conversation and at the same time enjoys the beauty of European literary prose, might never have come into existence.

(Aryanpur 1961: I, 260)

In this evaluation, quite apart from appearing to contradict himself (how, for example, did translators who 'were obliged to follow the style of writing of the original texts' at the same time pay insufficient 'attention to observing the literary characteristics' of these texts?) Aryanpur does not, it seems to me, consider some basic questions concerning these early efforts. He treats all those mentioned as very much of a piece, taking no note of differences in style between translators and, indeed, between individual works; he fails to identify those 'classics' presumably worth translating, while declining to investigate the reasons for translating 'trivial' works or, indeed, to evaluate the effect of such translations; and he ignores the important question of reception: who, in fact, read these translations, and for whom were they intended? It is this question that I shall address first.

A substantial number of early translations appeared, or first appeared, in the burgeoning periodical press, not only following the Constitutional movement of 1906 but significantly earlier. As early as 1871 Muhammad Hasan's translation of Jules Verne's *Adventures of Captain Hatteras* appeared in instalments in the 'scientific part' of the journal *Iran*, an official Government organ devoted to court news and reports on the personal doings of the Shah (Browne 1983: 50). The much-maligned *Memoirs of Mademoiselle de Montpensier*, as Browne informs us, 'were translated and added as a supplement to the Year-book, or *Sal-nama*, of A.H. 1313 (AD 1895-6), and ... on their publication, aroused the extreme anger of Nasiru'd-Din Shah, who caused all copies of them to be confiscated and destroyed' (op.cit.: 22). *Tarbiyat*, published in 1896-7 and edited by Mirza Muhammad Husayn Zaka' al-Mulk Furughi of Isfahan was a journal which had, in Browne's words, 'a special literary importance in regard to its style, composition, and quality of eloquence... and enjoyed a considerable influence, though its practice of flattering and praising contemporary notables detracted from its literary value'. It featured translations, in the form of *feuilletons (pa varaqi)* at the foot of its pages, which included works by Bernardin de Saint-Pierre and Chateaubriand (op.cit. 61-2). The journals *Farhang*, which appeared in the 1880s, and *Ganjinah-i Funun*, published in the early 1900s, were also

Iran 49

important for their publication of translations. Indeed, it would appear that translations were a less important feature of the post-Constitutional press, which was characterized mainly by journalistic essays and editorials, political and social satire, and original poetic contributions. We can deduce from this that the readership towards which translators aimed their efforts, while drawn from wider circles than that of the court, was still limited to the educated classes and that, despite the increase in literacy during the period and the fact that literature was no longer restricted to aristocratic circles, this readership could hardly be said to be a popular one.

A glance at the list compiled by Muhammad Ali Tarbiyat of books produced (both translations and original compositions), during the period between the establishment of printing and the Constitutional movement, indicates the tastes of this readership as regards both original compositions, and translations and adaptations (op.cit.: 157–66). Several important tendencies are seen. First, in both categories prose works predominate; the major poetic composition is Mirza Aqa Khan Kirmani's (d. 1896) *Salarnamah*, modelled on the *Shahnamah* of Firdawsi. Second, in both categories (exclusive of scientific and technical works) pride of place goes to works of historical import, both factual histories and historical novels, though science fiction novels (chiefly those of Jules Verne), also figure importantly. Third, the primary source language of translations and adaptations is French; curiously, no mention is made of the translations of the Arab novels of Jurji Zaydan by 'Abd al-Husayn Mirza Qajar which appeared during this period, nor of the *Thousand and One Nights*, though the translations from Azari Turkish of the plays of Akhundzadah are included, as are a number of translations from the Russian by 'Abd al-Rahim Taliboff. Fourth, original works show little if any influence of the translations, but are mainly based on traditional models; they do, however, betray a common interest in historical and ethical matters (admittedly traditional Persian preoccupations) as well as with new scientific achievements and accounts of travel to strange lands.

We may deduce from this that the translators of this period directed their efforts at a steadily, if slowly, increasing reading public interested not so much in European literature as such – much less in its 'masterpieces' or 'classics' – but rather in what that literature might offer in terms of information about the historical past, of Iran as well as of Europe (we may note a concurrent trend in Arabic literature reflected in the historical novels of Jurji Zaydan), and about European scientific progress (a topic of ever-increasing practical as well as intellectual concern). They were also concerned to satisfy the hunger of this growing reading public who were interested not only in serious matters but in being

50 *Modern literature in the Near and Middle East*

entertained and who were turning, for that entertainment, not merely to traditional verse romances and anecdotal compilations but to newer and more exotic sources; and they were undoubtedly curious as to what European literature might provide in the way of models for the achievement of their dual purpose of instruction and delight.

One point emerges clearly: that interest in the West, while concerned with adapting those materials which were of immediate relevancy or utility, also carried with it a strong element of 'exoticism' in its curiosity about an unfamiliar culture. In the light of this, Aryanpur's objection that early translators were as inclined (if not more so) to translate trivial works as they were the classics requires some re-evaluation. The scandal produced by the publication of such a 'banal' work as Ponson de Terrail's *Memoirs of Mademoiselle de Montpensier* would seem to indicate that its translation was not undertaken without some forethought: of interest because of its ostensible 'historical' content, it presumably also provided sufficient revelation of the strangeness of Western ways both to titillate the seekers after exotic entertainment and to shock those with more straight-laced or orthodox inclinations. Clearly such considerations provide the focus of interest here, rather than any 'literary' merit such works may possess. (One may compare similar trends in European literature, where the 'exotic' East was portrayed, graphically if unrealistically, as a land of fleshy delights and sensual enjoyments beyond the reach of the more 'enlightened', if more stolid, Europeans.) Further, then as now one may detect an obvious and understandable tendency to translate popular and exciting best-sellers (such as the novels of Ponson de Terrail) rather than classics, many of which enjoyed little popularity among their native readership during the period in question.

As for Aryanpur's second objection – that translators wrote seemingly incongruous 'prefaces and introductions to trivial, commercial crime novels, in which they discussed the necessity of spreading knowledge and acquiring education and skill,' as well as praising their royal patrons – this too would seem to testify to their dual goals of instruction as well as entertainment. Praise of patrons was undoubtedly dictated by economic and political necessity; but that such prefaces contained more serious discussions suggests that the translator, having found, so to speak, a captive audience attracted to the book because of its entertaining qualities, took advantage of the opportunity to deliver a didactic message. Didacticism, in any case, is by no means foreign to the Persian literary tradition.

Another factor influencing the choice of works translated was the extent to which translations or adaptations might lend themselves to treatment of the specific political and social circumstances of Iran. A case

Iran 51

in point is the translation of Morier's *Hajji Baba*, first published in Calcutta in 1905. As H. Kamshad has shown, the Persian version of this work is more an adaptation than a translation; 'the translator,' he observes, 'has shown no scruples in altering or supplementing the story whenever fancy takes him, or rather, as is mostly the case, whenever the changes suit his purposes.... Compared with the English text, the Persian reveals many minor alterations on almost every page' (Kamshad 1966: 24). Passages are also added or omitted at will. The existence of such often radical modifications would seem to leave the translator of Hajji Baba open to Aryanpur's criticism that early translators paid scant attention to following their originals, to the extent that they even 'adorned them with Persian verses' in traditional fashion. Leaving aside the question of poor translation, which is not unknown in any age, one is tempted to ask whether such 'adaptations' did not speak more directly to an Iranian audience than would a more literal but less readily grasped rendering.

This appears all the more likely when we recall that many of these modifications were intended to present criticism of the Persian scene. As Kamshad states:

> In his description of court manners, his exposure of *mullahs*, dervishes, and so on, and with his own additions, the translator has in fact made the Persian text much more subtle and funny than the original. Another great distinction of the Persian edition is the wealth of well-known and proverbial poems that are fitted into appropriate places. This, together with a multitude of popular, everyday sayings and the frequent verses quoted from the Koran and the Traditions, indicates the translator's mastery of Persia's literature, life, and language, as well as his knowledge of Islamic institutions.
>
> (op.cit.: 26)

It is quite likely this very aspect of the book which made it play an influential role in the Persian cultural awakening; and its style, as several scholars have noted, has had a lasting effect on the development of modern Persian prose (op.cit.: 27; Bahar 1337: 366).

But did such prose translations indeed stimulate writers to emulate the models they provided during this early stage? The fact is that, with isolated exceptions, the true impact of this 'age of translation and adaptation' was not felt until the succeeding period. The exceptions anticipate the area in which this impact was first perceived: that of the development of the novel.

The first major attempt at an Iranian novel was the *Siyahat-namah-i Ibrahim Beg* by Hajj Zayn al-'Abidin Maraghah-i (1837–1910), the first volume of which appeared in Cairo, presumably some time prior to its

52 *Modern literature in the Near and Middle East*

publication in Istanbul, in 1888. Generally considered to be the first novel composed on the European model,[3] the fact that it is, like many European novels of the nineteenth century, a work in three volumes would appear to support this notion. But while it indeed suggests an attempt to imitate European pedagogical novels such as Fénelon's *Télémaque* (and was perhaps modelled on the Arabic translation of that work),[4] it also demonstrates the re-forming of foreign models into Eastern modes, the 'Orientalization' of style and the concern for the native past which are typical features of much of the literary production of this period. It bears close affinities with Muhammad al-Muwaylihi's *Hadith 'Isa b. Hisham*, which began serial publication a decade later, and testifies to shared preoccupations, if not, indeed, to common sources. (In this connection it may be recalled that it is from Egypt, not Europe, that Ibrahim Beg – unlike his spiritual kinsman in Jamalzadah's 'Farsi Shakar Ast' two decades later – returns to Iran, only to find that promised 'Paradise', that Eastern 'best of all possible worlds', woefully imperfect.)

The Islamic literary tradition does not lack for models for this sort of social criticism, presented within the framework of an imaginary journey which is at once physical, spiritual and educational; al-Ma'arri's *Risalat al-Ghufran* provides an obvious example, but the Persian tradition also boasts many didactic works which incorporate social criticism along with their pedagogical function. It is, in fact, carry-overs from the Islamic tradition which account for the 'weaknesses' which, in Kamshad's view, affect the work (Kamshad 1966: 19–20): Ibrahim Beg's 'fantastic illness', dealt with in the second volume, which modifies, by transferring to a non-courtly context, a recurrent topic of Persian historiography (the king, distressed by the evils afflicting his domains, falls ill and dies of grief), and the collection of maxims, poetry, proverbs and the like (another favourite device of Persian historical and ethical writing) which make up its third volume. Such features proclaim the author's indebtedness to his native tradition as well as to European models; and if he failed to achieve a fully satisfactory synthesis of these elements, it is scarcely surprising in view of the great diversity of elements represented in this work.

A more tangible example of the influence of translations may be seen in the development of the historical novel, the first efforts towards which appear in the period of political crisis between the Constitution and the coup of Reza Shah, and which again exemplifies the blend of newly awakened interest in, and nostalgia for, the historical past, with the use of European models for the treatment of such material. Of these early efforts, Aryanpur states that since their authors were 'stimulated to novel-writing solely through reading ... foreign novels,' and lacked themselves a thorough knowledge of novelistic techniques, 'most novels which

Iran 53

appeared were imitations of foreign novels, and so weak and without substance that they are not worth the effort of reading' (Aryanpur 1961: II, 238). The earliest of these works, however – Muhammad Baqir Khusravi's *Shams u Tughra*, a three-volume novel published in Kirmanshah in 1909–10 and based on life in thirteenth-century Fars under the Ilkhanids – was described by Jamalzadah as 'unequalled among the literary works of the recent centuries. Without doubt the only book worthy of translation into foreign languages as a model of modern Persian literature' (Kamshad 1966: 45).

Though such praise may seem excessive, *Shams u Tughra* is a milestone in modern Iranian literature. An important feature of the work is its accuracy of historical detail in portraying the typical characters, customs and localities of the time in which it is set, and the accounts of which are, as Kamshad observes,

> based on historical data, often quoted word for word by the author and cited by him in a bibliography. In his care for historical accuracy, Khusravi made a completely new departure from older Persian literature: he brought to his work what may be described as a Western approach, engaging in extensive researches before committing pen to paper.
>
> (op.cit.: 44)

In this respect Khusravi's method recalls that of the historical novels of Walter Scott or Alexandre Dumas (of which latter author's works Persian translations were published beginning in the 1890s). It also parallels the similar efforts of Zaydan in Arabic; and Zaydan's example may indeed have influenced the author of *Shams u Tughra*, particularly since Khusravi's novel (unlike those of his successors in the next decades) dealt with medieval, not pre-Islamic, Iran, and he himself had translated Zaydan's 1898 novel *'Adhra' Quraysh* into Persian. His goal, like Zaydan's, appears to have been primarily instructive: the presentation of history by means of an entertaining story. The style is, in Aryanpur's words, that of Iranian story-tellers, 'in the form of quotations and anecdotes, with events in chronological order,' heavily larded with Arabic and with poetic quotations – features which 'place it out of reach of the majority of Iranian readers' (Aryanpur 1961: II, 251), supporting the contention that literary production at this stage was still not destined for the 'masses', and that it represents a blending of native and foreign in which traditional literary elements are still strongly represented.

The succeeding decades saw the publication of more historical novels: Shaykh Musa Nasri's *'Ishq u Saltanat*, on Cyrus the Great, in 1919, Hasan-i Badi's *Dastan-i Bastan*, drawn chiefly from the Shahnamah, in

54 Modern literature in the Near and Middle East

1921, and San'ati-zadah Kirmani's *Dam-gustaran ya Intiqam-khakan-i Mazdak*, on the last days of the Sassanian empire, in the same year. All these depart from the model provided by *Shams u Tughra* by going to the pre-Islamic past for their historical inspiration, while the first betrays its reliance on European sources, as well as models, by its use of transliterated French forms of the Old Persian names. All exemplify the desire to escape from the limitations of contemporary political and social life and to identify, on the one hand, with the glorious past, as contrasted with the repressive and backward present, represented by their sources, and on the other with the 'progressive' West which furnished their generic and stylistic models.

The development of the short story also owes much to the influence of Western models, although the way opened by Jamalzadah in 1921 was not to be well-trodden until some time later, beginning with Sadiq Hidayat, and did not become truly popular until after the Second World War. Few examples of either translated or original short stories can be found during the early period (with the exception of political satires, which constitute a different *genre*), and they appear to have been outnumbered by both translated and original novels, at least prior to 1921. Although a discussion of Jamalzadah's achievements is beyond the limits set for this paper, it is necessary to point out that his appears to be the first programmatic attempt to make literature – which he, no less than his predecessors, viewed as possessing a vital pedagogical function essential to social and cultural progress – accessible to a wide reading public, by treating the concerns of this public in a language, and through subjects, readily familiar to them. In so doing he managed to achieve a fruitful blending of native and foreign elements; for although story-telling is an ancient Persian art, its traditional forms could not produce dramatic effects comparable to those achieved by nineteenth-century European short stories, with their increased attention to plot, character, and realistic detail. Jamalzadah was able to combine the stylistic features of the European short story with materials drawn from Iranian life to create a truly Persian form that appealed to a wide readership. That his work had little immediate effect was largely due to the hostile political climate of the times; but his efforts represented the culmination of this early period of literary revival and paved the way for that which followed.

The other two categories of literary translation and adaptation, drama and poetry, are of manifestly less significance in this period, and will be given a correspondingly briefer treatment. Interest in the drama began, significantly, with the foundation of the *Dar al-Funun*, in one corner of the grounds of which a small European-type theatre was erected.[5] Tarbiyat's list mentions translations from the French of several plays of

Molière, as well as the Persian rendering of seven Turkish plays by Akhundzadah, examples which call attention to a basic problem during this early stage: the fact that Iran possessed no native drama of the European type, and (unlike the case with prose) had few useful indigenous models upon which to draw. Native dramatic forms included various types of comic sketch as well as the more important *ta'ziyah* religious drama based on the events surrounding the martyrdom of Husayn but incorporating other topics as well. While exposure to European culture caused an increasing awareness of the potentials of drama both for entertainment and as a vehicle for social and political criticism, many of the models popular in Europe failed to strike a responsive chord, especially among audiences unaccustomed to their conventions. This situation is perhaps best illustrated by the example of the translations of Molière.

Early renderings of Molière were in fact adaptations rather than translations, and contained many alterations intended to make the plays more attractive and comprehensible to Iranian audiences. Aryanpur observes that 'not only in the period of Nasir al-Din Shah, but afterwards as well, the taste of Iranian translators was such as to adapt the comic themes of Molière and others, and render them freely, so that they would correspond to the tastes of Iranian readers and audiences' (Aryanpur 1961: I, 342). Browne, however, considered that the translation of *Le Misanthrope* attributed to Mirza Habib Isfahani and published at Constantinople in 1869–70 under the title *Guzarish-i Mardum-Guriz* followed the original quite closely, despite the Persianization of its characters, the substitution of Persian idioms or proverbs for French and the clear influence of contemporary Turkish translations of Molière (Browne 1928: IV, 459). A reading of this translation, however, conveys an impression of intense artificiality and lack of relevance to the Iranian scene, despite the efforts of its translator to make it meaningful to its Iranian audience.

One cause of difficulty for such translations may have been, in some cases at least, the use of verse, giving a stilted quality to the dialogue as well as having unavoidable associations with both court poetry on the one hand, and folk poetry on the other which inhibit its creative use in this unfamiliar *genre*. Prose translations of Molière fared little better, however, and it may well be that the comedy of manners of seventeenth-century France was transferred with difficulty to nineteenth-century Iran. For whatever reasons, Molière's plays had little appeal to audiences who were, admittedly, little prepared for the reception of drama in general.

Somewhat more successful were the translations by Mirza Ja'far Qarajahdaghi of the plays of Mirza Fath 'Ali Akhundzadah from Azari

56 *Modern literature in the Near and Middle East*

Turkish into Persian which appeared in Tehran in 1874.[6] Dramatic writing and production had begun in Turkey earlier than in Iran and provided a model for many Persian writers, especially those who resided in Turkey at one time or another – not least because conditions in nineteenth-century Turkey were far closer to those of contemporary Iran than were the manners of seventeenth-century French aristocrats. The plays of Akhundzadah are among the earliest dramas written in imitation of European styles. The translator's introduction – which begins with one of those irksome encomiastic passages, dedicated to Nasir al-Din Shah – reflects the didactic preoccupations that have traditionally characterized Iranian literature:

> The purpose of this compilation and translation is moral instruction, contained in a comic discourse in simple, colloquial style, on the model of European theatre, in the practical form of representation: that is, the recognition of what is good and bad in man's nature, by means of observing types and resemblances, and hearing lively, unexaggerated, and natural speech.
>
> (Akhundzadah 1970: 64)

The comparatively greater realism in these dramas as compared with adaptations of Molière, testifies to the desire to represent contemporary conditions faithfully; it also reflects the author's familiarity with contemporary Russian literature, as well as his experience of performances of Russian and European drama which he witnessed while in Tiflis, and which inspired his own dramatic efforts. This greater awareness of the technical, as well as the literary and didactic, requirements of drama undoubtedly contributed to the greater success of Akhundzadah's plays, not least because in them, for the first time, the problem of representing direct and natural speech on the stage was directly confronted.

Akhundzadah's plays, far better received by Iranian audiences than those of Molière, led to imitations, for example by Mirza Aqa Tabrizi, the author of several plays first published in 1909 (though composed around 1870) and formerly attributed to Mirza Malkum Khan.[7] These plays lack the attention to the technical requirements of drama which marked those of Akhundzadah, and are therefore difficult to perform. It should be noted, however, that performance was not the only purpose of such compositions; indeed, political and social conditions did not often favour performance, and many of the dramas of this period – which in Browne's opinion were 'primarily political pamphlets rather than plays' (Browne 1928: IV, 463) – were not only seldom performed, but were probably intended more to be read than seen. In any case, the drama failed to become firmly established in Iran during the period, and it was only considerably later that new efforts succeeded in bringing more vigour and more popularity to this *genre*.

The third and final category of literary translations, and perhaps the most limited in scope during this period, was that of poetry. Interest in translating poetry began late, towards the end of the nineteenth and particularly after the beginning of the twentieth century. As translations of poetry are difficult to locate and identify, being scattered through various works including anthologies, the collected works of various writers, periodicals and the like, it is correspondingly difficult to form an accurate assessment of them or of their contribution to poetic modernization during this period; on the basis of the limited evidence available, however, that contribution seems to have been minimal. Poetic translations appear to have been directed towards an even more limited audience than were prose translations; they still retain the élitist aura which characterizes much of the poetry of the period, even, unfortunately, that dedicated to political and social reform.

The difficulties involved in translating poetry are, of course, far greater than for prose forms such as the novel, for the translator has three equally unsatisfying options: to translate the original verse into prose (the simplest but least effective, and least aesthetically pleasing, method); to render it in a traditional verse form (in which case he is more likely to produce an adaptation than a translation); or to develop new poetic styles or modify existing ones in such a manner that they will correspond more closely to the characteristics of the original. This is the most difficult task of all, and it requires that verse translation and poetic modernization take place simultaneously.

As is well known, throughout the Middle East it was poetry, with its long-established traditions, which most firmly and for the longest time resisted modernizing influences. Early efforts at modernization were largely confined to the subject matter, rather than the form, of poetry; although as early as 1870 there were, for example, discussions in the periodical press concerning 'prose poetry' (*shi'r-i mansur*),[8] these seem to have had little effect on actual composition or, for that matter, on translation. The feeling that the traditional poetic forms require no modification, while the traditional content is unacceptable and must be radically altered, was enunciated by Mirza Aqa Khan Kirmani (1853–96) in the preface to his *Salarnamah*. Referring to his conclusion of this work 'with an epic ending, after the fashion and method of the poets of Europe,' he proceeds to castigate the traditional poetry of Persia, not on the basis of its formal or stylistic conventions – the eloquence and beauty of which he is at pains to praise – but with regard to the moral effects of its content:

58 *Modern literature in the Near and Middle East*

The result of [the poets'] exaggerations and hyperboles has been to concentrate falsehood in the simple natures of the people.

The result of their praise and flattery has been to stimulate kings and ministers to the commission of all manner of vile and foolish actions.

The result of their metaphysics and mysticism has been nothing but a crop of brutish idleness and sloth, and the production of religious mendicants and beggars.

The result of their odes to roses and nightingales has been nothing but the corruption of our young men's morals, and the impelling of them towards smooth cheeks and red wine.

The result of their satires and *facetiae* has been nothing but the diffusion of vice and immorality and the promotion of sinful and reprehensible practices...

[By contrast] the poets of Europe ... have brought poetry and the poetic art under so sound a scheme of arrangement, and have made their verses so conformable to the laws of logic that they have no other effect than to illuminate men's ideas, dispel vain legends, endow their minds with insight, admonish the careless, educate the foolish, castigate the ignorant, incite men's souls to virtuous deeds, reprove and turn aside their hearts from vicious actions, admonish them and inspire them with zeal, patriotism and devotion to their people.... Of the Persian poets the only one whom European men of letters praise is that same Firdawsi of Tus, the verses of whose Shah-nama, although in some places they are not free from hyperbole, do nevertheless in some degree inspire the hearts of Persians to patriotism, love of their race, energy, and courage; while here and there they also strive to reform their characters.

(Browne,1928: IV, xxxiv–xxxv)

It was to fulfilling this didactic function of poetry that many of the early translations and adaptations, like many original compositions, were directed, as they addressed contemporary political and social issues. Due to the predominance of the classical forms, however, much of this poetry (with the notable exception of that intended for publication in the periodical press) was inaccessible to audiences who lacked the high standard of education required for its appreciation. The relative scarcity of poetic translations during this period also suggests that little of the poetry of nineteenth-century Europe lent itself to the depiction of the Iranian situation; and such poems as were translated were, in general, so 'Persianized' as to lose all sense of the original.

A number of poets representative of various poetic tendencies of the period became translators and adaptors of European poetry, including Adib al-Mamalik Amiri (1866–1917), whose own poetic style was influenced by European poetry to the extent that he introduced foreign words and motifs and images drawn from European literature into his poetry; Yahya Dawlatabadi (1864–1940), who experimented with European rhyme schemes as well as with syllabic versification, and whose translations from French poetry are some of the earliest in Persian; and Abu al-Qasim Lahuti, an important political poet.[9] The example of Iraj Mirza (1874–1924) provides an illustration of this early stage of poetic translation.

An important poet who employed traditional forms, Iraj Mirza knew several Eastern and European languages, and became one of the chief translators of European literature. Of his efforts F. Machalski states, 'He translated Schiller and La Fontaine, and his interpretations although somewhat free, enriched the treasury of Persian literature with new and lasting values' (Machalski 1965: I, 129). Indeed Iraj's translations are so free, so liberally Persianized with regard to both style and content, as to defy recognition as examples of European poetry. His consistent use of *masnavi* verse is perhaps justifiable in the case of translations from La Fontaine, where it provides a form analogous to that of the original; but the renderings themselves retain few of the characteristics of the original texts, and are virtually indistinguishable from the kind of exemplary tales characteristic of the medieval *masnavi* tradition. In short, while they are successful Persian poems, there is little to suggest their value as translations. The same is true of the unfinished verse romance *Zuhrah u Manuchihr*, a free adaptation of Shakespeare's *Venus and Adonis* which, while closely following the original text with respect to its episodes, descriptions and so on, transforms the mythological tale into a typical Persian verse romance, though without either the stylistic sophistication or the ethical relevance of medieval representatives of that *genre* or, for that matter, of Shakespeare's Renaissance adaptation (Aryanpur 1961: II, 401–13).

Iraj's translations and his original compositions demonstrate his commitment both to traditional forms of poetry and traditional conceptions of story-telling for didactic ends. It is not for nothing that, in one of his *qit'ahs*, he boasts, 'when I mount the steed of discourse, my stirrupmate is Farrukhi and my fellow rider 'Unsuri,' and concludes, 'I am the seal of the poetic art, as Muhammad was of prophecy' (Mirza, n.d.: 174). His own efforts at poetic innovation did not go beyond the introduction of foreign words and phrases into Persian poems, and an experiment with rhyme which – while announced as 'the foundation of a new poetic style' – is, as he himself notes, a variant on the *mukhammas* form which in truth required no special European inspiration (op.cit.: 9).

60 *Modern literature in the Near and Middle East*

Thus it cannot truly be said that in this period poetic translations played an important role in the literary revival; moreover, the effect of European influence on the Persian poetry of the time is negligible, and is generally restricted to attempts to adapt European (chiefly French) rhyme schemes into Persian in place of the monorhyme or couplet. The efforts at greater realism which were often confused with the insertion of European words and phrases in a Persian poem of traditional form, was a practice which must certainly have placed such productions even further beyond the reach of a broad segment of the public. It is only at a later stage, beginning chiefly with the efforts of Nima, that significant attempts at poetic modernization are seen.

This admittedly brief and general survey suggests that the role of translation and adaptation in introducing new *genres* and creating new literary styles must be thoroughly re-evaluated upon a systematic basis. Certainly the dissatisfaction with the florid style of courtly writing exemplified by such writers as the Qa'im Maqam Farahani and the Amir Kabir was intensified by increased contact with the outside world (and not only with Europe) as well as by the needs of educational institutions and, later, of the periodical press.[10] Such factors undoubtedly contributed to an increased concern with finding new stylistic and generic models to meet these new needs and to increased receptiveness to foreign models from the 'progressive' West.

No comprehensive assessment of the precise contribution of the movement of translation and adaptation to the literary revival can be attempted, however, until a thorough analysis of the materials involved has been accomplished. This presents a number of difficulties. First and foremost, the accessibility of the translations themselves is greatly limited, due largely to the circumstances surrounding their publication. Many works were published abroad, in Egypt, Turkey, India and Europe, and must be sought in a variety of locations. Many were published in ephemeral form, in the periodical press or as *feuilletons*, or privately printed, and are thus not recorded in bibliographical sources. In the case of poetic translations, such examples as have been published in the *divans* of their translators (as in the case of Iraj Mirza) are often without date, attribution, or indication of the language of the original (and sometimes not identified as translations at all).

Some attempt to survey and classify these translations and adaptations must, however, be made before embarking on an analysis of their contents and style, or a comparison with their originals. In this connection, special consideration must be given to translations from languages hitherto largely ignored, such as Arabic (an especially rich field for comparative studies) and Russian. Another question which has received little attention is the

Iran 61

extent to which Persian renderings of specific works were themselves based on translations, and the degree to which this influenced their perception and treatment.

A final important problem is that of reception. The readership for which translations and adaptations were intended obviously determined their selection; equally obviously, the audience for such works was by no means a unified one, though a certain standard of literacy was clearly assumed. Selection determines the availability, and hence popularity, of certain *genres* as opposed to others; to what extent did this affect the general perception of European literature, or, for that matter, of European customs and *mores*? An investigation of this question involves sifting through a great variety of potential, and largely ephemeral, documentation – diaries, journals, letters, as well as the more obvious book reviews and introductions to translated and original works – before one can answer both this and the related question of what works Iranian writers might have been familiar with either through translations or direct contact. What led Aqa Khan Kirmani to conclude that European poetry is highly moral but classical Persian poetry is not, and to find in this a justification for his own imitation, not of European models, but of the *Shahnamah*? What inspired Iranian writers to consider certain European works as morally instructive whereas contemporary European critical opinion might well deny such a quality to the very same works? Was it European technical progress which led Akhundzadah to consider European drama an educational tool leading directly to such progress, or Jamalzadah to find its secret in Europe's devotion to narrative fiction? Was it, in fact, the influence of European literature, or the basic preconceptions of such writers, arising largely from their own indigenous literary tradition, that led them to the opinion that any literature which is worthwhile must be didactic, despite what might be considered abundant evidence to the contrary from European literature itself, not least from those very works which found greatest popularity in Iran? Few of these questions have even been asked; much less has an attempt been made to answer them; but only when such issues have been dealt with, and when detailed analysis has been made of the entire field of literary translation and adaptation during this period, can a valid assessment of its impact both on its own time and on future generations be made.

NOTES

1 To the works listed here should be added Alavi (1964); for bibliographies see especially Kamshad (1966) and Rypka (1968).
2 Cf. the works cited by Professor Pierre Cachia in Chapter 3, pp 35 ff.

62 Modern literature in the Near and Middle East

3 Kamshad terms it 'the first attempt to write a Persian novel on the European model' (1966: 17); Aryanpur calls it 'the first original social novel on the European model in Persian' and compares it with Gogol's (then unfinished) *Dead Souls* (1961: I, 315). On the difficulties surrounding the dates of composition and publication of this work, see also Bakhash (1978: 359, n.2).

4 This translation, by Rifa'ah Rafi' al-Tahtawi, appeared before the Persian rendering by 'Ali Khan Nazim al-Mulk, published in 1887.

5 See Aryanpur (1961: I, 336–7). Nasir al-Din Shah founded the *Takiyah-i Dawlat*, modelled on the Albert Hall in London, in 1869. Theatre was severely opposed by conservative elements and most theatres were forced to close or converted to other uses.

6 The original was published in Tiflis in 1859; a Russian translation by the author of several of his plays had appeared even prior to their publication in Turkish, in 1853, in a Russian periodical (Aryanpur 1961: I, 353–4).

7 See Aryanpur (1961: I, 358–61); see also Browne (1928: IV, 463) and Kamshad (1966: 14) for the attribution to Malkum Khan.

8 The *Ruznamah-i 'Ilmiyah-i Dawlat-i 'Aliyah-i Iran* for 27 Sept. 1870 contained a discussion in an earlier issue of the *Ruznamah-i Millati*; see Browne (1983: 95–6).

9 See Machalski (1965: I, 50) on Amiri, (62–63) on Dawlatabadi, and (140) on Lahuti.

10 Kamshad suggests the widespread introduction of printing techniques resulted in a decline in 'decorative' aspects, not only of book production, but of literary style: 'With lithography, the art of decorating the written word started to decline, and the movement began to make communication simpler and more direct' (1966: 11).

5 Modern Hebrew

Tudor Parfitt

The very title of this chapter suggests that in some sense we are here dealing with a rather special case. Side by side with 'Turkey', 'The Arab World' and 'Iran' one might have expected some other geographical entity. It is clear that for the period under discussion this entity could hardly have been Palestine or the 'Land of Israel', but, as we shall see, it could not have been anywhere else either. Thus the title of this deliberation is merely 'Modern Hebrew'. From the second half of the eighteenth century when modern Hebrew literature can best be viewed as having originated, to the outbreak of the First World War, it enjoyed no exclusive association with any one geographical location. Indeed, at any given time there was a variety of geographical locations for the production of this literature throughout the Jewish diaspora. Not all of the locations were of any real significance: at the end of the eighteenth century, for instance, London was home to one fine Hebrew poet, Ephraim Luzzatto (1729–92), who certainly had no literary circle with which he could share his literary passions. Yet at the same time Hebrew literature had real centres of production elsewhere which included publishing houses, a periodical press, groups of Hebrew writers and critics, and so on, but these centres moved from time to time for political or social reasons (Abramson and Parfitt 1985). Indeed, one of the most remarkable things about the early history of modern Hebrew literature is its peripatetic nature.

The first centre of production of a body of modern, secular Hebrew literature reflecting European *genres* was Prussia, where in the second half of the eighteenth century an effort was made to adapt the German *Aufklärung* for Jewish consumption while adapting Jewish social and religious practices to facilitate the absorption of these Western ideas. The most important vehicle for the Jewish enlightenment (the *Haskalah*) at this time, was a Hebrew monthly, *Ha-Meassef,* which was published intermittently in Koenigsberg between 1784 and 1811 and which included numerous translations from world literature.

64 *Modern literature in the Near and Middle East*

Hebrew literature on German soil was to be short-lived. In 1783 Moses Mendelssohn (1729–86), the leading figure of the German *Haskalah*, finished his famous *Biur*, the translation of the Pentateuch from Hebrew into German with a Hebrew commentary. This translation may have had the effect of binding German Jews to the Hebrew Bible but it also introduced them to the pleasures of reading German, for certainly many German Jews learnt German from the *Biur*. In any event, no sooner had German Jewry been introduced to a secular literature in Hebrew than they started abandoning it for German literature, so much so that a hundred years later one would have been hard-pressed to find any German Jew capable of writing Hebrew *belles lettres*. However, the *Haskalah* and the Hebrew literature which was its most significant expression were to find more fertile soil further east, first in Galicia, then in Lithuania and Belorussia, and towards the end of the nineteenth century in the Black Sea port town of Odessa, which became the principal centre of Hebrew creativity until after the Russian Revolution of 1917 when Palestine became the only important centre of Hebrew literary activity (apart from a few years in the 1920s when Berlin became the short-lived home of a number of expatriate and mostly East European Hebrew writers).

If, then, the first point of significance is that Hebrew literature had no one centre of production with which it was exclusively associated, the second point is that for the majority of the period its geographical location was not primarily in the Middle East, even though the importance of Palestine as a centre of Hebrew writing grew dramatically from the 1890s on. To what extent then can Hebrew literature be viewed as an oriental or Middle Eastern literature during this period? Do the factors which influenced the development of the indigenous literature of the Middle East also affect Hebrew? Indeed is the title of Part I: 'The Age of Translation and Adaptation' as relevant to Hebrew as it is to Arabic, Turkish and Persian?

Clearly there are points of difference which must be stressed before any comparative conclusions can be drawn. The geographical difference is clear: for the majority of our period, Hebrew literature was primarily produced in Europe. The periodization of modern Hebrew literature is also quite different from that of the other literatures under consideration. The renaissance of Hebrew as a modern literary language began in 1750 and perhaps even earlier. Similarly the processes of translation and adapting Western literature and adopting its *genres* had been under way for a hundred years before the same processes started in the Middle East. Consequently, the period under discussion, notwithstanding the fact that an enormous amount of translation and adaptation was still taking place, was also a period in which Hebrew literature in its modern form saw its

Modern Hebrew 65

first flowering (a flowering which inevitably owed much to the work of the translators and adaptors of the previous century). Thus it was that the first Hebrew novel, Abraham Mapu's (1808–67) *Ahavat Tziyyon* (The Love of Zion) was published in 1853 (Patterson 1964a), while the great classics of this modern literature – the works of Mendele, Ahad Ha-Am, Bialik and Tchernikhovski were to be written over the next fifty years. In other words modern Hebrew literature was reaching something akin to maturity at much the same time as other Middle Eastern literatures, in their modern form, were beginning their developments.

It is tempting to view Hebrew literature, at least until about the turn of the century, as a European literature *simplicitur*, but this would be misleading in a number of ways. Until 1914, modern Hebrew literature, no matter where it was written, was addressing itself to a readership which was primarily located in the Russian Pale of Settlement – the strip of land between the Baltic and the Black Sea where Jews were permitted to reside. The Jews of the Pale were in many respects an oriental community. Until the end of our period they were the product of a traditional Jewish education in which pride of place was given to the study of the Hebrew Bible and to the Hebrew and Aramaic commentaries on it. The *Haskalah* was thus addressing a potential constituency whose intellectual formation had been moulded by ancient literatures of the Near East. The Jews of the Pale said their prayers in Hebrew; if they were educated they wrote in Hebrew and enjoyed an intellectual life which was based upon the Aramaic of the Talmud; of course, they spoke Yiddish but only infrequently did they have any competence in the languages of the countries in which they lived. Their seasonal festivals were in response to climatic conditions prevailing not in Russia but in Palestine. In addition, it was common for Jews to have an immeasurably sounder grasp of the geography and natural history of the Land of Israel than those of their European environment. Classical Hebrew is rich in words describing the natural phenomena of ancient Israel, but the lack of interest of the Yiddish-speaking Jews of Eastern Europe in their natural environment can be adduced from the paucity of such words in Yiddish. The Hebrew literature of the nineteenth century frequently alludes to both the Jews' ignorance of the natural world and their ignorance of the geography of Europe. Yet clearly almost every Jew had some idea of the importance of the mountains, rivers and plains of Palestine.

It can be said then that the Jews of Eastern Europe, at least in some intellectual sense, inhabited a world which had more to do with the Land of Israel than with Berdichev, Brody, Lublin, Pinsk, Shklov and the other cities of the Pale. But naturally the Land of Israel which, in this limited sense, they inhabited, was an idealized one. There was certainly an almost

66 *Modern literature in the Near and Middle East*

total ignorance of the conditions prevailing at the time in the real Palestine. This can be illustrated by a correspondence which took place in the pages of *Ha-Maggid*, the first Hebrew weekly journal, which had been founded in Lyck in 1856 by Eliezer Silbermann. The correspondence, which was protracted and scholarly, was between two rabbis who were discussing the ways in which the Jerusalem Temple would be reconstructed once the Jewish people had been restored to the Land of Israel. The correspondence came to an abrupt end when a reader pointed out that two not insignificant Islamic structures stood on the site of the Temple Mount! The image of the Land of Israel projected by the sacred writings of Judaism was to be more important than the reality for some time to come. Even when, in the 1880s and 1890s, Jewish writers living in Palestine, such as Yoel Moshe Salomon, A. M. Luncz, Ze'ev Ya'avetz and Shmuel Raffalowich started writing short stories on Palestinian topics, the old diaspora image of *Eretz Yisrael* was much more potent than the perceived reality of Ottoman Palestine (Yardeni 1967). The stories seem to be drawn directly from the Hebrew pastoral tradition: the Arabs are barely mentioned. In view of the centrality of *Eretz Yisrael* in the imagination of the Jews of the Pale it is perhaps no coincidence that the first Hebrew novel, a work which was to draw more Jews to secular literature than any other Hebrew book in the nineteenth century, was a romantic tale set in Israel at the time of Hezekiah. Much of the above is surely sufficient justification for the treatment of modern Hebrew literature side by side with the literatures of Iran, Turkey and the Arab world in this symposium. Certainly the Hebrew literature of the period was addressing a readership which in a number of ways was not dissimilar to the consumers of the new Westernized literatures in the Islamic world. A major difference was the incidence of literacy which was extremely high among the Jews of central and Eastern Europe and low in the Muslim world.

The main objective of the literature of the *Haskalah* was to encourage the Jews of the Pale in the paths of reason, good taste, and the enjoyment of the beauty of the natural world. One of the curious features of this literature is that reason was being upheld by Jewish writers as a panacea for the ills of mankind at more or less the same time as in Western Europe new philosophies and systems were beginning to replace those based primarily on rationalism. 'Good taste', the expression used by the *maskilim*, was intended to indicate correct modes of behaviour, dress, speech and deportment, all of which were modelled on Western European norms. The obsession with nature came about through the belief that the Jews over the centuries had cut themselves off not only from the outside world in terms of ideas but also from the outside world in literal terms.

Modern Hebrew 67

Often the outside world was perceived as the world outside the *yeshivah* or *beit ha-midrash*. What the *maskilim* sought then was to change Jewish ideas, morals, sensibilities and behaviour in the light, largely, of eighteenth-century ideas. Naturally, not only the original literature of the *Haskalah* but also the translations and adaptations into Hebrew were to serve these objectives.

One of the chief weapons in the armoury of the *maskilim* was a belief in the connection between ethics and aesthetics. It was believed that exposing the Jews to beauty in whatever form would lead to a regeneration of the Jewish spirit. It was largely for this reason that the chosen vehicle for the ideas of the *Haskalah* was the Hebrew of the Psalms and Prophets rather than the Rabbinic Hebrew which had been in use for most written purposes for centuries. The deliberate exclusion of the later forms of Hebrew placed unnecessary limitations on the emergent literature. The language of the Bible was simply incapable of transmitting the fruits of the European renaissance without violence being done both to itself and to the subject matter. Mapu, whose first novel represents the highest literary achievement of the neo-classical period, was one of the first to recognize that if it were to survive, the literature would have to harness all the linguistic resources available: the Hebrew of the Mishna, the Talmudim, the medieval period. The process of adapting the linguistic resources of the various strata of Hebrew for the purposes of creating a viable modern literature of original work as well as translations went on for much of the nineteenth century and well into the twentieth. Yet by the end of the nineteenth century a workable synthesis had been created. The new style, referred to at the time as the *nusah*, was a flexible and expressive tool which carried with it rich possibilities of allusion.

There was one respect in which the language of many of the important Hebrew works of this period was deficient: there was still no spoken language from which to draw dialogue, slang usage, folk expressions and the like. However, from the 1880s onwards Palestine became the centre of the revival of Hebrew as a spoken language chiefly as a result of the activity of Eliezer Ben Yehudah (1858–1922) (often called the reviver of the Hebrew language), and partly as a result of the linguistic diversity of the Jewish communities in Palestine which created the need for a common spoken language. The *Biluim*, a pioneering group of Russian Jews who settled in Palestine in 1882, and the settlers who followed them became the keenest supporters of Ben Yehudah's attempt to revive Hebrew as a language of speech and it was in the schools of the early colonies that the phenomenon of spoken Hebrew spread most rapidly. Although the possibilities of a totally 'revived' language were only exploited fully in the Hebrew literature of the 1920s and 1930s, even in the period before the

68 *Modern literature in the Near and Middle East*

First World War a body of Hebrew drama and, of some significance for our present purposes, a body of translated drama, was produced in Palestine reflecting nascent speech patterns and helping to spread and encourage the rise of spoken Hebrew.

In medieval times a prodigious amount of material was translated from Latin and Arabic into Hebrew, but for two hundred years or so before the beginning of the *Haskalah*, a period during which there was little symbiosis between the great centres of Jewish population in Europe and the non-Jewish world, very little was translated into Hebrew. But during the period of the *Haskalah*, translation was consciously viewed as a tool of the greatest possible importance and there were frequent calls in the Hebrew periodical press for more and better translations from Western literature (e.g. *Bikkurei ha-'Ittim* (1827–8). Thus from around 1780 until the end of the period under discussion there was an enormous amount of material translated from English, French, Italian, Spanish, Russian and, particularly, German. In the early years of the *Haskalah* the translations which appeared in *Ha-Meassef* and elsewhere were chosen, seemingly, on the basis of the literary importance of the writers concerned. Thus early issues of the journal from the 1780s included poems by some of the outstanding writers of the eighteenth century, such as the dramatist Petro Metastasio (1698–1782), the biologist and poet Albrecht von Haller (1708–77) and the rococo writer Salomon Gessner (1730–88). Thereafter there was a general tendency until the end of the *Haskalah* period for the quality of the translations to improve but for the quality of the original literary matter to deteriorate. Perhaps this was because in the first years of the *Haskalah* its aims were served rather precisely by the best of the literature which was being written at the time whereas later, although the aims of the *maskilim* had not substantially changed, the central preoccupations of European literature had. A further reason was perhaps that as the *Haskalah* moved east, it moved further and further away from the sources of Western culture, and few of the later Hebrew journals of the nineteenth century seem to have had their finger on the literary pulse of Europe as surely as did *Ha-Meassef*.

For all its revolutionary quality, the purpose of the *Haskalah* and the movement that followed it was to modify Judaism and 'Jewishness' not to destroy it. Even the 'enlightened' were obsessed and driven by their Jewishness. Thus even while the *maskilim* were looking at the intellectual products of the Western non-Jewish world, they were anxious, perhaps more than anything, to see what that world had to say about Judaism. Consequently it is not surprising to discover that a large proportion of the literary works which were translated or adapted into Hebrew during this period were dealing with Jewish themes. In the post-*Haskalah* period,

Modern Hebrew 69

when many Hebrew writers were affected to some extent or another by the ideas of *Ḥibbat Zion* and later Zionism, many works in European languages reflecting these ideologies were published in Hebrew. Thus translations were made of Disraeli's *David Alroy* (tr. by Abraham Rekowski in 1880) which dealt with the leader of a messianic movement which flourished among the mountain Jews of Persia in the twelfth century, and *Tancred* (tr. by Judah Levin in 1883) which, beside its strong messianic elements, had on offer the compelling personality of the Jew Sidonia, one of the novel's more attractive characters. George Eliot's so-called 'Zionist' novel *Daniel Deronda* was translated by David Frischman in 1894 and Israel Zangwill's *Ghetto Tragedies*, with its obvious relevance for central European Jewry, was translated by S. L. Gordon in 1896. Needless to say, Theodor Herzl's works were translated: *Der Judenstaat* by M. Berkowitz in 1896 and *Das Neue Ghetto* by R. Brainin in 1898. Most of these works have some literary merit. The same, however, cannot be said of *The Jew*, a cumbersome novel by the eighteenth-century English writer Richard Cumberland (1732–1811) which was translated by Joseph Brill in 1878. Its only importance is that its central character, a Jewish moneylender called Sheva, insulted in the book as 'the merest muckworm in the city of London', is finally revealed for what he really is: a protector of widows, a friend to orphans and a lover of humanity at large.

European poetry on Jewish and biblical themes was translated with equal enthusiasm. Menahem Litinsky translated Klopstock's *Der Tod Adams* which appeared in Prague in 1817. In 1843 a dramatic poem on the life of Moses by the French poet Madame S. F. de Genlis was translated by David Zamoscz under the title *Ro'ot Midyan o Yaldut Moshe*; in 1845 the Austrian poet Ludwig August Frankl's (1810–94) cycle of poems entitled *Rachel* was translated by M. E. Stern; in 1884 Byron's *Hebrew Melodies* was translated by the talented Hebrew poet Y. L. Gordon (Yalag) (1830–92) (some had been translated in 1824 by M. Letteris (1800–71) in his *Ayyelet ha-Shaḥar*); while in 1892 S. Raffalowich published in Jerusalem a translation of Milton's *Paradise Lost*, making its relevance to his Jewish readership obvious by calling it *Toledot Adam ve Ḥava* (the story of Adam and Eve). In view of the dubious worth of almost all *Haskalah* verse, it is perhaps significant that throughout the nineteenth century there are no Hebrew volumes devoted to the poetry of, for instance, the great English metaphysical poets or the French imagists.

Two of the more successful translations into Hebrew during the period of the *Haskalah* were in the realm of drama. Lessing's *Die Juden* and *Nathan der Weise* were widely read in their Hebrew translations. *Nathan der Weise* was translated sensitively by A. B. Gottlober (1810–99) in 1874, although it had already been translated in 1866 by Simon Bacher (or

70 *Modern literature in the Near and Middle East*

Bacherach) (1823–91). The play was ideally suited for the purposes of the *Haskalah*. Nathan, a character inspired by Lessing's friend Moses Mendelssohn, is made in the play to uphold the principles of tolerance, brotherhood and humanity against the relatively bigoted spokesmen for Christianity and Islam. *Die Juden* translated by Gottlober in 1873 never achieved in Hebrew the popularity of *Nathan*. Nonetheless, its significance from a Jewish point of view is considerable. Its publication in 1749 marks the first time that a Jew was presented in a more or less favourable light in a European play. Racine's *Athalie* is another play with an understandable attraction for Jews influenced by the *Haskalah*. Based on the biblical story of Ataliah it is almost bleakly moral in tone. It was first translated into Hebrew in 1770 by the Dutch Jewish writer David Franco Mendès. In his translation, as Glenda Abramson has put it, 'he constructed characters similar to Racine's, dressing them, however, in the spiritual garments of Jewish thought and including elements typical of the Jewish literature of that period' (Abramson 1979: 22). A further free adaptation of *Athalie* was done by Letteris in 1835. Entitled *Geza Yishai* it was subtitled 'an imitation after Jean Racine'. Perhaps the freest of all the Hebrew adaptations of Western literature is Letteris's working of Goethe's *Faust* which was published in Vienna in 1860. Entitled *Ben Avuyah*, the original is completely transformed: the play is Hebraized in every sense: the characters and their *milieu* are Jewish and anything of Christological significance is of course omitted. It was not unusual for Judaization to affect both the title and the contents of translations: Salkinson's able translation of Shakespeare's *Othello* (1874) and *Romeo and Juliet* (1878) were respectively entitled *Itiel* and *Rom ve-Ya'el*!

The process of Judaization was clearly calculated to make the products of Western literary culture acceptable to the readership of the Pale of Settlement. Jews had fairly severe misgivings about the gentile world at large and knew nothing of its *literati*. It is said that Rabbi Zevi Hirsch Chajes of Zolkiew was so distressed at hearing about the death of Goethe that his congregation became aware of his sadness if not of its cause during the morning prayers in the synagogue. Eventually the rabbi told them what was the source of his unhappiness: that Goethe had passed away. Needless to say no one in the congregation had ever heard of Goethe; but they took it for granted that some great Jewish sage had departed this life. So this news spread all over the town that Rabbi Goethe had died – and everyone said the proper benediction!

During the earliest stages of the *Haskalah*, *Ha-Meassef* had included a large number of translations from Western, and particularly German literature, of a morally edifying character. This trend was to continue throughout the nineteenth century with the publication of endless

Modern Hebrew 71

translations of works whose message was consonant with the didactic aims of the *Haskalah*. Thus English poetry of the Age of Reason continued to be read in Hebrew translation after it had been forgotten in its native land. Edward Young (1683–1765) was particularly popular. The sentiment behind his well-known line 'Reason the root, fair faith is but the flower' was close to the *maskil's* heart. Similarly, literary works of various sorts that stressed the central place of nature in man's affairs were translated avidly. Many of the nineteenth-century collections included poems by Ewald Christian von Kleist (1715–59), a friend of Lessing's, whose best work was a celebration of the world of nature. Another popular work was *Harmonie de la Nature* by Bernardin de Saint Pierre, translated by Joseph Hertzberg and published in Vilna in 1850. It is no coincidence that the greatest *belle-lettristic* Hebrew writer of the nineteenth century, Mendele Mokher Seforim (Shalom Ya'akov Abramowitsch) (1835–1917) produced an enormous Hebrew compilation of western works on scientific subjects entitled *Toledot ha-Teva'* (The History of Nature) which was published in three parts between 1862 and 1873.

Notwithstanding the specific interests of the *maskilim* before 1880, and the ideological stance of the Hebrew writers and translators thereafter, the range of the material that was translated into Hebrew throughout the period of the *Haskalah* and in the years prior to the First World War was extremely wide. In 1845 a Hebrew translation of Bunyan's *Pilgrim's Progress* translated by S. Hoga was published in London; Defoe's *Robinson Crusoe* (translated by M. Rumsey) was published in Vilna in 1861. Translations appeared of Victor Hugo: *L'Âne* by W. Gronich, Vienna, 1881; *La Guerre Civile* by J. Lewner, Warsaw, 1896; *Le Dernier Jour de la Vie d'un Condamné*, Warsaw, 1898. Jules Vernes was also translated: *Vingt Mille Lieues sous les Mers* and *Voyage au Centre de la Terre* by Issac Wolf Sperling; *The Divine Comedy* was published in Trieste in 1869, *Don Quixote* in Lemberg in 1871, Frug's poems in Warsaw in 1898, and so on. A comprehensive list clearly lies beyond the limited scope of this paper. But probably the most popular literary work to be translated into Hebrew during the nineteenth century was Eugène Sue's novel *Mystères de Paris* translated by the prolific *maskil* author Kalman Schulman (1821–99) and published in Vilna in 1857. Sue's treatment of the Christian legend of the wandering Jew, his *Le Juif Errant*, translated by Simhah Posner and published in Warsaw between 1856 and 1873 also had something of a following. But it was *Mystères de Paris* which really captured the imagination of the Hebrew readers of the Pale. It is often said that it was this novel, along with Mapu's *Ahavat Zion*, which formed the most effective gateway from the traditional texts of the *yeshivah* to the new secular literature. Sue's contrived and labyrinthine plots had a very

72 *Modern literature in the Near and Middle East*

considerable influence on the Hebrew novelists of the late *Haskalah* period. Mapu, indeed, considered Sue to be the greatest exponent of the art of the novel. Nonetheless, Mapu had considerable reservations about the translation of Sue's novels into Hebrew. It has been suggested that his own novel, *Ahavat Zion*, owed so much to *Mystères de Paris* that he feared that the publication of Sue's work might damage his reputation (Patterson 1964a: 103).

The amount of Western literature which was translated into Hebrew between 1850 and the 1880s was so enormous that it has led one critic to conclude that during this period Hebrew literature was an *übersetzung-literatur* (Meisels 1922). This is to some extent true although it must not be forgotten that during this period there was a very considerable production of original Hebrew literature as well: indeed it was a period in which the Hebrew novel made enormous progress with works by Mapu, Smolenskin, Braudes, Leinwand and Sheikewitz (Patterson 1964b).

One of the more curious features of the development of modern Jewish literary languages is the connection between the revival of Hebrew as a literary language and the parallel revival of Yiddish. Clearly the revival of Yiddish had a great deal more in common with the other revivals which took place in nineteenth-century Europe (e.g. Slovak, Croatian, Estonian, Bohemian, Norwegian etc.) insofar as in the case of Yiddish a commonly spoken mother tongue was turned into a language of literature, whereas in the case of Hebrew a literary language which had been used in the main for religious, scholarly and administrative purposes, was adapted for use as the vehicle for a modern secular literature. One of the ways in which this was achieved was via a symbiosis between Hebrew and Yiddish. This can best be perceived in the work of Mendele Mokher Seforim who has the unique distinction, perhaps, of being considered the father of two modern literatures. In 1863 Mendele published his first Hebrew story, *Limedu Hetev*, which was expanded into a novel, *Ha-Avot ve-ha-Banim*, which was published in Odessa in 1868. It had been argued that the latter was modelled on Berta Friedrich's *Zwei Geschlechter* which appeared in 1863. However, the following year, Mendele, unwilling perhaps to contend any longer with the difficulties imposed by trying to write modern literature in classical Hebrew, abandoned Hebrew for Yiddish. The Yiddish novels he wrote over the next twenty years still stand as arguably the greatest monuments of Yiddish literature. However, between 1890 and 1911, Mendele undertook the task of recasting these novels, notably *Dos Vinshfingeril* and *Fishke der Krumer*, into Hebrew. The first appeared as *Be-Emek ha-Bakha* in 1904 and the second as *Sefer ha-Kabtzanim* in 1909. The task of adapting into Hebrew Yiddish novels about the impoverished Jewish masses of the Pale, which were written in an

Modern Hebrew 73

appropriately earthy and colloquial Yiddish, forced Mendele to find strata of Hebrew that would serve as the basis for colloquial dialogue and perhaps even more significantly to find linguistic strata which could reflect the quite remarkable capacity of Yiddish for expressing a certain sort of self deprecating humour. A few examples can illustrate both points. In Yiddish the Hebrew word *peger* (literally 'corpse') is used as a verb *pegern* with the sense of 'to kick the bucket'. By using the Hebrew word in an incorrect context he was able to invoke the slang sense of the Yiddish. Or similarly the Hebrew word *nevelah* which also means 'corpse' is used in Yiddish with the sense of a 'lazy good for nothing'; again by using the Hebrew word in an unlikely context Mendele was able to convey the Yiddish sense of the word. Or take this example: *A Yod Fahrt! In der Erd mit dem kof fart er!* (A Jew on the move! What an idea! If he moves his head into the earth he'll be lucky!). This is conveyed effectively into Hebrew via direct translation: *Yehudi nose'a! Im ha-rosh ba-adamah nose'a hu!* If direct translation, or readaptation of Hebrew words used in Yiddish did not work, there was a further device of some importance. The device could be called the de-sanctification of the Hebrew sources. Take the following example: *Er iz given a heisser, begrattener a breendigger Yud!* (He was a warm, roasted, fireburnt Jew!). As a direct translation of this into Hebrew fails to convey anything of the earthiness of the original, Mendele was forced to something else. Thus: *Hu haya yehudi nilhav, me'yn nitzutz meshalhevet yah nitznetz bo.* The elevated nature of the Hebrew with its strong biblical allusions and formal repetition of the root *nitznetz* is so incongruous in the context of the indigent world that Mendele is describing, that a rich comic effect is achieved. The unexpected, ironical or inapposite use of biblical Hebrew words and expressions is one of the most productive peculiarities of Hebrew still today. Mendele constantly reworked both the Hebrew and the Yiddish versions of his novels. There is much to support the view that Mendele's reworking of each text in the light of the other had a significant effect on the development of both literary languages.

By the first decade of the twentieth century Hebrew literature had more or less caught up with the literature of Europe. Western literary *genres* which had not previously existed in Hebrew literature, such as the novel and the play, had been absorbed. Contemporary techniques such as stream of consciousness had been introduced in the early stories of Brenner. Of perhaps greater significance is the fact that almost all Western ideology from positivism or Tolstoyan socialism, to extreme forms of romantic nationalism, were reflected in this literature. Klausner, the historian of modern Hebrew literature, concluded his monumental study by saying that there was no literary tendency or political doctrine which

74 *Modern literature in the Near and Middle East*

did not affect the literature in some way and that it was precisely these influences which, to use his phrase, were *sod kiyyumah* - the secret of its existence (Klausner 1950: 513).

This was partly due, no doubt, to the extensive *oeuvre* of translation and adaptation which had been undertaken throughout the eighteenth and nineteenth centuries. But there were other channels, too, which cannot be ignored. Most of the Hebrew writers of the period were conversant with a number of European languages particularly, of course, German and Russian. Thus many Western works such as the novels of Dickens, which were not immediately translated into Hebrew, were accessible to Hebrew writers in translation. Dickens's novels were published in serial form in Russian literary journals, in some cases within months of their original publication in English, and can be seen to have had a very considerable impact on the development of the social novel in Hebrew. Even though Hebrew was the only means by which thousands of Jews could find access to Western literature none the less only a small proportion of the flow of Western ideas reached the Jewish intelligentsia via Hebrew translation. Because most of the writers enjoyed access to Western literature in European languages, it could be that the effect of the body of translations upon the development of modern Hebrew literature was not as great as all that.

If this suggests that the literature of translation was in some sense peripheral, the same can be said in a rather different context. The literature of the Jews has a long and honourable tradition, and it is in many ways tempting to view modern literature in Hebrew as being an integral part of that tradition, notwithstanding its Western appearance. Agnon, the greatest writer to have been produced by the modern literature, was far more influenced by traditional Hasidic literature, for instance, than he was by any Western literature, notwithstanding his consummate modernism. Bialik and Mendele, too, owe far more to the literature of the Jews than they do to the literature of Christian Europe. Ahad Ha-Am, the severest critic of the Hebrew writing of the nineteenth century, criticized much of the *Haskalah* literature as being '*Mikra* for boys rather than Talmud for men'. By this he meant that the real literature of Israel, as he might have put it, should draw on altogether deeper and more substantial sources than Eugène Sue. There is much to support the view that the finest products of the new literature have been those which ignored the blandishments of the West and stayed very firmly within the tradition.

Between the turn of the century and the First World War, Hebrew literature improved out of all recognition. The new quality of the literature was matched by the quality of a great deal of the translating which by now could be judged on purely aesthetic criteria. One of the great modern

Hebrew poets Saul Tchernikhovski (1875–1943) had a vast and impressive output. He translated Longfellow's *Hiawatha* and *Evangeline*; the Epic of Gilgamesh (from a German translation); the Finnish epic *Kalevala*; Sophocles's *Oedipus Rex*; Molière's *Le Malade Imaginaire*; Shakespeare's *Macbeth*; Goethe's *Reinike Fuchs,* and a great deal besides. During the First World War Tchernikhovski served as a medical officer in the Russian army and was attached to a mobile unit which was stationed for much of the time just behind the front lines. During the period of widespread starvation, political violence and terror which followed the Revolution of 1917, Tchernikhovski travelled, much of the way on foot, from St. Petersburg to Odessa. The privations he suffered during this period can scarcely be imagined. None the less between 1917 and 1919, in addition to composing some of the finest sonnets ever to have been written in Hebrew, he managed to translate a good deal of the *Iliad* and the *Odyssey*, Anacreon's lyrics, Plato's *Symposium* and a substantial work on human anatomy. For those of us who have ever worked as translators he can stand as a model!

PART II

FROM ROMANTIC NATIONALISM TO SOCIAL CRITICISM 1914–1950

6 The political setting 1914–1950

Charles Tripp

The First World War witnessed an unprecedented intrusion of European military power into the Middle East. This not only led to the collapse of the imperial orders of the area, but also brought with it the means of asserting the European conception of the state form as the proper way of organizing political communities. The significance of this development was that it came after a century or so of European economic, cultural and at times military penetration, during which the old forms of authority may have been preserved, but attitudes towards their legitimacy had undergone a gradual transformation. Ideas of popular sovereignty, however imperfectly expressed or realized, had arisen to challenge the absolutism of the Ottoman Sultan and the Qajar Shah in the early 1900s. Similarly responses to the power and inspiration of Europe had led to attempts to redefine the nature of the political community itself. For some the answer seemed to lie in the revitalization of the Islamic community, the decline of which was all too apparent in the fact that the Sultan-Caliph in Istanbul could maintain his position and the territories of his domain only on the sufferance of the European powers. For others, the model of European nationalism appeared to provide a pattern which might usefully be followed if the peoples of the area were not to lose all sense of identity in a world dominated by the interests of others.

The consequences of the First World War, therefore, permitted and in some senses compelled people in the Middle East to think about the ways in which new foundations for political community could be devised. These would replace the old imperial systems and either safeguard that which they valued in the old existing order, or allow the emergence of new forms of order, hitherto retarded by the delayed collapse of the Ottoman and Qajar dynasties. However, these experiments were to be conducted within a framework of states which owed more to the beliefs and needs of French and British imperial administration than to any other principle. Consequently they were expected to conform in their territorial shape and

80 *Modern literature in the Near and Middle East*

their political organization to the interests of those powers. The lesson for those who wanted to avoid such a degree of foreign control, and who had the resources to do so, was to adopt a similar pattern of administration within their own territories, and from that consolidated base resist further European encroachment.

The fate of both the Tripolitanian Republic in Misuratah and the Sharifian administration in Damascus demonstrated that such resources would have to be considerable. In Anatolia, Mustafa Kemal was able to marshal a sufficient counterforce to establish the Turkish Republic. This meant defying simultaneously both the plans of the Allied powers for the partition and control of the Turkish-speaking heartland of the Empire, as well as the authority of the Sultan-Caliph who had lost the power to resist the Allies' intentions. In this project of state formation, Mustafa Kemal was able to benefit from a preponderant military-bureaucratic class formed by the Ottoman Empire itself. This largely Turkish-speaking élite had been engaged not only in the state reforms of the preceding century, but also in the debate about national identity which had tended inevitably, if disruptingly for the Empire itself, towards the formation of linguistically based Turkish nationalism. The war had served to reinforce this identity by removing the major part of the non-Turkish provinces, leaving only the Kurds and Armenians as minorities in a state founded on the homogeneity of its Turkish-speaking majority.

In Persia, Reza Khan was able to profit from the hiatus between British and Russian power and the collapse of the central authority to begin the military reconstruction and consolidation of a centralized state. It was a somewhat conditional project, since it was perforce conducted under the watchful eyes of both the newly formed Soviet Union in the north and the British in the south. At the same time, Reza Khan could not depend upon the same feelings of common identity that had worked to the benefit of Mustafa Kemal in Turkey, in that the state he envisaged would have to include a multitude of relatively autonomous and distinct ethnic groups. Nevertheless, there was sufficient sense of common purpose to allow him to carry out piecemeal the establishment of a unitary Iranian state which would, in turn, provide the ambiguous framework for the elaboration of a specifically Iranian nationalism.

Among the Arab lands of the defunct Ottoman Empire, Egypt was exceptional in having enjoyed a long history as a unitary state. However, in 1882 it had lost its independence to Great Britain while nominally remaining under the rule of the dynasty of Muhammad 'Ali, which in turn derived its authority from the Sultan-Caliph in Istanbul. These particular circumstances had led to a specific form of Egyptian nationalism under the slogan of 'Egypt for the Egyptians'. In the aftermath of the First World

War, it challenged not only the right of Great Britain to control the country, but also implicitly the right of the dynasty to rule without the consent of the people. These challenges found expression in the formation of the Wafd and the events of 1919. Even if imperfectly understood by some of the instigators of the national movement, these events at least convinced the British that Egypt would be ungovernable without some measure of consent from the Egyptian political class, leading to the grant of limited independence to Egypt in 1923 and the establishment of a constitutional system of government for the state.

This was to be paralleled by similar developments throughout the newly created states of the mandated territories. Great Britain and France required, and found, a degree of acquiesence to the state and political structures they had erected among the economically and socially powerful strata within these newly defined political entities. In the Levant and Mesopotamia, bureaucracies, military organizations and political institutions were brought into being. Their form and extent were determined by the mandatory powers, as were the conceptions of the machinery and territorial identity necessary for the definition of a modern state. Political community would, it was assumed, follow later, crystallizing around the given same structures, creating a sense of common purpose that would in time overcome the forces of social rejection which necessitated direct mandatory control in the formative years. These processes, together with their underlying assumptions and their social and economic implications, were to generate considerable conflict, the effects of which are still visible in contemporary politics. In this radically altered framework of politics one can discern three major themes, corresponding to varying attitudes towards the nature of political endeavour and to the different groups which espoused them.

In the first place there were those who might be considered either as enthusiastic partisans of, or as collaborators in, the state venture. Animating these groups was an idea that the state structure and administrative machinery was the best way of realizing national or dynastic interests, or of preserving and advancing particular social and economic interests. In general terms, these comprised the narrow political élites which had been the dominant elements in the society and administration of the Ottoman Empire, Khedival Egypt and Qajar Persia. The state seemed the best means of guaranteeing order, as well as of permitting the élites to secure the interests which the faltering hold of the previous autocracies had either kept in check or directly threatened. The conflict, in this respect, was to be a political one for the control of the state itself. In Turkey and Iran it was characterized by a clash between the increasingly autocratic methods believed by both Kemal Atatürk and Reza

82 *Modern literature in the Near and Middle East*

Shah to be the *sine qua non* of the establishment of a modern state, and the resentment of those who rejected such methods. For many who supported these leaders' earlier efforts to rid their countries of foreign control and curb the power of those who resisted the call of modernization, there were grave doubts about the propriety, and indeed wisdom, of concentrating absolute power in the hands of one individual.

In the Arab world, where the foreign presence was still a military and political reality, the political struggle was marked firstly by the attempt of these élites to rid themselves of the irksome fact of European control. Secondly, it was evident in conflicts among the notables who formed that élite for such control of the administration of the state as French or British policy allowed. Whilst the future character and extent of the community underpinning the state might yet be left open to question, there was little doubt that the administrative structures themselves were largely determining the focus and form of political activity. For those engaged upon this activity, the structures of the state were taken for granted and the more pressing problem was to establish the authority of those who would control them, as well as the purposes they would ultimately serve.

To some extent, these attitudes were challenged by the second major cluster of interests affecting the development of politics within the given framework of states. These were the groups who rejected the idea of political community represented by the state itself, and who regarded, therefore, the states that had been established as legitimate entities, as having no authority to command obedience. Underlying the rejection were a number of strands of thought, based on the common belief that political power and the instruments required for its exercise could only be sanctioned by service to those principles of authority, whether divinely or communally defined, which the states erected after the First World War seemed to negate. Consequently, it became the task of the proponents of such definitions of authority to advance their cause in defiance of the order imposed on the region, setting them against both the European powers and the local partisans of the state venture.

Islamic rejection of secular ideas of state and nation was evident in both Turkey and Iran. Both Kemal Atatürk and Reza Shah had to cope with the power of this legacy in the societies they intended to control. The increasing forcefulness, if not to say brutality, with which they faced up to the challenge represented by this idea was testimony not simply to their individual political styles, but also to the capacity of such an idea, if left unchecked, to subvert their whole project. In other areas of the Islamic Middle East, deference to Islam by those seeking political authority evidently sat uneasily with the requirements of governing a modern state. Whilst a variety of means were employed temporarily to overcome this

The political setting 1914–50 83

contradiction, the contradiction itself remained. In doing so, it retained a capacity for weakening the allegiance of many to states and rulers alike, leaving an unsettling item on the political agenda which would return to haunt their successors.

At the same time, strands of nationalism, evolving since the late nineteenth century, were to develop with disruptive effect for those states which appeared to divide these imagined communities. Arab nationalists had seen their hopes for a transcendant pan-Arab political order dashed by the intrusion of the European powers. This very fact tended to obscure the extent to which such a sense of political community had in reality existed among the very Arabs who were the object of the nationalists' attentions. Nevertheless, the given states and the élites which both ran them, and to a large extent profited from them through the various discrete administrations, were indicted for their betrayal of a supposed common ideal. The same could be said, on a geographically more limited scale, of the Syrian nationalists who espoused a secular Syrian identity, hoping thereby to overcome the confessional differences of the inhabitants of that area. From this perspective, the administrative divisions imposed by the French seemed both to reinforce the patterns of communal conflict and to guarantee the continuation of foreign domination.

The perspective was rather different, although no less subversive of the state, from the point of view of the sects and communities themselves. Fearing for their future security and identity in states dominated by their historical enemies, they revolted in many instances against the attempt to destroy their earlier precarious autonomy and to subject them to the centralized control of an alien state. Such a reaction was perceptible among the 'Alawis, the Druzes and the Kurds. Although, in these cases, there was scarcely an articulate nationalism in the modern sense, there was nevertheless a deeply felt resentment at their inclusion in states which demanded a degree of commitment lacking in the looser structures of empire. The use of force could temporarily limit their capacity actively to disrupt the functioning of the state, but it could not eradicate either their awareness of separate identity, or the conviction that the state, as it was then constituted, represented a permanent threat that must either be resisted or suborned.

In Palestine, the state as defined by the British authorities contained a lingering ambivalence regarding its ultimate form, since the intention seemed to be that it would be based on two communities claiming exclusive right to control their own affairs. Zionism was founded on the idea of Jewish self-determination, implying for many that the ultimate aim was the creation of a distinctly Jewish state. For the Arabs of Palestine, this was a threat to their own control of the territory of Palestine and of the

84 *Modern literature in the Near and Middle East*

state which Great Britain had been given a mandate to establish. Although there was as yet little articulation of a distinctively Palestinian nationalist idea, their identity as Arabs and – predominantly – Muslims seemed to be in danger were they to acquiesce in the definition of a state based not on an aggregate of their interests but on that of an alien community. The strength of the latter was that it not only enjoyed initial British encouragement to expand, but also, in the Zionist movement itself, possessed a leadership and a growing sense of national purpose which the Arabs of Palestine found difficult to match.

These conflicts about the ultimate form of the ideal political community and about the control of the existing state structures were underpinned, and in some senses exacerbated, by the transformations of the societies in question. This represents the third major current affecting politics and political conflict during this period. It was partly a result of the direct incorporation of these societies into the international economy, and in a more peculiar respect, it stemmed from the changes which the very demands of statehood itself worked upon hitherto neglected communities. It was characterized by the politicization of ever larger sections or strata of the societies bounded by these states. Economic transformation had been speeded up by the state formation and by the forces which had brought those states into being. As a result, new patterns of agriculture and of industry were established, to the detriment in many cases of those sections of society dependent upon traditional, artisanal industry and commerce. The integration of local economies into the capitalist world economy not only had dislocating effects, since it required new and exacting standards of competitiveness, but it also imposed radically different relations of production, and subjugated these societies to the fluctuations of an international economic system over which their members appeared to have little control. For those who did not wish to remain victims, this created a strong incentive to gain greater social control over the resources of the state, bringing them into conflict not only with the external powers, but also with the élite who had succeeded in exploiting the possibilities of the capitalist system to their own advantage, if not necessarily to that of the general public. At times, this impulse showed itself to be strongly influenced by the desire to recreate the economic and social certainties – imagined though they may have been – of a pre-capitalist world. However, the challenge to the dominant order was also manifest both in a form of economic nationalism that questioned European domination of local economies, and in a developing critique of the social and economic inequalities of the existing order.

These trends were given further impetus by the effects of economic transformation and of state creation on the composition of the political public itself. Rapid urbanization, the beginnings of mass education, the

The political setting 1914–50 85

extension of face-to-face encounters between individuals and the organs of the state as well as the cultural conflicts this process implied, were creating a new mass constituency for those who sought to act within the political conditions of the time. It was a constituency far outnumbering the traditional élites which had hitherto monopolized political power. The nature of the developing mass awareness of the possibilities of political action, the socio-economic situation of those who were beginning to think of these things for the first time, as well as their ambivalent situation between the values of a traditional society and the attractions of the new, were throwing into question the very authority of those élites. The state was a more intrusive mechanism than the old looser empires had been: it compelled people to join armies, it taxed them, it staffed and deployed a burgeoning bureaucracy on a scale not seen before. In short, the obligations of the individual towards central authority increased, as had the capacity of central authority to enforce compliance. At the same time, the obligations of central government towards the people were proclaimed to be of a radically different kind than had hitherto existed. Those who made a claim to power, claimed also that the sole justification of that claim was service to the people as a whole. When it became apparent that this was largely rhetorical and that those in authority were considerably less concerned about fulfilling their own obligations than in enforcing the obedience of their subjects, the latter quite naturally began to question the right of their ruler to do so.

This was neither a sudden, clear-cut development, nor one which had yet touched the major part of the populations of these states. However, within a relatively short period of time, it had succeeded in engaging significantly larger numbers than hitherto, in the guise both of those who acted as the footsoldiers of urban mass politics, and of those who saw themselves as the leaders and organizers. Equally, the very speed with which this was occurring, and its accompanying social dislocations, was adding to the contradictions and tensions within political discourse itself. The encounter with the alien culture of Western Europe and its portrayal as something which must be adapted or resisted at varying rates and at varying levels, had gone far beyond the restrictive élites who still held political power. The themes which they had been debating amongst themselves, as part of an almost private discourse within an exclusive governing stratum, had now gained mass currency, and in the process were being transformed by the very preoccupations of the hitherto excluded. In such circumstances, one could say that a popular political culture was in the making, increasingly requiring the attention of those who would seek power, but with highly ambiguous consequences both for the nature of the state and for the forms of political authority through which the state would be ruled.

By the 1930s, the pressures generated by those conflicting groups and

86 *Modern literature in the Near and Middle East*

themes were beginning to challenge the political structures established by the mandatory powers and by the strong centralizing autocrats. Whilst the power of these authorities was still sufficient to contain the challenge, there were signs of strain in the political society. In Turkey and Iran, the consolidation of the state seemed to lead inexorably to the concentration of political power in the hands of those who had founded the state. Under the banner of consciously developed nationalism, Atatürk and Reza Shah were claiming an exclusive right to interpret the will of the nation and the absolute powers which they demanded to ensure its realization. Inevitably, this led to the suppression of the alternative visions of the nature of the national community, of the ordering of national priorities, and of the means by which this could be secured. For many, therefore, the challenge to absolutism became enmeshed in the ideas of greater social as well as political justice. In this respect, there was a growing awareness of the limitations of nationalism: whilst it might unify a people against a foreign threat, it seemed to contain no necessary prescription for the way in which that people would be ruled. Some clearly took it as a mandate for dictatorship, but many others saw it merely as granting the right of every individual within the national community to control his own fate. However, whilst the agenda for debate may have been changing, debate itself became increasingly a suppressed activity which by diverging from the dictates of the President or Shah, respectively, was proscribed. Nevertheless, ideas concerning the alternative ordering of the state and society were biding their time, becoming correspondingly more attractive with the perceived failings of the political and economic system.

In Egypt, where debate was more open, and political activity permitted within certain limits, the fact of British power remained, and the Wafd continued to be the main vehicle of challenge. Nevertheless, the authority of the Wafd to represent the Egyptian nation was repeatedly thrown into question, since it appeared constantly to neglect the material grievances of the majority of those who constituted that nation. Rivalries within the élite over this issue, unchecked by any sense of constitutional propriety, had led to a devaluation of parliamentary life, as the King, the Wafd and other groupings of notables engaged in a struggle for power which seemed increasingly remote from the needs of the population. This led to the emergence of organizations outside the parliamentary framework, advocating the radical social and economic reform which the existing parties seemed to neglect. Whether the critique was based on the principles of Islam, of a corporatist nationalism, or of Marxism, there was an increasing tendency to indict the failures of the older generation of nationalist leaders and to advocate the use of force in order to bring about the political changes that would allow social reconstruction.

The political setting 1914–50 87

Similar organizations of a parliamentary and radical nature were also appearing in the Levant and in Iraq. Frustration at the failure of traditional leaders to gain the complete independence they claimed to champion, combined with a suspicion that their privileged economic and social position compromised their commitment to the national cause, was creating a growing constituency for the idea that violent action might be necessary to change the bases of the orientation of political society. Where violent political change occurred, as in the repeated military interventions in Iraq, it became apparent that this was not of the radical nature believed necessary to set a proper course for the future, but simply represented the manoeuvres of the dominant élite, leaving social relations unaffected. Although some in the Ahali group may have believed that the military would provide the necessary vehicle for the implementation of their own programme of social reform, they soon realized that the price they had to pay for this allegiance was their own subordination to intra military rivalries and the abandonment of their political and social agenda.

In Palestine, the Zionist movement had concentrated in the main on the creation of a social and economic community which would act as the framework both for the reception of growing numbers of Jewish immigrants, and seemingly for the establishment of an exclusively Jewish state. British recognition of the direction in which this was heading led to the Peel Commission report. For the first time it recommended the partition of mandated Palestine into two separate states: one Jewish and one Arab. The reaction of the Palestinian Arabs to this proposal and to the general threat which the establishment of the Yishuv represented for their own political future could not be contained for long. It erupted into the General Strike of 1936, followed by more widespread and violent revolt. The vehemence of the social rejection of British plans for the territory as well as the increasing engagement of other Arab states on behalf of the Palestinian Arabs in the name of Arab nationalism, led eventually to a reversion of British policy back to the original idea of encouraging the emergence of Palestine as a unitary state. It would be a state necessarily dominated by the Arabs, with the Jewish community existing as a minority within its borders. This left two important legacies for the future: first, it increased the determination of the whole Zionist movement to secure its existing position, and to seek to provide a haven for the persecuted Jews of Europe, by aiming single-mindedly at the creation of a Jewish state; secondly, in a perilous manner it linked the legitimacy of many of the Arab states' governments to their capacities to prevent such a development from occurring.

These were the main currents and trends within the Middle East on the eve of the Second World War. Just as the First World War had been a

88 *Modern literature in the Near and Middle East*

dramatic historical event which had stimulated competing visions about the political future of the Middle East, so too did the Second World War have equally momentous consequences. First the demands of the war intensified the intrusion of the European powers into the states of the region as they sought to mobilize the political, social and economic resources required to secure their respective strategic positions. Although in the short term this appeared to redouble the assertion of European control, on the pattern of the First World War, in the longer term it signalled the end of European Imperial power. In the aftermath of the war, the exhausted states of Europe lacked both the means and the will to maintain the kind of hegemony over the Middle East that had once seemed vital to the security of their interests.

Secondly, the war had had a marked and sometimes disruptive effect upon the states of the region. In some areas, the economic consequences of the war itself had led to considerable hardship and inequalities, as some groups exploited the disruptions in world trade to build up local industry or to accrue substantial profits, whilst those not in a position to do so suffered severely the effects of shortages and profiteering, leading to malnutrition and serious epidemics. At the same time, a series of political developments had thrown into question the ability and the right of existing political orders to maintain themselves in the post-war world. In Iran, the forced abdication and exile of Reza Shah had severely weakened the autocratic system he had created and opened up new possibilities for Iran's political future. In Turkey, the death of Atatürk in 1938 had diminished the perceived legitimacy of the authoritarian regime which İnönü had originally enthusiastically reinforced, facing the President in 1945 with a crisis of authority. In Egypt, the Wafd had been returned to power in 1942 as a result of a British military *coup d'état* against the King. In Iraq, the Regent, the King and the notables surrounding them had been reinstalled following successful British military action against the self-proclaimed 'nationalists' around Rashid 'Ali al-Gaylani. In Palestine, the Arab political leadership was divided and dispersed, whilst inexorable pressure built up to allow the immigration of the half million survivors of the Nazi attempt to destroy European Jewry.

Consequently, after the war, new possibilities emerged in politics as the old methods were discredited and their European protectors retreated from the area. On the agenda of political debate, there was a growing resentment of the neglect of political liberties and of social justice, coupled with a diminished acceptance of the authority of those who had hitherto ruled the state. The intolerance of the latter to the new demands being made upon them, and their entrenchment in the political structure of the state, inevitably led to ideas about the ways of overturning the *status*

The political setting 1914–50 89

quo, if necessary through violence, by those who felt excluded from power. Social inequalities seemed to underpin political inequality, yet the former could be redressed only if the latter were attended to. Furthermore, nationalism, as articulated in the preceding decades, had provided little idea of how to cope with either.

In many respects, the war in Palestine of 1948 seemed to many in the Arab world to be a means of restoring a lost unity. For the rulers, aware of the increasingly precarious foundations of their authority, this was to be a means of exercising their states' newly found independence, creating through collective action a sense of the utility and legitimacy of the state in realization of goals sanctified by a range of highly charged principles which had pushed them into battle. The establishment of Israel and the dispersal of much of the Arab population of Palestine was a constant reproach to the order for having failed to protect the Arab homeland. They had failed on their own terms as leaders of states and as nationalists. It was therefore open to call into question the social and political order which had allowed such a catastrophe to occur.

For many in the Middle East there were too many social discontinuities and too few political bonds of rights of loyalty for the rulers to escape unscathed. Increasingly, they were indicted for having failed to serve the interests of the community, whether this was defined as its collective well-being or its collective identity. In some cases they fell victim to assassination. In others, they were removed from office with the active participation of the armed forces. The latter, having been intimately involved in the war of Palestine, had felt the defeat most sharply. Many of their officers began to see themselves as the guardians of the national idea as well as the rightful initiators of a long overdue reform of the social and political order. The period ends, therefore, with a spate of acts of political violence which demonstrated how thin and contentious the myth of unity fostered by nationalism had become, and how divisive the issues in the politics of these states were to be. A new cycle of illusion, and eventually of disillusion, had begun throughout much of the Middle East: the entry into politics of army officers claiming to be champions of radical reform.

7 Turkey

Geoffrey Lewis

There is no shortage of nationalism in Turkish writings of the First World War and the 1920s, but romantic nationalism is harder to find. Turkish national feeling arose only when the sun was setting on the Ottoman Empire, and most intelligent writers were too preoccupied with the struggle for national survival to take any but the most realistic view of nationalism. The most highly esteemed member of the group known as *Millî Edebiyatçılar*, the exponents of national literature, was Ömer Seyfettin (1884–1920). He formulated his ideas on nationalism in a short story called *İlk Düşen Ak*, 'The First Grey Hair':

> 1 People who share a language and a religion are of one nation (*millet*). The Turks too are a nation, but because they have hitherto lived within the framework of a religious community (*ümmet, umma*) they have neglected their own nationhood and culture and tried to be like the Arabs and Persians.
>
> 2 On becoming a nation, it is necessary to modernize. They set out to imitate the Europeans.
>
> 3 The Turks, however, like other nations, have a distinct personality of their own, in every area of culture. They will be able to progress when they discover this personality.
>
> (Alangu 1962: III, 68)

Nationalist he certainly was, but his sense of humour was too keen to permit him to be a romantic. Some of his most successful satires were those in which his victims were Europeans, especially those who took a romantic view of Turkey. But he also satirized those Turks who persisted in writing Ottoman instead of plain Turkish, those who were fanatical about their religion, and those who blindly admired everything European. As an example of his treatment of the last named class we may take his two short stories *Fon Sadriştayn' ın Karısı* (1917) and *Fon Sadriştayn' ın Oğlu*

(1918), 'The Wife of von Sadristein' and 'The Son of von Sadristein' (Seyfettin 1970). This character is a Turk, whose real name is Sadrettin; his nickname derives from his inordinate affection for everything German. Leaving his wife at home, he goes on a long visit to a friend in Germany, where he admires all that he sees. His German friend explains:

> This comfort, this prosperity, this excellence, is not inherent in the soil or stones or geography of Germany but in the German woman. It is the German woman who creates the prosperity, the luxury, the wealth of Germany. Let's find a German girl for you. Marry her. Go back to Istanbul. You will live in the same orderliness and ease that exist in Germany.

He follows his friend's advice and returns home with his new German wife, to find that his 'wretched, smart, Turkish wife has fallen in love with a monocled gentleman as smart and as fashionable as herself'. At her request they obtain a divorce. Twenty-five years pass. For our hero, life with his German wife has been no bed of roses. Apart from anything else, their only son has gone to the bad, finally absconding to America with their life savings. But one day von Sadristein is stirred out of his normal misery and lassitude, because a new national holiday has been proclaimed, the birthday of the brilliant young nationalist poet Orhan. Every newspaper devotes a special issue to him. One critic, renowned for disapproving of everything and everybody, writes:

> I revere the genius of Orhan Bey. Before him, no works so sublime have been written in such natural language... . Before him, everyone aped either the Persians or the Europeans. He has looked towards neither... . He has turned his gaze inwards, to his own soul ... He has found his heroic deeds, his stories, his themes, his language, entirely in the Turkish consciousness.

Like everyone else, von Sadristein is carried away by his enthusiam for this wonderful young man. He calls at the poet's house (where he lives with his mother, his father having fallen at Gallipoli) to pay his respects. The poet is not at home, but the poet's mother receives him graciously and, of course, turns out to be his former wife (Seyfettin 1970: 96–125).

There is no doubt about which author to consider if our starting point is to be romantic nationalism. These words at once call to mind the early works of Halide Edip, particularly her novel *Ateşten Gömlek*, first published in 1922 (Kitabevi 1943). The title, literally 'The Shirt of Fire', connotes a prolonged agony, a Nessus-shirt. The story tells of three youngish men, Peyami, Cemal and İhsan. Twelve years before the story opens, Peyami's mother had wanted him to marry her young cousin Ayşe, Cemal's sister. He scornfully refused: 'Lord have mercy on us! An Izmir

92 *Modern literature in the Near and Middle East*

girl called Ayşe! I packed my bag and fled to Europe'. He did not return until hearing, six months later, that she had married someone else and gone back to Izmir. After the Greek landings at Izmir, in May 1919, news arrives that the Greeks have cut her husband into pieces and shot dead her five-year-old son. Ayşe manages to get to Istanbul, and some days later she goes with Peyami and Cemal to a great meeting held in Sultan Ahmet Square to protest against the Greek action and the Allies' connivance. Peyami says:

> That day I saw the real Turkey for the first time. That dark mystery which is the far side of Istanbul, its real quarters, had opened its mouth and poured forth its inhabitants... The frowning, silent, and unseen old people of Istanbul. Scrawny, wrinkled necks were rising out of strange frock-coats and morning-dress of unguessable antiquity, and tears were openly raining down onto their white beards from beneath their spectacles. Grandmothers were coming in ample silken *charshafs*, with tears on their wrinkled cheeks. There were hosts of women dressed in red and yellow, newly emerged from the *charshaf*, red-eyed, their faces visible through the mesh of their lacy veils, like the painting of the horde of women storming Versailles at the French Revolution.

One cannot help feeling that if Peyami thought that lacy veils, silken *charshafs* and morning dress, however old, were the real Turkey, he still had a lot to learn.

The crowd was so dense that Peyami and the others could not get close to the small platform which had been put up for the speakers. He says:

> We could not distinguish the people on the platform, nor could we hear what they were saying. Sometimes the high-pitched voice of a woman rent the square, sometimes it was the deeper words of a man that were scattered abroad.

What lends piquancy to those words is that most readers would know, though Peyami and his friends did not know, that the woman who spoke at that meeting, and, it is said, spoke very effectively, was the author Halide Edip herself.

Ayşe is invited to the house of Salime Hanım, the chief of a group of fashionable ladies who want to dismember, hang and burn the Union and Progress leaders who had brought Turkey into the First World War on the losing side. Their policy apart from that is to conciliate the Allies, Britain in particular. Salime Hanım's purpose in inviting Ayşe is for her to meet Mr Cook, an important British correspondent, and tell him about the Greek atrocities at Izmir. The description of Mr Cook is a fine piece of invective:

He sat as though he were the only person in the room, his long, skeletal legs and kneecaps discernible through his trousers, ceaselessly swinging his huge, skinny feet. His head with its sparse hair was like that of an ancient hunting bird whose feathers had moulted. His nose was enormous, aggressive, and raised in the air. His small, close-set and clouded eyes gazed like two blue beads, quite devoid of feeling. But his most striking peculiarity was the drooping moustache, of indeterminate colour, which covered his lips. One could not tell whether the mouth behind these ugly whiskers was smiling, mocking, or speaking. What most exercised the beholder was that mysterious mouth, which every now and then would reveal, in a bloodthirsty sneer, yellow teeth like pickaxes. He was a deeply ignorant and base example of the colonialist tyrants of the British Empire, trampling under its boots the colonial peoples which it always maliciously termed 'the natives': arrogant, full of himself, sarcastic, his triumph gone to his head.

Mr Cook tells the company that their only course is to seek British protection. He does not know whether Britain would grant it, particularly as the Turks killed sixty thousand British soldiers at Gallipoli, but she might forgive them if their repentance was sincere. Salime is assuring him that they would indeed try to win Britain's forgiveness, when she is interrupted by Ayşe:

Let the British grant their forgiveness to those who want it! It is not for tyrants to forgive, but for their victims! You must ask our forgiveness. Yesterday you signed an armistice, today you send murderous brigands into our country, under the protection of your once honourable Navy.

She then tells him what she herself has witnessed at Izmir, including the killing of her husband and son. Mr Cook leaves without shaking anyone's hand. Peyami politely sees him to the door and returns to find all the officers present, young and old kneeling at Ayşe's feet, vowing, 'We shall not sheathe our swords until all our limbs are severed on the road to Izmir.' It would be churlish to wonder what they were going to sheathe their swords with.

The men go to join the fight in Anatolia, and Ayşe goes to nurse the wounded. Peyami and İhsan both fall in love with Ayşe, but she and İshan are killed in battle and are buried in adjacent graves. Cemal and Haşmet Bey, another of the officers who made that vow to Ayşe, try to comfort Peyami, but by now he is quite crazed:

I see it all now ... I see what they all mean to do. It is a crafty plan, to get to Ayşe before me. But can this be? Is she not now lying side by

94 *Modern literature in the Near and Middle East*

side with İhsan? ... I have a brilliant idea. I shall be the first to enter Izmir. Ayşe told İhsan that if he got into Izmir she would marry him. But she didn't love İhsan. I know. She didn't love anyone. She was going to love only the man who would enter Izmir. Haşmet is going to carry out his crafty plan; I find that amusing. I shall be carrying the Turkish flag on the quay at Izmir before he gets there.

That might have been a good place in which to end the book, but there is an odd epilogue, in which two doctors discuss the case of Peyami, who died while a bullet was being extracted from his brain. One of them has been trying to identify the people named in Peyami's scribblings, but can find no record of an Army nurse called Ayşe (a wild improbability, one would have thought). His cousin Cemal fell in battle. Cemal had a sister, of whom not even the name is known. The doctor puts the whole story down to the effect of the bullet in Peyami's brain. After a protracted scientific discussion, the two doctors find a complicated Latin name for Peyami's shirt of fire. This outline should serve to show that the book is stronger on the romance than the nationalism. The nationalism is there all right, but the author chose to couch the story in terms of personal relationships. Besides the identity of the woman who spoke at the Sultan Ahmet square meeting, the book exhibits another curious feature, a consummate example of how vain authors can be. In the preface, which she addresses to her friend and fellow writer Yakup Kadri, Halide Edip explains that she decided to call her book *The Shirt of Fire* after he had told her that he was writing a book of the same name.

> The characters who suddenly presented themselves to me kept calling their story, with childlike persistence, 'The Shirt of Fire'... . Your wearers of the shirt of fire are not the same as mine.

So Yakup Kadri had to find another title for his book; he chose *Yaban, The Stranger.*

The reason that I have devoted so much space to *Ateşten Gömlek* is that it is the most successful full-length novel by a writer of the first rank which explores the theme of romantic nationalism. It is probably true to say that this emphasis was an aberration, in that the strongest tide running through Turkish literature since the late nineteenth century had been that of social criticism.

The War of Liberation (1919–22) brought the intellectuals into Anatolia, where for the first time they saw the benighted existence of the great majority of their fellow-countrymen, whom a few of them might previously have idealized but most had either despised or simply never thought about. Once the war was won, no writer of any sensibility could

Turkey 95

possibly have gone back to Istanbul or Ankara and romanticized what he had seen. Romanticism took wings and fled, and the targets of social criticism changed. They were no longer rich *parvenus,* comic Levantines and Frenchified or Germanizing *poseurs,* but uncaring intellectuals, self-important bureaucrats, grasping landlords, and other enemies of progress.

Yakup Kadri's great Anatolian novel did not come out until 1932. But his novels had been appearing for ten years before that. The one that attracted most attention was *Nur Baba, Father Light,* a *roman à thèse* (1922). It has been suggested that he wrote it to pave the way for Atatürk's outlawing of the dervish orders, which happened in 1925. Whether he did so or not, it was certainly effective anti-Bektashi propaganda. The eponymous Father Light, a Bektashi sheykh, is a dedicated seducer of women. He brings to the depths of degradation, and then casts aside, a high-born lady who visits his lodge at first purely out of curiosity. The Bektashi background is of great interest, and the writing, as always with Yakup Kadri, is masterly, but this is not an attractive tale.

In 1932 he published *The Stranger,* which he had intended to call *The Shirt of Fire* (Kitabevi 1945). It tells of Ahmet Celal Bey, an officer who lost his right arm in the First World War and quits Istanbul to settle in the native village of his batman Mehmet Ali. He believes that Anatolia is the home of the true Turkish nation, men and women with splendid hearts free of the hypocrisy and turpitude of the capital. When he realizes his mistake, he bitterly apostrophizes the Turkish intellectual:

> You are to blame for this! What have you done for this ruined land and these destitute human masses? After sucking their blood for centuries... now you think you have the right to come here and find them disgusting.
> The people of Anatolia had a soul, which you have not enlightened. They had a body, which you have not been able to feed. They had a land on which they lived; you have not let them work it. You have left them in the grip of brutishness, ignorance, poverty and famine. They have grown like weeds between the hard earth and the parched sky. Now, sickle in hand, you have come here for the harvest. What have you sown? So what do you expect to reap?

He had had few illusions about the physical environment he was going to, but the reality turned out to be worse than anything imaginable. He had hoped that the villagers would appreciate that he had lost his arm in fighting for them, but none of them cared; they scarcely even noticed, because lameness and other deformities were so common among them: there was a hunchback, two lunatics, a dwarf, and so on. Everything he does seems to fascinate them; they watch him as if he were a clown at the

96 *Modern literature in the Near and Middle East*

circus, they follow him about and spy on him in his room. Mehmet Ali eventually tells him why:

> Sir, stop shaving every day. Sir, on this mountain top what's the point of brushing your teeth night and morning? Sir, among us only the women comb their hair. Sir, why do you keep reading all night? They think you are casting spells.

He falls in love with a girl from the next village, but she is betrothed to Mehmet Ali's loutish brother. And one day the Greek Army arrives, in retreat after being defeated by the Turks at the Battle of the Sakarya (September 1921), and all is blood and fire. Afterwards, the Turkish authorities send a commission to look into reports of Greek atrocities. In the rubble of the devastated village they find an exercise book, scorched and torn, containing the officer's diary. They ask the surviving villagers what has become of the owner of it.

> None of them knew where he had gone, although it was they who had told the commission that he had lived in the village for two or three years and had been there until the final catastrophic day. A member of the commission, astonished at their lack of concern, asked, 'How can this be? A man who has lived with you for years; is it possible that no one knows where he has gone, what has happened to him?'
> The villagers shrugged their shoulders resentfully and began to move away. But one of them, a puny, dropsical man of indeterminate age, turned and said, 'Well, he was a stranger. Like you.'

The book raised powerful emotions. Many criticized it for its hostile depiction of peasant life, although the author had unequivocally absolved the peasants of responsibility for the awfulness and hopelessness of it. Yakup Kadri himself denied that his novel was objective. In his preface to the second and subsequent editions he described it as 'the heart-rending cry of a fevered soul, of a consciousness and a conscience suddenly confronted by a painful and dreadful truth.' It was objective enough for most readers, however, who, whether or not they discounted the obvious emotionalism of the book, were made aware through it of that painful and dreadful truth. It inspired many writers to write their own Anatolia books, though not all of them felt obliged actually to go and live in an Anatolian village before doing so. One distinguished exception was Sabahattin Ali (1907–48), who had seen something of the way of life of his peasant compatriots even before serving ten months in prison (1932–33) for a poem held to be libellous of Atatürk (see Halman 1982 for a translation of one of his best-known stories: *Kağni*, 'The Cart'). To find a work as effective and influential as Yakup Kadri's *Yaban*, we have to wait until

1950, when Mahmut Makal published his non-fictional *Bizim Köy, Our Village*, subtitled 'A Village Schoolmaster's Notes'. There is no doubt that the impetus to rural improvement in Turkey owes much to these two books and to the climate of opinion which they generated. But by no means all the writers of the period were interested in social criticism for its own sake. Many were content to tell stories, and no blame to them for that. Among the names in this category which should not be omitted from any survey are Memduh Şevket Esendal (1883–1952), Sait Faik Abasıyanık (1906–54), and Reşat Nuri Güntekin (1892–1957). Sait Faik was the most gifted short story writer of his generation (see Halman 1982 for a translation of *İki Kişiye Bir Hikâye*, 'An Episode of Two').

I shall not give you a sample of the work of Aziz Nesin (1915–), because the full flowering of his satirical gift did not occur until well after 1950, and none of his earlier work is all that remarkable. But for social satire, Haldun Taner (1915–86) is, to my mind, unbeatable. This judgement may surprise some Turkish readers; not because they would deny his supremacy but because his satire is so gentle and his humour so subtle that he is generally thought of simply as a writer of short stories (as well as a playwright), rather than as a satirist. As a sample of Haldun Taner, I give an abridged translation of his *Sonsuza Kalmak*, 'To All Eternity'. There were still quite a few Union and Progress men around in 1948, when the story was written.

The narrator, Sunuhi Bey, is a schoolmaster who has never had a house of his own. In his last year before retirement, his brother-in-law Razı Bey, a successful businessman, offers him a share in a new housing cooperative at a bargain price, and by cashing in all their savings he and his wife manage to find the necessary deposit. The builders start work. One morning the foreman comes and tells him that some big stones are turning up in his plot. He has a look:

And what do you think I saw? A relief of an old woman holding a child.
That evening I told my wife about it. 'These may be classical antiquities,' I said. 'We might show them to Şükran Hanım at the Museum.'
'Oh come on! Don't make life more complicated!'
My wife has got it in for Şükran Hanım at the best of times, the way every woman who hasn't had an education feels about the woman who has, and has made a career for herself. Yet Şükran Tur is an inoffensive bit of a girl; short, skinny, silver-rimmed spectacles, never married nor likely to at this rate, with a degree in archaeology. Hardly opens her mouth. Doesn't smile much. Reads English books.
'What harm will it do if she sees them?' I said. 'What if they're antiquities?'

98 *Modern literature in the Near and Middle East*

'And will you get a reward if they are?'

'I'd just like to do my duty as a civilized human being.'

That day I cleaned two more stones. A ceremonial procession: four people with offerings in their hands and sandals on their feet.

Early next morning, Razı Bey came and asked to see them. I showed them to him. 'They're not antiquities,' he said. 'And suppose they were; would that be your business?'

'Isn't there such a thing as one's duty to mankind, to civilization? What if they are the work of some great artist? What if they're masterpieces, calling out from centuries past to centuries yet to come?'

'You say the weirdest things, Sunuhi Bey. Seeing they've been underground for centuries, where's the harm if they go on staying there?'

'But humanity ...'

'Now you're on your humanity line. I'm not a complete ignoramus, you know. You haven't mentioned this to anyone else, have you?'

'No.'

'Well, don't. In particular, that know-all Şükran Tur mustn't hear about it. If any word gets out about antiquities, the State will requisition the land and get excavations going. The cooperative will be finished. This isn't just between the two of us. The interests of forty-seven shareholders are involved. If you don't keep your mouth shut, it's all done for; all the money and all the hope.'

When Razı Bey had gone, I said to my wife, 'Was it you who put him up to it?'

'What was I to do? I was afraid you'd go and do something crazy.'

I said,'When a man gets to my age, he lives to gain immortality. Either he can have children or he can leave his mark on the world some other way. And how is this done? It can be done with some masterpiece that calls out from centuries past to centuries yet to come. Why did the Pharaohs have the Pyramids built? Why did Michelangelo do his statue of David? Why did Sinan the Architect build the Süleymaniye Mosque?'

'They all had a home to lay their heads in, replied my better half. 'Have you ever owned a house till now? Cut out the rhetoric and stick to the facts. I'm in no mood to listen to you binding on, I've got a headache without that.'

I could see that I had more chance of being struck by lightning than of persuading her of the immortality of art, so I shut up.

Next day I was accosted by that great hulking Nuri İskeçe and Sırrı Erdem, the retired superintendent of police. Nuri İskeçe was breathing heavily through his nose. 'There's some daft gossip going round town,' he said. 'Or have some antiques really been found on the property of our cooperative, or what?'

Turkey 99

I don't know if you've noticed, but these chaps just don't know the word 'antiquities'.

'I haven't said anything to anybody yet,' I said.

'Someone has, because people have heard about it.' He gave a long sigh. He shook his head from side to side perhaps ten times and muttered, 'God give me strength!' Then he said, 'If anyone mentions antiques again, I'm not kidding, there'll be bloodshed. We've put exactly fifteen million into this business. It's no joke.' He then looked me full in the face with his bloodshot eyes and said, 'Friend, I'm an old Union and Progress man; Razı may have told you. Yesterday in the café I swore an oath on my pistol.' And off he went.

Three more days passed. Nuri Bey's terrorist pistol kept getting mixed up in my dreams.

One evening my wife said to me, 'Razı Bey wants the stones.'

'What does he think he's going to do with them?'

'How do I know? He said he was going to take them off in a lorry.'

'Where to?'

'Somewhere where they'd be safe, he said.'

(About that time Sunuhi was taken ill and by the time he had got over it the building work was finished.)

Thanks to Nuri İskeçe's intimidatory tactics, one didn't hear much talk in town about antiquities. Anyway, we're all going to be neighbours; there's no room for tension and ill feeling. Recently, Sırrı Erden married off his daughter and we all went to the wedding. There was a great deal of drinking. When everyone was merry, Razı, Nuri, and Gavsi took me by the arm and we all embraced.

'We were on the point of falling out over nothing at all,' they said. 'Anyway, it's all over and forgotten.'

'It's true it's all over, but what I said wasn't wrong. What does man live for?'

'To be able to call out for centuries past to centuries yet to come,' said my wife in a fair imitation of my way of speaking.

Gavsi Bey said, 'Don't worry. Those masterpieces that call out from centuries past to centuries yet to come, we didn't throw them away or sell them or smash them into little bits. They're in a very secure place.'

'Where's that?' I asked.

'They're all in a very safe place; they're still looking to the centuries yet to come and calling out to them.'

'Where are they?' I asked.

Proudly Gavsi Bey replied, 'We used them to line the walls of the cooperative's septic tank.'

100 *Modern literature in the Near and Middle East*

'What!' I roared. 'Shame on you!'

Gavsi Bey retorted, 'Credit us too with a modicum of respect for art, of intellect and right thinking. It would have been wrong to defile the faces of those lovely ancient reliefs. We turned them all backwards. Cheer up! Their faces are to the earth, they are still looking into eternity.'

'I give up,' I said. 'I mean ...' What else could I say? Throughout my life, the expression 'I give up' has been the one I've used most often. It's only three syllables, it's easy to say and it does help relieve your feelings. Up to a point.

(Taner 1983)

When we come to poetry, we must bear in mind the dichotomy between popular poetry, in syllabic metre and plain Turkish, and *Divan* poetry, which uses the Arabo–Persian system of prosody and a plethora of Arabic and Persian words. Popular poetry has never stopped, whereas *Divan* poetry is virtually dead. The one twentieth-century exponent of it whose work is represented in all the modern anthologies was Yahya Kemal (1884–1958), a Chestertonian figure who used to hold court every evening in the old Park Hotel in Istanbul. His early work is almost as incomprehensible to the Turk in the street as that of any of his sixteenth-century predecessors, but later he approximated to the speech at least of educated people. Here is an example of romantic nationalism, the opening lines of his *Açık Deniz*, 'The Open Sea', an attractive bit of youthful *Weltschmerz*:

> While my childhood passed in Balkan cities,
> There burned in me a longing like a flame.
> In my heart the melancholy that Byron knew.
> I wandered the mountains, dumb in my day-dreams.
> I breathed the free air of the Rakofcha plain
> And felt the passion of my raiding ancestors,
> Heard in my heart the echoing thunder of their charge
> Ever northward, in many a hundred summers.

(Kemal 1963: 14)

Nâzım Hikmet (1902–63), received his university education in Moscow (1922–4) in economics and social science, and came back a convinced communist. He had an extraordinary poetic talent. In 1929 he wrote several articles on the theme that with changing social conditions the old poetry, both *Divan* and syllabic, must inevitably give way to free verse. Some of his work sounds heavy to modern ears and some of the literary devices seem too obvious, notably the repetitions. But he intended his poetry to be read aloud, and read aloud it was, to such effect that in 1938

Turkey 101

he was sentenced by a military court to twenty-eight years' imprisonment for sedition. Not long after being amnestied in 1950, he left Turkey, to live in Warsaw, Sofia and Moscow, in which last city he died. The following is from his *Benerci niçin kendini öldürdü* (1931), 'Why Banerjea Killed Himself', about an Indian nationalist who committed suicide in prison:

> When the light of the star which flows into my eyes as a drop of gold
> first pierced the darkness in space,
> there was not a single eye on earth looking at the sky...
> The stars were old, the earth a child.
> The stars are far from us, but how far, how far...
> Among the stars our earth is small, but how small, how small.
> And Asia, which is one-fifth of the earth's surface.
> And in Asia, India is a country.
> Calcutta is a city in India,
> Banerjea, a man in Calcutta...
> And I tell you that
> in India, in the city of Calcutta, they stopped a man on his way,
> a man who was walking they cast into chains...
> And I do not condescend to raise my eyes to the radiant void.
> The stars are far, we are told; the earth is small, we are told. I don't
> care. I am not concerned.
> I want you to know that for me, more marvellous, more powerful, more
> mysterious and enormous, is the one who was stopped on his way, the
> one was cast into chains, the man...
> (Hikmet 1963: 96–7)

The next step forward was taken by Orhan Veli (1915–50). In 1941 he wrote as an introduction to a book of poems about himself, Melih Cevdet and Oktay Rifat, a manifesto entitled *Garip*, meaning 'a stranger in a strange land'. It begins, 'Poetry, that is to say, the art of speaking.' Of rhyme he says, 'It was invented by primitive man to make it easy to remember the second line; then he found a certain beauty in it... But mankind has progressed since then.' He goes on, ' The people who fill the modern world are winning the right to live, after a ceaseless struggle. They have a right to poetry, as to everything else, and poetry will address itself to their tastes...' (Uyguner 1967: 11–12).

And in the remainder of his short life he turned out poems in accordance with that specification, and he drank. He was a thin, bony man, never robust. In 1939 he lay in a coma for three weeks after a car accident. In 1950 he fell down a hole which some workmen had dug and neglected to put lamps round, and he died a few months later of a cerebral haemorrhage while the doctors were treating him, not unreasonably, for

102 *Modern literature in the Near and Middle East*

alcohol poisoning. Dylan Thomas at once springs to mind, but Orhan Veli was not such a larger-than-life figure, and the sort of people who here would not be seen dead with a poetry book, even by Dylan Thomas, read and love Orhan Veli. One of his poems, *Vatan için*, 'For the Motherland', has become almost proverbial:

> What have we not done for this land!
> Some of us have died,
> Some of us have made speeches.
> > (op. cit.: 48)

No less trenchant is *Cevap*, 'Answer,' subtitled 'From the Butcher's Cat to the Alley Cat':

> You speak of hunger;
> That means you are a communist.
> That means you are the chap who's been starting all the fires.
> All the ones in Istanbul,
> All the ones in Ankara.
> What a swine you are!
> > (op. cit.: 49)

His poem which shocked most respectable folk was *Eskiler Alıyorum*, 'I buy old things', which may be why it is not to be found in all editions of his works:

> I buy old things,
> I buy them and make them into stars.
>
> Music is food for the soul;
> I'm crazy about music.
>
> I write poems,
> I write poems and buy old things.
> I sell old things and buy music.
>
> And if only I were a fish in a bottle of booze!
> > (Veli 1973: 157)

One could carry on indefinitely about Orhan Veli, but there is another poet whose genius is universally acknowledged, and that is Fazıl Hüsnü Dağlarca, a former Army officer (1914–).Here are two stanzas from his *Çakırın Destanı* (1945), 'Çakır's Epic', which he describes as 'the story of observing the individual in his society and of abandoning the individual for the sake of the community.' I give them as translated by Talât Halman, who elegantly reproduces the cadences and the rhymes:

I decided I shall die
In the midst of mighty rivers, without fear.
In the light and with remote inscriptions,
The fact will hang and stay around my neck
Like an amulet with a prayer.
Years ago, before the blue age of the seeds,
I decided, with the consent of the birds of night,
I shall surround myself with big empty beakers,
And with the thirst of dried up corpses,
Like a sultan I shall stare at them in delight.

> (Halman 1969: 19)

With his cycle of poems *Üç Şehitler Destanı*, 'Epic of the Three Martyrs' (1949), Dağlarca harks back to the War of Liberation, but he is no more of a romantic nationalist than Siegfried Sassoon. Here is one of the poems, *Şehitlerle Ölüler*, 'Martyrs and Corpses', again in Talât Halman's version:

On the Hill of the Three Martyrs our faces light up
In the distant glow of the soldiers who lie slain.
What, after all, is death compared to this?
Each breath we take is smoke or poison or pain.

Suppose our war is ended here, my friend.
Say we are discharged and back in the village again.
How can a man return to his mother,
His face smeared with a dismal stain?
That there is no way out changes nothing.
Thank heaven, we shunned the lowliness we disdain.
Answer me, did all these heroes
Sacrifice their lives in vain?

> (op. cit.: 35)

It is not surprising that he went on from there to take up the theme of social injustice. In *Toprak Ana*, 'Mother Earth' (1950), he tells of the tragic plight of Anatolia, the theme which we first saw dealt with by Yakup Kadri. That was not the end of Dağlarca's poetic development, but here we are at 1950 and it is time to pause.

8 The Arab world

Robin Ostle

In the Arab World, the Age of Translation and Adaptation revealed the extent to which it had borne fruit when the novel *Zaynab* was published in Egypt in 1913. It was not the first original novel to appear in Arabic, but more than any other work of its type it established this *genre* as a serious and permanent feature of modern Egyptian and indeed of the whole of modern Arabic literature. It was written by Muhammad Husayn Haykal (1886–1956), the son of the *'umda* of the village of Kafr Ghannam in the delta, and a totally typical member of that new Egyptian meritocracy which was rising to prominence in the first decade of the twentieth century. Many of them were the products of the institutions of non-Azhari education which had received such a boost to their development during the Khedivate of Isma'il (1863–79): the government schools, *dar al-'ulum*, and the Egyptian University itself which was founded in 1908. From such places there began to emerge in increasing numbers the equivalent of an Egyptian liberal *bourgeoisie*: the professional groups of doctors, lawyers, teachers, engineers, journalists and administrators who were to supersede the power groups which had held sway in the nineteenth century, namely the court circles and the Turko-Egyptian aristocracy. These were the characters who had been both described and satirized at the turn of the century by Muhammad al-Muwaylihi in his *Hadith 'Isa b. Hisham*, a book which is both the death of an old literary form and the birth of something new. Both the language and the inner structure of this work indicated that the traditional *maqama* was not to be the literary form which would express the visions of the new *bourgeoisie*, but at the same time the book makes it quite clear that the future of the country depended on the eventual success of their efforts to emancipate themselves from both British imperialism and the old court aristocracy.

Thus it was that in 1913, Haykal proposed a dramatic new departure with that most supple and formless of all the literary categories, the novel. With *Zaynab*, modern Arabic fiction gained its own version of *La*

Nouvelle Héloïse, because it encompasses the dreams and visions of Haykal's class in a manner strikingly reminiscent of Jean-Jacques Rousseau. The book was actually written while its author was in Paris, and so foreign was it in form and content to the current standards of literary taste in Egypt, that initially Haykal was unwilling to acknowledge its authorship. The book consists of all the classic elements of its·European models: long, sustained idylls about the Egyptian countryside, episodes of romantic passion, the struggle to adhere to the accepted patterns of social virtue as against following one's natural, instinctive, inclinations. The real significance of this novel lies not so much in its intrinsic literary qualities – indeed from the point of view of structure it is an odd, incoherent creation – but in the fact of its existence and the subsequent patterns which it established in Egyptian fiction throughout the 1920s and the 1930s. The main feature of the book is the vision of Haykal's romantic nationalism. He is totally imbued by the ideals and aspirations of the new generation of secular liberals, many of whom were attracted to Ahmad Lutfi al-Sayyid, the *Hizb al-Umma* Party, and its newspaper *al-Jarida. Zaynab* was the result of Haykal's attempt to relate the visions of the person that he had become to the society from which he originally came. He was only one of many writers who were exposed to the results of education and culture as it had developed in the societies of Western Europe, and who then returned to the Arab world and attempted to get to grips through literature with what they saw as the realities and potentials of their own original situations.

The two elements in Haykal's book which were seminal for the subsequent development of creative prose writing for the next three decades are pastoral, and satire. Together these express the aspirations and the revulsions of Haykal's time. In *Zaynab* it is the first which predominates: the long sustained passages of idyllic description of scenes of the Egyptian countryside represent the author's dream visions about his society. The *fellahin,* the peasant characters, including Zaynab herself, take on almost heroic dimensions. At a time when Haykal and his generation were trying to create new political and social identities for their community, it was natural that the countryside should become a vital ideological necessity for the discourse of politics, and for the imagery of the new literature of national authenticity. After all, the countryside did contain the vast majority of the population. The second element, that of satire, is somewhat muted, but it is undeniably present. There is just sufficient of a grasp of some of the realities of life in rural Egypt, with its poverty and oppression, to give one a strong sense of how severely circumscribed are the possibilities for individual freedom and liberty. So Ibrahim, whom Zaynab really loves, is unable to pursue their relationship

106 *Modern literature in the Near and Middle East*

because it is the parents who do the match-making. He is driven away from the village and the girl that he loves because of military service, which he cannot avoid because of his humble social origins. Zaynab ultimately pines away and dies in final scenes of intense sentimental emotionalism. The double-edged message of Rousseau, that of natural idyll and social critique, is now firmly established in the Arab world.

Haykal's novel was one of the more dramatic examples of the formal transformations which had been affecting prose literature since the late nineteenth century, but the case of Arabic poetry was very different. The external façade of poetic form was to endure well into the twentieth century, long after the *maqama* had become irrelevant in artistic terms. An inevitable result of the impatient Europeanizing policies of the Khedive Isma'il in Egypt was to create cultural polarities within society, and on the scale of these polarities, poetry was ranged on the side of the traditionalists. Indeed, it was one of their most powerful weapons. Poetry was, and is, the supreme Arab art, and even at the turn of the century, the *qasida* form was still eminently recognizable as that which had been used by Imru'l-Qays some thirteen centuries ago. Poets such as Mahmud Sami al-Barudi (1839–1904), Hafiz Ibrahim (1871–1932) and Ahmad Shawqi (1868–1932) were the equivalents in literature to the followers of Sheikh 'Ali Yusif and Mustafa Kamil in politics. They were fiercely anti-British and dedicated to the maintenance of indigenous values and traditions, while Haykal and his colleagues were ardent nationalists, and at the same time enthusiastic proponents of Westernization in Egyptian society. Faced with the apparent omniscience and omnipotence of Western Europe, Arabs could feel that at least in the realm of poetry they had no reason to feel inferior as their poets continued to display a tenacious self-confidence in the pride of past achievements. It is hardly surprising that where Shawqi and Hafiz Ibrahim struck the widest response, both inside Egypt and beyond, was in their satirical attacks upon the British presence; it was in the realm of political poetry in general, that these neo-classical poets achieved particular renown, and nowhere was this more so than in Iraq where Ma'ruf al-Rusafi (1875–1945) and Muhammad Mahdi al-Jawahiri (b. 1900) turned their highly talented artistic invective against corruption, social injustice and British imperialism. Both Hafiz and Shawqi remained ardent patriots until their deaths in 1932, and although Shawqi in particular was subjected to bitter attacks after the First World War by a younger generation of writers, he had the ultimate satisfaction of knowing that he was an incomparably greater poet than any of his detractors.

The cultural polarities which took root in key parts of the Arab world during the nineteenth century, continued to affect both the discourse and the practice of literature, and nowhere were the debates pursued more

The Arab world 107

vigorously than in Egypt in the 1920s. Ahmad Shawqi was attacked by al-'Aqqad and al-Mazini, not so much because of the quality of his poetry, as because of the particular image of traditional Arab-Islamic culture which his poetry represented. Taha Husayn called into question the authenticity of some pre-Islamic poetry, not because he was against pre-Islamic poetry, but because he was anxious to introduce into an Egyptian forum some of the methods and standards of Western criticism. It is wrong to think of such literary radicals as 'anti-Islamic', as their opponents usually claimed, but they were certainly against a vision of Arab–Islamic tradition which they thought of as ossified and reactionary, and which they held responsible for the disparity which existed between their own societies and those of Western Europe. In this context we may now consider a poet from a region of the Arab world which has but few claims to eminence in the history of the Arabic literature produced between 1914 and 1950, a poet who died prematurely in 1934, just two years after Ahmad Shawqi, but who belongs to a very different world of poetry: the Tunisian Abu'l-Qasim al-Shabbi (1909–34).

In Tunisia in the 1920s and 1930s the prevailing political and social realities must have been especially depressing for a young man with vision and aspirations such as al-Shabbi. New political groupings were still very much in their infancy, and the grip of the French Protectorate seemed ominously permanent. In 1927 al-Shabbi swept into the Khalduniyya institute in Tunis where he delivered a long lecture entitled 'Poetic Imagination and the Arabs'. It represents a bitter and extreme attack on certain aspects of traditional Arab–Islamic culture:

Arabic literature no longer suits our present spirit, temperament, inclinations or aspirations in life... . It was not created for us, children of these times, but for hearts that are now silenced by death... . We must never look upon Arabic literature as an ideal which we have to follow, or whose spirit, style and ideas we have to imitate, but we must consider it simply as one of those ancient literatures which we admire and respect, and no more... .

(translation by M. M. Badawi in von Grunebaum 1973: 196)

This lecture is extreme in its views and quite unscholarly in many instances. To derive any value from it, we must see it as an emotional reaction of extreme frustration, a loud rhetorical protest against the travesties of Islamic values and civilization as they existed in the sorry state of his own society, or as they had been distorted in the ossified, irrelevant instruction which al-Shabbi had received in the then archaic system of the Zaytouna mosque-university. In the same lecture, he objects with vehemence to the manner in which much of classical Arabic literature had portrayed women:

108 *Modern literature in the Near and Middle East*

The attitude of Arabic literature to woman is base and ignoble, and sinks to the lowest depths of materialism. It only sees in woman a body to be desired and one of the basest pleasures in life to be enjoyed... . Have you ever heard anyone among them (the Arab poets) talk about woman who is the altar of love in this universe, in the way a devout worshipper talks about the house of God?

(ibid.)

Al-Shabbi is largely correct when he makes this 'accusation', because apart from some of the poetry written back in the Umayyad period, most Arab poets in their treatment of women had concentrated heavily upon the physiological constants rather than the psychological variables. He reacted against the heavily physical conventions of the traditional portrayal of women's attributes in pre-modern Arabic poetry, and in so doing he created an excess of platonic spiritualism. In this trend he was accompanied by the majority of Arab romantic poets in the 1920s and 1930s, particularly by the Apollo poets in Egypt led by Ahmad Zaki Abu Shadi. They took as their models and their inspiration the highly idealized, spiritual representation of love and women which had been characteristic of European literature in its more intensely romantic phases. In his famous poem 'Prayers in the Temple of Love', he elevates woman to a plane of ethereal adoration, compensating in his eyes for her centuries of degradation at the hands of Arab–Islamic tradition. Such celebrations of the female ideal which one finds in the poetry of al-Shabbi and some of his Egyptian contemporaries are mostly devoid of any elements of physical or psychological realism. The majority of the women in this romantic poetry of the 1920s and 1930s are, like Caesar's Octavia, of holy, cold and still dispositions. While one would have to make an honourable exception of some of the more sensual pieces of amatory poetry written by the Egyptian 'Ali Mahmud Taha or some of the earliest poems of the Syrian poet Nizar Qabbani, on the whole these images of women are statuesque rather than warm and living. The issue of women's emancipation in the 1920s and 1930s remained a subject of hot debate, as it had been ever since the nineteenth century, but in the majority of Arab societies, the debate was not accompanied by dynamic processes of rapid social change on a wide scale, directed specifically at transforming the lot of women. Poetry responded to a relatively static situation by replacing one set of symbols by other symbols, which, ironically, in some respects were even further removed from reality than their traditional classical counterparts.

The work of al-Shabbi provides some of the best examples of Arabic romantic poetry produced during the period under discussion. The tragedy of

The Arab world 109

this time was that for writers, intellectuals, and for many politicians, it was an age of idealism and aspiration which all too often lacked any concrete form of fulfilment in individual or societal terms. In al-Shabbi's verse there is a constant transition from the mimetic to the symbolic. Suffering as he did from a fatal illness, his own struggle for life is transformed into a struggle for a new existence on the part of his whole nation:

If the People one day desires to live, then fate must needs respond.
(al-Shabbi 1966: 240)

Imagery drawn from nature dominates his work, and a recurrent theme is the traditional antithesis between aridity and luxuriant verdant growth: the former is the waste land of time present, and the latter is the vision of the future. There is a constant alternation between visions of nightmarish horror, associated with darkness and evening, but these give way to the dawn in which the poet finds refreshment, relief and renewal. It is through the symbol of the re-birth of morning that he expresses most frequently the expectation of redemption both for himself as an individual, and for his nation as a whole:

Wounds be calm, and sorrows be silent
The time of lament and the age of madness are dead
Morning has peered out beyond the peaks.
(op.cit.: 234)

The Egyptian poet 'Abd al-Rahman Shukri died in 1958, but most of his significant work was written at least a decade before that of al-Shabbi. Although he does not quite scale the same intensely spiritual, platonic heights as al-Shabbi, his sense of the harsh duality between real and ideal, ugliness and beauty, the sordid and the sublime, is much more acute. Throughout Shukri's *diwan*, there is a tortuous flow of aspiration and disillusion, of frustration which is born of an impotence to realize ideals. His poetry is corroborated by the largely autobiographical *Confessions*, which he claimed were a record of the thoughts and feelings of a young Egyptian facing up to the problems of his existence. The book was published in 1916, and the young Egyptian is pessimistic about the changing forms of tyranny which his country endures. He has grandiose hopes and dreams, but also a chronic incapacity to put them into effect. He is a prey to doubt and bewilderment, and is torn between the old and the new. He is uncertain as to which ideas and customs are harmful fantasies, and which are the proper bases for development. In his poetry, Shukri veers so sharply from ecstasy to despair, that much of his work reflects a manic-depressive quality. In the final line of this poem 'The Poet and the Vision of Perfection', he virtually writes his own epitaph:

110 *Modern literature in the Near and Middle East*

> May God have mercy on a poet, who perished a victim to lofty desires.
> (Shukri 1960: 130)

At its worst the Arabic romantic poetry of the 20s, 30s and 40s illustrates literary forms of facile, subjective escapism, in which highly nebulous concepts such as *al-majhul* (the unknown) were accorded a significance which they did not deserve, and in which a strong sense of cultural alienation was cultivated *ad nauseam*. At its best, in the hands of the Tunisian al-Shabbi, the Syrian 'Umar Abu Risha, or the Lebanese *poète maudit*, Ilyas Abu Shabaka, it becomes a splendid artistic extension of the painful dilemmas which gripped individuals, societies and nations. Not the least of its contributions was to the continuing development of Arabic poetry itself. On the surface, in the majority of cases, the lines of regular length remained, end-stopped rhyme remained, and the conventional metre continued to be employed. But within the outer frame of these time-honoured forms, the language and imagery of the Arab romantic poets amounted to nothing less than a revolution.

Although the appearance of *Zaynab* in 1913 had established the novel as a permanent feature of modern Arabic literature, the progress of this new literary form was anything but rapid and dramatic. In Egypt, Haykal's lead was followed by Ibrahim al-Mazini, 'Abbas Mahmud al-'Aqqad, Taha Husayn and Tawfiq al-Hakim, who were responsible for a number of novels which appeared from the mid-1920s through to the 1940s. One problem that these writers faced was the fact that a virtually conventional feature of the European novel was passion, either in its romantic or in its more animal forms. Haykal's book had been particularly *avant-garde* for its time in this respect. The plots of novels such as al-Mazini's *Ibrahim al-Katib* (probably written in 1925–6) or al-'Aqqad's *Sara* (1938) are catalogues of the amorous adventures of the central characters, which proceed by a series of unconvincing coincidences, and which come perilously close to the world of facile escapism purveyed by popular romantic magazines. However in the case of al-Mazini in particular, important technical advances were made in the use of dialogue, and the humour of his writing is another vital element which helps to make the improbable sequences of events more palatable to the reader. Yet these books make it clear that the theme of the love story was not one which could be transposed easily into an Arab society in the 1920s and 1930s along with the novel form. In the meantime, the short story was making rapid strides towards artistic maturity: already back in the 1880s and the 1890s 'Abdulla al-Nadim had played a pioneering role with the original short stories which he published in his Cairo periodicals *al-Tankit wa'l-Tabkit* and *al-Ustadh*. This *genre* was also able to build solidly on certain

The Arab world 111

elements in the classical Arabic literary tradition, and the masters of the short story in French, Russian and English literature were increasingly well known to Arab writers as the twentieth century progressed.

The group of writers who became known as *jama'at al-madrasat al-haditha* (The New School) were particularly instrumental in establishing the short story as the most technically accomplished of the prose *genres* in this period which we are discussing. They were active in Cairo in the 1920s, and their number included such major writers as Muhammad and Mahmud Taymur, Ahmed Khayri Sa'id, Mahmud Tahir Lashin and Yahya Haqqi. Yahya Haqqi in particular greatly expanded the formal and the thematic possibilities of the short story with his early writings in the 1920s, most of which were published in *al-Fajr* magazine, and concentrate on the numerous types and variety of human kind amongst the poor classes of society in both rural and urban environments. Some of the better-known stories of Mahmud Taymur and Mahmud Tahir Lashin recall the preoccupations of Haykal in *Zaynab. Al-'Awda* by Taymur continues the theme of the pastoral idealization of rural Egypt, while the city is a symbol of vice and corruption. More seriously, Lashin's story *Hadith al-Qarya* exposes mercilessly the dilemma which had faced writers ever since Haykal placed the *aryaf* and the *fellahin* at the centre of Egyptian literature: the dilemma was, how did the new meritocrats relate the theories and visions of their liberal educations, absorbed in Cairo or in Europe, to the situation of their compatriots as a whole, who had little or no point of contact with that culture. The problem was acute, because it was the new educated élite which had formed the new generation of political power groups. In this particular story, there is no meaningful contact between the *fellahin* and the well-meaning young liberals from the city. The story ends in complete mutual incomprehension.

Of especial interest in this period under discussion is the technical success of one or two outstanding examples of the *novella,* a sort of half-way house in formal terms between the short story and the full-blown novel. Once again the writer in question is Mahmud Tahir Lashin with his novella *Eve without Adam* published in 1934. Here he develops even more fully the theme of incompatibility between traditional and modern culture, as his heroine, Eve, struggles to exercise some control over her career, and her personal and emotional life. Eve's tragedy is the tragedy of this whole period, when ideas and ideals could be pursued and even realized in certain individual cases, but the individual achievement was not accompanied by wider social transformations, which might then allow the individual to be fulfilled also in terms of society as a whole. This work is a classic literary representation of cultural alienation, and the heroine personifies a number of the principles which had long been preached in

112 *Modern literature in the Near and Middle East*

Egypt and elsewhere: the need for education, the elimination of social inequalities, and the emancipation of women. In spite of all Eve's qualities and the development of her social and intellectual talents, she is unable to exploit these properly in the wider framework of society. Thus she fails as a woman, a teacher and a potential social reformer. Less pessimistic both in outcome and underlying philosophy is Yahya Haqqi's *novella*, *The Saint's Lamp* published in 1944 (see Badawi' 1973). Here again the theme is that of the clash between modern science and traditional beliefs, but there is ultimate symbiosis between the two to the benefit of all concerned. The protagonist Isma'il is one of the few characters in modern Arabic literature who, on occasion, identifies positively and sympathetically with the urban *milieu* which has been a vital formative element in his personality.

Ever since the inauguration of the Royal Opera House in 1869 as part of the festivities which accompanied the opening of the Suez Canal, the theatre had become part of the life of the more affluent members of society in Cairo and Alexandria. Although the prolific 'Abdallah al-Nadim had written an original play entitled *al-Watan wa'l-'Arab* during the Khedivate of Tawfiq, it was not until the second decade of the twentieth century that successful original playwrights such as Muhammad Taymur and Muhammad Lutfi Jum'ah began to emerge. Another important pioneering Egyptian dramatist was Ibrahim Ramzi (1884–1949) (see Badawi (1988: 74–101). But it is the name of Tawfiq al-Hakim which dominates the development of the drama throughout the period under discussion. Ever since the publication of his first play in 1919, *The Unwelcome Guest*, he played a central role in the rise of the modern Arab theatre during the 1920s, 1930s and 1940s. The year 1950 saw the publication of a volume of his plays which ran to almost 800 pages: it contains no fewer than twenty-one separate plays, all of which had been written since 1945! Although one may have reservations about the practical problems involved in actually staging many of al-Hakim's plays, few would deny that works such as *People of the Cave* (1933) or *Shahrazad* (1934) have become the classics of the modern Arab theatre. It does not diminish his achievement to suggest that it is only since 1950 that the drama in Egypt and numerous other Arab countries has achieved a genuinely widespread balance between inspired writing and the more refined techniques of stage production. This is a process in which the ever youthful al-Hakim played a full part before his death in 1987.

A surprising statistic indicates that writing for the theatre represents less than half the prodigious amount of Tawfiq al-Hakim's creative writing. In 1933 he produced in the form of a novel his version of the mood of romantic nationalism which had gripped Egypt prior to the 1919

The Arab world 113

Revolution: this was *'Awdat al-Ruh (Return of the Spirit)* But it is with his *Yawmiyyat Na'ib fi'l-Aryaf (Diary of a Country Lawyer)* published in 1937 that we return to the themes which had obsessed Haykal in 1913. Now there is a significant change of emphasis: the idyll has all but disappeared and it is replaced by the biting satire which condemns the folly of applying laws to peasants who have no understanding of the laws or of the processes of applying them. The reader is brought up against the dichotomy in mentality and lifestyle which exists between urban administrators and the rural recipients of the doubtful benefits of this administration. Between the court officials and the *fellahin* there are whole worlds of difference in their codes of honour, and in their cultural mythologies. Through this book, al-Hakim reveals that he himself is no nearer to solving the dilemma which the countryside posed for writers and for Egypt as a whole. He is essentially an outsider, observing the *aryaf* across the chasm which has been created by his own cultural formation and experiences. It is true that the angle at which al-Hakim refracts his visions of reality is much narrower than it has been in the work of Haykal, but he remains an outsider. This was a theme to which he returned with considerable success in his short play *Ughniyat al-Mawt (Song of Death)* published in 1950.

With the 1940s the novel in Arabic finally comes of age, and it does so in a setting which is urban. The transition from dreams of romantic nationalism to nightmarish visions of social reality is illustrated graphically in novels based on life in the city. The work of Yahya Haqqi had turned the attention of creative literature towards the lower strata of urban society, and along with the novel *Millim al-Akbar* (1944) by 'Adil Kamil this leads directly to the drug addiction, pimps, prostitutes, poverty and petty crime in the world of Naguib Mahfuz. If the real hero of *Zaynab* had been idealized visions of the Egyptian *aryaf* then in the novels of Mahfuz published in the 1940s, it is Cairo which is the protagonist, although hardly the hero. The titles themselves give an accurate indication: *Khan al-Khalili* (1945), *al-Qahira al-Jadida* (1946), *Zuqaq al-Midaqq* (1947). The human characters are dominated by the *milieu* which is all-embracing and usually malevolent. The humour with which writers such as al-Mazini and al-Hakim had accompanied their satire in the 20s and 30s here has a sharpening rather than a mitigating effect. These extremely large-scale works by Mahfuz are the nearest equivalent in Arabic to what one might describe as the 'classical' phase of the development of the novel in nineteenth-century Europe, where the city was frequently a symbol and a setting for chronicles of dramatic social mobility. So also in Mahfuz, all the classic elements are present: avarice, a desperate obsession with money, and a willingness to embrace all manner

114 *Modern literature in the Near and Middle East*

of immorality to achieve upward social mobility. The fatal difference is that in the Cairo of Mahfuz, the means of achieving such mobility are cruelly limited, and such as do exist, tend to degrade the characters, thus precluding dimensions of grandeur or heroism. Hilary Kilpatrick (1974: 79) observes in a study of *Zuqaq al-Midaqq* 'only the dead have anything material to steal'. The protagonists of the books go to exaggerated lengths to transform their existences, and the end results mock their futile efforts. Thus Mahjub 'Abd al-Da'im in *al-Qahira al-Jadida* begins his career with lofty ambitions but in the end he can only gain a position in a ministry by marrying the mistress of one of the higher officials, this being a convenient way of maintaining her while the affair with the higher official continues. In *Khan al-Khalili,* Ahmad 'Akif is a symbol of the numerous civil servants who are victimized by the lack of any opening or opportunity in society. His initial hopes and ambitions gave way to the depressing reality of a lowly bureaucrat, who has no future in his professional life or in his personal relationships. *Zuqaq al-Midaqq* records the frustration of Hamida with the alley, and her determination to avoid the mundane fate which will be hers if she stays there. The only means of transformation available to someone in her position lies in the possibility of sexual exploitation: she gambles with this, her only asset, and falls under the control of Ibrahim Farag, the pimp who runs a brothel patronized mainly by foreign soldiers.

The city, which was a traditional setting for many of the great novels of Europe, was a symbol of social mobility, a symbol which in Europe was not divorced from social and economic reality for a significant number of people who did not exclude the *petite bourgeoisie*. In the modern Arab world the city is no less a symbol of social mobility, and a focal point for ambitions and aspirations. But for the vast majority of people these extremely powerful symbols are not supported by reality. The means whereby they may transform their circumstances according to their expectations simply do not exist. The cities from Casablanca to Cairo and elsewhere are more like monuments to *immobilisme* for too many of their inhabitants. In the Cairene novels of Mahfuz, most of the characters are blocked. They suffer from an inability to transform their fate by normal endeavour and action. Ambition and reality are somehow incompatible.

After the First World War, the hopes entertained by the new nation states in Egypt and the general area of the Levant, on the whole were not realized. The initial optimism of the immediate post-war years soon gave way to the realization that the colonial powers did not intend to abandon their positions of power in the region without a longer struggle. At the same time, it proved much easier to preach the principles of social reform and economic justice, than to put them into practice. For the Arab states of

The Arab world 115

North Africa, the situation was even less ambiguous. The period which we have been discussing is one which may be characterized as beginning with optimistic hope and ending in despair and frustration, whether one is considering literature or politics. On the political front, the period ends with the first Arab–Israeli war and its immediate aftermath. What many think of in positive terms as the creation of the State of Israel, is seen by Arabs as an act of destruction. Both as an historical fact and as a symbol, it concludes a period which began with high hopes and ended in the ashes of disillusion. I have tried to suggest how literature charted this cycle from idyll to nightmare. This student derives what comfort he can from the observation that literature remains one of the glories of a region which has more than its fair share of economic injustice, and political perfidy which is both international and domestic.

9 Modern Hebrew

David Patterson

The rubric 'from romantic nationalism to social criticism 1914–1950' is perhaps less applicable to modern Hebrew literature than to the other literatures under review. As in many areas of Jewish experience, modern Hebrew literature does not conform to the more usual patterns of development. Indeed, both romantic nationalism and social criticism are firmly rooted in earlier patterns of modern Hebrew literature. For something like a hundred years, approximately 1790–1890, Hebrew literature attempted to come to grips with the modern world first in central, and then in Eastern Europe. Its avowed aim to serve as a bridge in order to facilitate the entry of the Jewish people to the world of European culture was diametrically at odds with a literary theory which attempted to express a widening range of ideas in a neo-biblical Hebrew. These two contradictory forces which characterized most of modern Hebrew literature throughout the nineteenth century may perhaps be conveyed in the image of a 'phoenix in fetters' which symbolizes the lofty aspirations of a literature chained by the shackles of a restricted vocabulary and a classical structure. Again, the didactic tendencies of the authors were accompanied by plot elements of adventure and intrigue to engage the reader's attention. Two such disparate aims, however, frequently made strange bedfellows, and tended to subject the reader's credulity and patience to some considerable strain.

As Dr. Parfitt has shown (see Chapter 5, pp 65ff) the novels of Abraham Mapu were informed by a romantic nationalism, while social criticism permeated both his novels and particularly those of his successors such as Peretz Smolenskin, Reuben Asher Braudes and most of their contemporaries. In spite of the influence Mapu's tales exerted on at least two generations of Hebrew readers, the aesthetic qualities of nineteenth-century Hebrew literature left much to be desired. The great leap forward took place in the twenty-five years prior to the First World War, which represented the classical period in modern Hebrew literature. The advance

Modern Hebrew 117

was heralded almost simultaneously by Chaim Nachman Bialik in poetry, Mendele Mocher Seforim in fiction, Ahad Ha-Am in the essay form, and a host of other talented writers. After lagging behind European literature to the extent of several decades, modern Hebrew literature caught up in one fell swoop. For the first time in the modern period, the literature became interesting not only from the point of view of the history of literature and the development of language, but aesthetically for its own sake. The whittling away and gradual deterioration of the great cultural and educational institutions in Eastern Europe seem to have unleashed a wave of creativity, with Hebrew literature riding on its crest. By the outbreak of the Second World War Hebrew literature in Eastern Europe had increased dramatically both in quantity and quality. Within its framework, romantic nationalism was expressed by Bialik, Tchernikhovski, and such writers as Frishman and Feierberg, while strong social criticism characterized the novels of Mendele, Brenner, Gnessin and Berdichevski. It is remarkable, however, that in spite of the overall high quality, the writers criticized each other mercilessly, claiming – contrary to all the evidence – that nothing of worth was being produced in poetry or in prose.

From the first decade of the twentieth century, and particularly in the period between the two world wars, an extraordinary development occurred which can have few if any parallels in world literature. In the space of two or three decades, Hebrew literature uprooted itself from Europe and transferred itself bodily to Palestine or to use the term most frequently encountered, *Eretz Yisrael*, the land of Israel. It is important to recall that the term *Eretz Yisrael* reflects most accurately the image in the mind of most of these writers, in order to understand the processes involved. This extraordinary shift involved the transference of literature from a society in Eastern Europe comprising many millions of inhabitants to an extremely sparse Jewish population which in 1914 numbered scarcely 85,000 souls, a figure which was further reduced during the deprivation of the war years to less than 60,000 in 1918. The transition, not surprisingly, was neither smooth nor easily accomplished. The transference of the centre of Hebrew creativity from a solid base in terms of the size and social stratification of a closely knit and long established community to the flimsy and precarious structure of a numerically tiny population, much of it of comparatively recent vintage, gave rise to considerable stress.

A difficult process of adjustment is encountered by every writer, indeed by every person, who emigrates from one country to another and is forced to become acclimatized to a radically different environment. The physical, social and sociological upheavals involved in accommodating to radically new surroundings vary with the stage in life at which such a change is

118 *Modern literature in the Near and Middle East*

made. The ability to acquire and speak a new language like a native, for example, appears to reach a threshold at about the age of ten. Although prior to that age an immigrant can learn a new vernacular without accent, it becomes an extremely rare accomplishment in the case of older immigrants. A young immigrant is likely to absorb the social and cultural patterns of his land of adoption much more readily and thoroughly than the adult whose mind and attitudes have already been formed. For the former, the old country is merely a prelude to a new life, whereas for the latter the new country is largely a sequel to the really formative experiences already gained. Certainly, a harking back to origins, whether with admiration or disdain, is almost inevitable.

Admittedly, in the case of Hebrew writers migrating from Europe to *Eretz Yisrael* there were mitigating factors. Although their first vernacular was usually Yiddish, most had studied Hebrew as their first literary language from a very tender age. Immigration, in consequence, did not involve the acquisition of an entirely new language – as was the case with the vast majority of Jews migrating to the United States, for example, during the same period – but rather a different application of a largely familiar language. Again, the emotional ties and loyal devotion of a large section of diaspora Jewry to the holy land were deeply rooted and conducive to radical action – as witnessed by the extraordinary growth of national aspirations that fashioned the movement of Zionism. Far from imagining that they were migrating to a foreign land, Jewish immigrants to *Eretz Yisrael* were convinced that they were returning home, and that their title to the land was absolute.

The importance of this factor can scarcely be overemphasized. For the Jewish child in Eastern Europe, education began with the Hebrew Bible at kindergarten age, and his familiarity with the patriarchal narratives was constantly strengthened by their annual recitation in the synagogue. To many Jewish boys the exploits of their ancestral heroes in the ancient land of Israel seemed far more intimate and real, and certainly more appealing than the squalid misery of the hostile environment in which they lived. However harsh and long drawn out, the exile was a temporary circumstance, and redemption might occur at any time. The daily prayers were redolent with hope for the restoration to Zion, and there was no question that sooner or later it would come to pass. The religious festivals were related topographically and climatically to Jerusalem. The complex regulations governing the agricultural cycle, so important in both synagogue service and classroom studies, were geared entirely to the geography of *Eretz Yisrael*, regardless of the conditions of Eastern Europe or anywhere else.

Jewish entitlement to *Eretz Yisrael* seemed so natural and absolute that its exponents were long able to ignore almost entirely any unpalatable mention of other occupants, despite all evidence to the contrary. During the forty years from the appearance of Mapu's novel, *The Love of Zion* in 1853 to the publication of Ahad Ha-Am's searing articles 'Truth from *Eretz Yisrael*' in the years 1891–3, Hebrew literature contains scant reference to the real political and demographic facts of Palestine in the nineteenth century. Indeed, the following snatch of conversation from a novel by A. S. Rabinowitz is sufficiently uncommon to warrent special mention:

> In my view Smolenskin is quite correct in saying that there is no way out of our impasse other than settling in *Eretz Yisrael*.
>
> Ha, ha, ha! Settling in *Eretz Yisrael*! You would be better advised to say settling in Palestine, the land of the Turks, for the land does not belong to us now, but to the sons of Ishmael, the wild Turks who are quite uncivilized.
>
> (Rabinowitz 1887: 150)

It is no wonder, then, that Ahad Ha-Am's contention that the amount of good land currently unoccupied was not large and that the Arabs were not 'wild men of the desert' as was usually supposed, caused such consternation.

> The peasants are delighted when a Hebrew colony is founded in their midst, for they are well rewarded for their labour, and prosper from year to year, as experience has shown. And the big land-owners are also delighted when we come, for we pay a price for their wastelands such as they have never even dreamed about. But if in the course of time the Jewish holding in the country develops to such an extent as to encroach in some degree on the native population, the latter will not easily give up its position.
>
> (Ahad Ha-Am 1950: 24)

The clash of image and reality is a factor of central importance in the shift of Hebrew literature from Eastern Europe to *Eretz Yisrael*. The exponents of nationalism had viewed the land so consistently through blinkers which allowed little shift in perspective, that physical contact with the country would seem to imply only two possibilities. Either the vision would have to shatter against the harsh reality of Palestine, or an attempt would be made to make the land conform to the vision of *Eretz Yisrael*. But frequent resort was also made to a third possibility which demanded the simultaneous acceptance of both attitudes, however contradictory – engendering the kind of paradox not infrequently encountered where

120 *Modern literature in the Near and Middle East*

strong emotional factors are at work. The dilemma permeates much of the major writing of the period, as the stories of Brenner, Agnon and Hazaz – to mention only three of the more important authors – amply demonstrate. Indeed a detailed investigation of this phenomenon, as manifested in the work of each individual migrant author, is clearly a major pre-requisite for a proper understanding of the development of modern Hebrew literature – certainly from the early years of the century until the outbreak of the Second World War. Writer after writer left the shores of Europe in search of *Eretz Yisrael,* only to find themselves in Palestine.

The psychological stress resulting from the clash of image and reality was frequently the more disturbing for other reasons. The situation was aggravated by the nature of immigration which consisted largely of individuals rather than family units. This was particularly the case among young pioneers, who all too frequently found themselves without a single relative in their new land. When U. Z. Greenberg described his departure from his parents' home in the line from *Le-Margelotayikh Yerushalayim:*

> Father raged, mother wept, and a white bed was orphaned
> (Barash 1930: 400; Greenberg 1939: 39)

the poignancy is exacerbated by the knowledge that not only the bed, but the poet himself has been orphaned by his action. In great measure the collective settlement became a substitute for the lost family structure, and there can be little doubt that the rapid growth and success of the collective was due, at least in part, to its social function. Hebrew literature was conditioned, however, not only by the physical and psychological odysseys of the individual writers, but to some extent by the nature of the readership. It is important to recall that prior to the First World War, and largely – although in decreasing measure – in the period between the two world wars, the majority of readers of Hebrew literature lived in Eastern Europe, which also supported most of the Hebrew publishing houses and the leading Hebrew periodicals. The emotional expectations of these readers, who lived in conditions of extreme political and economic oppression, must be regarded as a powerful force. Cherished illusions die hard, and the reader's susceptibilities tend to be taken seriously, particularly when the writer has shared his convictions to the arduous point of himself settling in *Eretz Yisrael,* and remains anxious to encourage Jewish immigration – or at the very least not discourage it.

This geographical separation of author and readers is a most unusual if not unique circumstance and certainly worthy of consideration. The writer in exile is, of course, a common enough phenomenon, and his work is often directed to a mass readership in his lost homeland. But in the case of Hebrew literature in the period under review, the situation was reversed.

Modern Hebrew 121

Here, the writers who left Europe to settle in *Eretz Yisrael* regarded themselves as being in their real homeland, while their readers in Eastern Europe were regarded – and, indeed, looked upon themselves – as being in exile. Whereas the writer in exile in other literatures is concerned with the task of changing the conditions of his homeland so that he may himself return to his readers, the Hebrew writer in Palestine was concerned with the task of bringing his readers to him, and of helping to shape conditions to make such a major demographic shift possible. It was the case – if the metaphor may be pressed into service – of making the mountain go to Muhammad! The methods and degrees of subtlety employed towards this end vary greatly in the case of each individual writer, and the whole process again requires detailed investigation. But the inherent logic of the situation would seem to be compelling. The psychological pressures on any writer in such a situation, where ideology, emotional inclination and self-interest coincide, are clearly very great – hence the need to cherish the vision even in the face of harsh reality.

It is pertinent, perhaps, to quote a passage from Amos Oz's novel *Touch the Water, Touch the Wind* in which Kumin (the author's grandfather?) relates the following anecdote:

> My father was a kind of Hebrew poet, a kind of madman, a Zionist, a stray lamb in the streets of Odessa. All his life he wrote poems about Mount Carmel and Mount Tabor and Mount Moriah, and the wailing wall in Jerusalem, about the desert and the holy tombs... . A few years ago I packed him off to Palestine before it was the death of him or he was the death of me. And do you know...what became of him there in the land of his dreams in the twilight of his life? The old man settled down, no doubt on one of the hills to which he had always lifted up his eyes, among his holy tombs, and there, in his long-dreamed of Palestine, among the hills and tombs there the old man goes on to his dying day writing heart-rending poems of longing for some other Palestine, the real one. All with perfect faith. All in Hebrew. And in Biblical language.

(deLange 1976: 91)

Geography is responsible, too, for a further problem with which the immigrant authors were compelled to grapple. A writer's imagery is heavily dependent upon the impressions and associations gathered in his most formative years. The climate and landscape, the flora and fauna, the geography of town and country, as well as the civic and domestic architecture of the native land together form a basic environment from which the literary imagination draws its sustenance. The metaphors and similes, the colouring, the light and shade of description reflect the

122 *Modern literature in the Near and Middle East*

impressions of the outside world upon the tender mind of a growing child. They are what C. N. Bialik called 'pictures of my world in those first days... the soul's basic, elemental scenes'.

> How true the saying is that man sees and perceives only once; in childhood! The first visions, in that same innocence as on the day when they left the Creator's hand, they are the real essence and the very stuff of life; and those impressions that follow are secondary and deficient, seemingly like the first, but weak reflections of them, and not genuine... . All the sights of heaven and earth which I have blessed throughout my life, have received no nourishment except from the power of that first vision.
>
> (Patterson 1961: 55)

It is not difficult to imagine the shattering effect exerted on a writer when all the physical ties linking him to his native environment are abruptly and finally sundered. 'I am here, totally here', Leah Goldberg wrote, 'in a foreign city in the heart of the great alien motherland' (Goldberg 1970: 104). The point is forcefully portrayed in D. Shimoni's idyll *Yovel ha-Eglonim* ('The Waggoners' Jubilee'), in which a young poet describes the extent to which the radical change of landscape which he experienced in moving from Eastern Europe to *Eretz Yisrael* inhibited his poetic creativity.

> From the moment I came to the land my spirit was utterly downcast.
>
> Nature opened her book before me, but I did not know how to read.
>
> The letters were new and strange, their combinations oddly unfamiliar.
>
> I was captivated by their hidden beauty; I experienced the secret magic.
>
> But my heart did not leap for them as yet, like a bird for its nest.
>
> The full redeeming echo still did not well from the depths of my soul.
>
> And even in moments sublime, when the Muse descended upon me.
>
> And a torrent of feeling raged and blazed into vision before me –
>
> They were not the sights of the land of Israel. – No! But the distant sights of another land which had cradled my childhood... .
>
> My young bones were filled with the sights and sounds of the Russian landscape.
>
> The shadows of its dark forests and the majesty of its great rivers.

Modern Hebrew 123

The freedom of the green steppes and the gold of its wide meadows...

I saw a majestic palm and longed for the sad poplar;

The winter-blossom charmed me, but I dreamed of a wilderness of snow,

I recognized the beauty of the landscape, and knew that it was mine.

But it had not yet penetrated my innermost being, my very soul.

(Shimoni 1962: 96ff – my translation)

It takes a long time for a new country to start looking hospitable, even where the landscape is cultivated and gentle. In the wild harshness of what seemed a ravaged and neglected land, the process could be painfully slow.

But in respect to geography, as with so many aspects of this complex theme, it is also possible to discern sharp tendencies of an opposite kind. For many immigrants the romantic image of *Eretz Yisrael,* which had become so integral a part of their thinking, responded favourably to the geographic realities, and blended in the landscape, vegetation, contours and colouring of the adopted land. Such coalescence of image and reality is responsible, for example, for the appeal exerted by the poetry of Rachel (Blaubstein) for whom the process of fusion was so complete that the dividing line simply faded out of consciousness:

...my Kinneret, oh my Kinneret.
Are you real, or have I dreamed a dream?

(Blaubstein 1972)

A passionate desire to recreate the homeland and change the value of society served as a powerful source of inspiration for much of the Hebrew poetry of the 1920s. Total rejection of the exile, with its alien culture, implacable hatred and social and religious persecution spurred many writers deliberately to reject even those aspects of their native environment with which they had felt most in tune, and foster a positive relationship, however hard at first, with their adopted homeland. In this respect U. Z. Greenberg represents, perhaps, the most determined example. Again, for many writers the creative energies unleashed by pioneering and revolutionary fervour drew nourishment from the magical beauty and breathtaking variety of landscape, whose very strangeness and unfamiliarity appeared so well suited to the new forms and unfamiliar images increasingly employed in Hebrew poetry after the First World War. Even Shimoni's young poet ultimately felt in tune with his surroundings, and was able to draw inspiration from the landscapes of his adopted country:

124 *Modern literature in the Near and Middle East*

I stopped thinking of nature and its beauty, and had already laid down
my pen;
When one night as I sat idling near the stable door, quite suddenly
I felt the veil fall away from my eyes, and I saw the magic of the night,
Uncovered, exalted, and near.
I seemed to recognize it again after a long estrangement.
And now when I look at the heavens, they are near to me, yet sublime.
I remember the pain of estrangement, and I recall the delight of
recognition.
My heart is full to the brim, and I am drunk with excitement.

(Shimoni 1962: 97f)

Between the two world wars the Jewish population of Palestine increased
tenfold from about 60,000 to 600,000 souls, but it still comprised less than
5 per cent of the total Jewish population in the world at that time. For the
young immigrant writers the transition was difficult, and most of them
remained psychologically divided with one foot in both worlds and never
quite at home in either. There is, however, a marked difference in outlook
between the prose and poetry in these two decades. Prose writing in the
period is somewhat restrained. The overall effect is cultivated and
civilized, but it is characterized by an emotional restraint and a reluctance
to react strongly to the events of the outside world.

The poetry, however, is of a very different nature. The poets who made
the transition from Europe to Palestine in the early 1920s such as
Shlonsky, Lamdan, Greenberg and many more, came as revolutionaries
with revolutionary fervour. They had deliberately turned their backs upon
the diaspora and its values and they were motivated, in no small measure,
by the idealistic concepts associated with revolutionary movements in
Russia. They came to *Eretz Yisrael* with the deliberate intention of
changing their lifestyle and moving from a *bourgeois* to a working class
milieu. They worked on the roads in the *Gedud Avodah*, they became
members of collective settlements, and they involved themselves in the
process known as *Kibbush Avodah* (the conquest of labour) with the
purpose of cleansing the taint of diaspora rootlessness by physical
attachment to agriculture and the land. They began to produce poetry that
was ecstatic, messianic, which aimed at a transvaluation of values in
Jewish life by singing paeons to the idea of Jewish labour and Jewish
collective endeavour. The poetry was revolutionary in intent, in language
and in its use of imagery. From a literary point of view they were revolting
against the 'classical' poetry of the period prior to the First World War
which was largely rooted in the diaspora. Their revolutionary fervour was
translated into explosive, violent expressionism with a new kind of

Modern Hebrew 125

imagery and symbolism to suit their purposes. Houses in a collective settlement could, for example, be compared to Phylacteries and roads to the straps of *Tefillin*. Or a poet would exhort himself to don his 'coat of many colours' and go out to physical labour in the field (see Mintz 1966: 184). In this way ancient symbols and metaphors were given a new revolutionary and sometimes messianic context.

The poetry of the period was both lyrical and national. The poets regarded themselves as representing a new kind of Jew in a veritable Jewish renaissance, and they purported to speak for the new generation of workers – just as Bialik in his day had been the mouthpiece of the Jewish people in the diaspora. Revolution permeated their forms of poetry, their coinages, their imagery; and yet for most of them Hebrew was still an acquired literary language. For all the skill with which they used it, it was not their mother tongue. No matter how steeped in the traditional sources they were, nor how brilliant their handling of ancient materials in a modern context, it was not a language which they had used and spoken from their very first years. Indeed, it is in the difference between them and the poets and writers who were born in *Eretz Yisrael* or who arrived there in infancy that the great divide can be most clearly perceived.

In the 1940s, even before the creation of the state of Israel, a new phenomenon burst upon the literary scene in *Eretz Yisrael* in the shape of writers who had been born in the country or who had arrived there as young children and had grown up with Hebrew as their first language. They possessed a deep personal experience of the struggle of the Jewish population for survival between the two world wars, and the kibbutz (the collective settlement) and *Hagganah* (the defence force) were the factors which moulded their thinking. For these writers the landscape of *Eretz Yisrael* was natural, the only one they knew; and the language, too, was natural for them – the only one that they knew well. One of the first expressions of this new phenomenon appeared in a little magazine called *Yalkut Reim* which was published in 1946.

The Hebrew reading public which had grown up with 'classical' modern Hebrew or even the revolutionary poetry of the inter-war years, was suddenly confronted by a new kind of writing which, in its initial period, managed to emancipate itself to a large extent from the shackles of Jewish tradition, and which was written in the everyday language of the younger generation, with natural and free-wheeling rhythms, the like of which had not appeared in Hebrew literature prior to that time. It came as a veritable bombshell. For the first time the literature reflected the everyday language of current speech. And although in retrospect it has a certain naivety, it also possessed a number of very interesting qualities. These young *Sabra* writers – as they were called – had grown up in a

126 *Modern literature in the Near and Middle East*

harsh environment. Whereas the prose writers of the inter-war period tended to be restrained, inhibited and urbane, the *Sabra* generation reflected a rough, uninhibited, down-to-earth image. The writers were keenly aware of the little leaden bullet and very much involved in the physical dangers of a strife-torn land. Social and political realism informed their stories and novels. The style, however, was somewhat naive and unsophisticated.

The language they used provided an even greater contrast with that of their predecessors. In this new *Sabra* literature, the language conveyed a natural flavour. For more than a hundred years prior to 1948 the stories, satires and novels which were written in Europe and in *Eretz Yisrael* all contained dialogue, but of an artificial kind. Characters who in real life would have spoken Yiddish, German, Rumanian, Russian, or one of a number of other languages, were made to express themselves in a contrived type of Hebrew. Whereas in real life it is the character who creates the conversation, in literature it is the conversation which creates the character. If the conversation is stilted and artificial, the characterizations remain commensurately unconvincing. Here, for the first time, the characters speak in a real vernacular. Moreover, just as Mendele, some fifty years previously, had introduced Aramaic alongside Hebrew as a kind of racy colloquial, so the *Sabra* generation interspersed phrases drawn from Arabic for the same purpose. The language of the *Palmach* was an 'ingroup' language. It was a mode of expression which reflected a particular situation and which signified a feeling of belonging. All 'ingroups' have their own terminology, a fact which makes the members of the group feel different and special. As such, it injected a refreshing note into Hebrew literature. But, the language of any 'ingroup' is necessarily limited and indeed impoverished. Fifty to a hundred words at most could well cover the entire spectrum. The abandonment in great measure of traditional phraseology reflecting associations stretching literally over millenia in favour of a colloquial and 'ingroup' language soon proved to be unsatisfactory and insubstantial. A sharp reaction to its extreme forms was not long in coming.

A further characteristic of writing following the creation of the State which contrasted strongly with the literatures of England, the United States, and other countries at that time, lay in its conformism. The literature conformed to and accepted, by and large, the standards and ideals of the State. Indeed, the heroes of these early works tended to be collective heroes – the kibbutz or the *Hagganah*. Just when in Great Britain, for example, the novels of the 'angry young men' such as *Hurry on Down, Room at the Top* or *Lucky Jim,* and the play *Look Back in Anger,* were making their appearance, as an expression of revolt against

Modern Hebrew 127

the accepted standards of society, Hebrew writing reflected a positive conformity. The real angry young men in Hebrew literature appeared some five decades previously in Europe. Writers such as Brenner, Berdichewsky and Gnessin had then produced powerful literature of non-conformity and revolt.

During the 1950s, however, a reaction began to set in. Hebrew literature was still grounded in realism, but it became increasingly laced with irony and satire. The language was less a reflection of the everyday speech of the kibbutz or the *Hagganah* as the limitations of the colloquial rapidly became manifest. Just as one hundred years previously, Abraham Mapu had reached the conclusion that a neo-biblical Hebrew could not serve the demands of modern literature, so the writers of the first *Sabra* generation discovered that if they confined their writing to the colloquial language of everyday speech, they soon faced severe limitations which were too confining. They felt compelled to draw on deeper literary sources in order to create a new literary language.

In every society there is a gap between the language of the street and the language of the book, between the colloquial and the literary language. But at the creation of the State of Israel the divide was even greater than in most places. In the British Isles, for example, there is a large stratum of population that speaks – or at least is familiar with – what may be termed 'good standard English', the sort of English used by the BBC. The majority of the population would feel reasonably at home with it. They might not always use it in their own speech, but they would be used to hearing it and they would understand it. There is an equivalent 'good standard French', 'good standard German', 'good standard Spanish' and so forth. But in the years immediately following the creation of the State of Israel, a Jewish population of little more than 600,000 souls, most of which was itself of recent vintage, had to absorb twice that number of immigrants, the majority of whom did not know Hebrew, and who in the process of learning the language, infused Hebrew with all kinds of vocabulary, idioms and thought-forms from their native languages.

The differences between Indo-European languages and Semitic languages are well known, but the changes brought about in Hebrew in the first decade following the creation of the State were, perhaps, more radical than had occurred in the previous one hundred years. It was a remarkably telescoped process whereby elements from all kinds of languages invaded Hebrew; so much so, that articles in Hebrew newspapers began to resemble in much of their linguistic structure European languages in Hebrew vocabulary. The feeling became non-Semitic both in structure and in concept. Again, the writers were often unsure who their readers would be. The European readership had gone, while the whole readership in

128 *Modern literature in the Near and Middle East*

Israel during its first years was comparatively small because the majority of the population could not easily read what was being written. These factors brought about rapid changes in the nature and kinds of literary material which appeared during the early 1950s, while a concomitant change of ethos resulted in new attitudes towards the accepted values of society.

It is important to recall that at the end of the 1940s the ideal of the kibbutz was still so strong that people living in towns were often apologetic for not living in a collective settlement. kibbutz members were more or less regarded as the aristocrats of the country which helped to bolster their self-image in no small measure. Within the space of a few years, however, there was a flood of immigrants whose education, training and experience were far from conducive to kibbutz life. People who had grown up in Zionist youth movements and who believed that the kibbutz idea represented the best kind of social organization, entertained a very different concept of the word 'collective' from that which existed in the minds of people whose experience of collective life was obtained in Eastern and central Europe prior to, or during, the Second World War, and for whom the mere word was enough to send a shudder down the spine. As more and more immigrants entered the country with fewer and fewer holding collective life in high regard, the image of the kibbutz suffered proportionately. In the course of a few years, far from feeling the aristocrats of the new State, the kibbutz members were no longer sure of their position. It is one thing to enjoy universal esteem, which can help maintain ideals in the face of difficulties and hardships. If, however, that esteem rapidly dissipates, a very different attitude and self-image can emerge. This process soon became reflected in the literature in a revolt against conformism. The two great heroes of the first period of *Sabra* literature, the kibbutz on the one hand and the *Hagganah* on the other, began to lose their force, and the consequences of such change became increasingly obvious in Hebrew writings as the 1950s progressed.

The retreat from conformity in the 1950s and early 1960s may perhaps be illustrated in three skilful and humorous novels by Aharon Megged of which the English titles are respectively, *Hedva and I, Fortunes of a Fool* and *The Living on the Dead*. They all portray the gradual abandoning of the ideals which were so much in evidence prior to, and during, the early years of the State, and they all represent powerful exercises in demythology. The process may, perhaps, be best illustrated from the novel *Fortunes of a Fool*, which is reminiscent of Kafka in that the hero is caught up in a situation which he cannot understand, although the tone is much more lighthearted. The hero, who remains a somewhat naive idealist, reads of the death of a great legendary figure, Eli Brand, in the

Modern Hebrew 129

kibbutz of which he used to be a member. He decides to go back for the funeral. In the empty dining room he falls into conversation with the treasurer of the kibbutz who reminisces at great length about the extraordinary physical, mental and spiritual strength of the deceased, emphasizing his tremendous prowess as a worker and his gargantuan size and appetites. But when the hero becomes a pall bearer, he is amazed to find how light the coffin seems and the long episode concludes with the following paragraph:

> When we placed the coffin on the ground, I was again surprised by how light it was, because as it rested on the clods of earth it swayed a little and slipped. I was so shocked by this that I flashed a questioning glance at the three people with me, and my lips moved silently as if to say 'Look, Eli Brand is no longer with us,' but their furious looks silenced me. Around me was a dense, white, silent mass of people. For a long time everything was paralysed. There was a feeling of suspended anticipation in the air... . When we lowered the coffin carefully into the depths of the grave, I knew already that it was empty, because a hollow sound came from within when it lay at the bottom of the pit. A faint, muffled sound also came from it when I threw the clods of soil and grains of dust upon it with a spade, until it was entirely covered by them. I straightened up and whispered to those standing round me: 'The coffin is empty, Eli Brand is no longer with us'. But no one heard me. What a mighty army of people, united, its heart beating as one, in mourning for Eli Brand who wasn't there!'

> (Megged 1962: 83)

What the passage is really saying, of course, and very well, is that this great mythological figure, this mighty representative of all that was best in the ideology of the kibbutz has somehow crumbled away and nothing is left. It is an extreme statement and the satirical element is very strong. It remains, however, a kind of epitaph for the halcyon period which had gone, while Hebrew literature, in a number of different ways, prepared itself to come to grips with the harsh realities of the fledgeling state.

10 Iran

Homa Katouzian

INTRODUCTION

In their objectives, methods and results, revolutions are universal: they occupy not only the realms of politics, law and society, but also the domain of education, culture and letters. The form and content of literature – as a means of artistic, cultural and social communication – begin to be transformed as they can no longer serve, with sufficient ease and proficiency, those functions which they had hitherto fulfilled in harmony with the traditional social framework. The English, French, Russian and Chinese Revolutions all bear witness to this rule, and the Persian Revolution (1905–9) was no exception to it.

Historically, Persian literature had always been dominated by poetry, for Persian poetry had served a greater variety of purposes than its European counterpart. Apart from lyrics, epics and mythology, it contained mysticism, philosophy, religion, moralizing, eulogy and praise, naturalism, history, fiction of a special type, elegies, satire, pornography, abuse, invective and obscenity. Yet it excluded social and political analysis and criticism except in an occult and indirect fashion, and then only rarely. Prose, on the other hand, was confined to formal administrative essays, historiography and chronicles, *hikayat,* and occasionally long meditations. There was no prose fiction, satire and drama such as existed in Western European literature. And, once again, critical comments on politics and society were absent except, covertly, in such rare (but outstanding) examples as Baihaqi's *Tarikh* and Sa'di's *Gulistan.*

When the Constitutional Revolution broke out, the uses of prose and poetry were still predominantly the same as before. Classical Persian poetry is conventionally thought to have ended with 'Abd al-Rahman Jami, the fifteenth-century author. Likewise, the intervening Safavid period is almost universally held to be an age of decline and 'decadence', although it may look strange that three centuries of 'decadence' should have followed a rich and powerful literary tradition. It is also odd that in the course of a few decades this tradition should have risen once again, like the phoenix from the ashes, to give birth to a 'renaissance' in the nineteenth century. A critical reappraisal of those established schema of the history of Persian poetry is beyond the limits of this chapter, but, in any case, the neo-classicism of the nineteenth century did not innovate much in form or content, although its imitative nature and quality have been somewhat exaggerated.

Prose, on the other hand, had evolved more quietly and with much less fuss throughout the centuries, although here too, structure and purpose had seldom undergone paradigmatic transformation. Therefore, when the impact of Europe began to be felt, prose began to respond more readily than poetry, and with little conflict and opposition. Prose fiction, first in the form of the historical novel – a literary *genre* for which there had been some historical counterpart in the classics – began to emerge from the mid-nineteenth century. This prepared the ground for the later, and more advanced, works of writers such as 'Abd al-Rahim Taliboff and Zain al-'Abidin Maraghah'i who by then were openly concerned with modern ideas as well as social issues.[1]

The revolutionary process led to the transformation of the functions, purpose, and especially in the case of prose, form of Persian literature. The proliferation of popular newspapers played a crucial role in determining the style and direction of these literary developments. These newspapers were read by the ordinary literate public, who in turn read them out to a large number of the illiterate in public places. Therefore, the authors had little choice but to be simple in style, use common vocabulary, and write on social and political issues. On the other hand, radical writers and poets themselves were in the mood for such popular and progressive developments, both because of the growing impact of Europe, and because of the revolutionary movement. This led to a coincidence of expectation and purpose on the part of readers and writers alike. The names of 'Ali-Akbar Dehkhuda, Ashraf al-Din Husaini (Qazvini), Jahangir Khan Shirazi, poet-laureate Bahar, Abu'l-Qasim Lahuti, Farrukhi Yazdi, Isma'il Pur-Davud, Sayyed Hasan Taqizadah and even – in spite of his otherwise solid classicism – Mirza Muhammad Qazvini, describe but a few prominent and in some cases, outstanding *literati* who helped the process (see Browne 1914 and 'Abbasi 1958).

The Constitutional Revolution lacked an ideology in the specific sense as rendered by politics, sociology, and philosophy. The revolution's declared aims, and its short-lived achievements, were first, to abolish arbitrary rule, and secondly, to establish democratic government. The two

132 *Modern literature in the Near and Middle East*

objectives should not be confused. The Iranian state had been based on *istibdad*, that is both absolute and arbitrary rule, or absolute government by *fiat*. The revolution began by a demand for law (which would normally exist in any dictatorial system), and the further escalation of the struggle led to the further demand for democratic government. Constitutionalism (or *mashrutah*) implied both of these objectives, the first of which was absolutely indispensable to, but insufficient for, democracy.[2] Neither aim constitutes an ideology in the strict sense of the term, although the social and political implications of each of them were no less momentous for that.

The strong anti-Russian views and sentiments of the Constitutionalists were somewhat different in nature from modern anti-imperialist ideas, if only because the Russian troops attached to the despotic state simply made up part of the domestic forces of *istibdad* against which the revolutionaries were struggling. Nationalism, therefore, was not the dominant ideology of the revolution, and much (although not all) of the revolutionary propaganda was conducted in terms of religion, morality, natural justice, legal and political equity, and the like. Authentic nationalist concepts and ideas were rare, and debates and discussions on them were even more scarce.[3] Yet they soon began to conquer the social and political consciousness of the country's political and literary élites. To sum up, the revolution was accompanied by a democratization of literature. This literature was principally engaged in social and political criticism, indeed in struggle, but not in nationalist propaganda. Yet, the seeds of nationalism, and of romantic nationalism in particular, were quietly being sown, and they were to bear fruit before long.

THE HIGH TIDE OF ROMANTIC NATIONALISM: 1914–41

In 1914 the First World War broke out; in 1921 there was the *coup d'état* by Reza Khan and Sayyed Zia; in 1926 the Pahlavi state was founded; in 1941 war again entered Iran, and Reza Shah left. Not all the prominent writers of this period (and their works) may be described as romantic nationalists, as we shall see. Yet, in terms of both political and literary developments, the appellation is apt, especially as compared with the period 1941–50.

All nationalism is romantic: it glorifies the past and sometimes the present beyond the capacity of rational inquiry and appraisal; it proclaims hopes and aspirations far beyond the limits of existing socio-economic resources; it conceives of 'the nation' as an organic body, and so it underrates the importance of ethnic, linguistic and social divisions; it is aggressive and offensive towards other races and nations; it is associated

Iran 133

with authoritarian and dictatorial rules. However, what justifies the use of the term romantic nationalism is that 'nationalism' is widely used in inappropriate contexts, and the appellation 'romantic' helps it to regain its original meaning. Hitler, Stalin, Mao-Tse Tung, Chiang Kai-Shek, Musaddiq, Gandhi and Nasser cannot have all been nationalists, or the term itself would be redundant. More specifically, mere anti-colonialism or anti-imperialism is not sufficient proof of nationalism, as every country would defend its independence and territorial integrity. Yet it is so difficult to convince writers and readers of these simple truths that it looks as if journalism has gained the upper hand.[4]

The First World War brought Iran unmitigated ruin and unprecendented chaos. At one stage, there were even two governments in the country, one 'neutral', and the other pro-German. Hatred for Russia and suspicion towards Britain (dating back to the Iranian *Thermidor* of 1911) had led to almost universal pro-German sentiments. Taqizadah and his literary circle published the famous newspaper *Kaveh* in Berlin, with the blessing and financial support of the German government. *Kaveh* did not campaign for (romantic) nationalism, but the seeds of nationalism were one layer below its anti-Allies, patriotic and modernistic messages. In Iran itself, nationalism was being nurtured in both politics and literature. Experienced poets such as 'Arif, Lahuti and Farrukhi Yazdi were in the forefront, but younger talents (e.g. 'Ishqi) were not too far behind.

When the last guns of the war were silenced, the guns of Iranian nationalism began to be loaded. 'Arif and 'Ishqi even had to taste prison food during the campaign against the Anglo-Persian (1919) Agreement. Although the *coup d'état* of Reza Khan and Sayyed Zia had had foreign blessing and support, for many years the ground had been prepared for a fundamental shake-up in the directions of nationalism and modernism. That is why the *coup* was initially hailed by modern intellectuals and the educated middle classes as a great triumph. The declarations issued by Sayyed Zia and Reza Khan were tough and revolutionary in tone; and more significantly, their nationalist bombastics had had no precedent in the history of Iranian government (see Katouzian 1979; Bahar 1942; and Musaddiq 1986: I). Little wonder, then, that 'Arif and 'Ishqi, and even a less modern poet like Vahid Dastgirdi, sang hymns of praise for the new regime and its leaders. Some of them later fell out with the regime thinking that Reza Khan was not a true nationalist, but on closer examination they can be seen to be fighting the rise of his dictatorship which was quite consistent with the ideology of 'true' (romantic) nationalism. Even after Reza Shah's rise to total power, and the foundation of the Pahlavi state (1926), there remained a close

134 *Modern literature in the Near and Middle East*

correspondence between the basic values of official and intellectual nationalism, in spite of the opposition of many intellectuals to the new state because of its suppression of basic rights and freedoms in the country. Modernism was (romantic) nationalism's twin sister. It was not only the nationalists who wished to modernize the country. But whereas democrats and old Constitutionalists thought that this should be done with caution and suitable adaptation, the nationalist-modernists wished to lose no time in uprooting the old, and replacing them by Europeanist ideas, morals, institutions and techniques. (In their own fashion, socialists and communists shared the same attitude, but, at the same they were a small minority with few roots in the society.) Modernism came to mean turning Iran into France – the favourite European country – overnight.[5]

The tides of nationalism and modernism in politics and sociology coincided with the winds of change in literature. In the 1920s, an apparently curious debate broke out on how to bring about a 'literary revolution', when it had already been in progress for a few decades.[6] On close examination, however, 'literary' turns out to refer to poetry alone, and the fact that in spite of so many changes (which were not sufficiently recognized) it was still based on the classical structures, metres and rhymes. But European poetry was not like that: metres were open and numerous, rhymes less perfect, and infrequent, metaphors more distant and abstract, formal logic and rationality unnecessary. Hence, the question which was implicit in this search for 'the literary revolution' was how to write European poetry in the Persian language. The search proved to be in vain at the time, partly because of an as yet insufficient assimilation of European poetry. It fell to an unknown and reclusive young poet, Nima Yushij, to tread this path alone in the 20s and 30s, and to found the modernist school of Persian poetry which became dominant in the 40s and 50s.[7]

But another literary revolution had already occurred without a shot being fired. It shows the relatively subordinate position of Persian prose that the movement for 'the literary revolution' was simply concerned with poetry. As mentioned above, prose had begun to break new ground several decades earlier, and by the 1920s it had gone much further along the road of innovation than poetry. The great achievement of Persian prose in the '20s was the fruition and maturity of modern prose fiction. The fact that prose fiction had no precedent in classical Persian literature was an important factor in its unhampered and undiluted success: it did not change or replace any existing traditions; it created a new and socially relevant channel for literary expression; it hurt no artistic prejudice, nor did it threaten any vested interest. No wonder that Qazvini (the devout classical scholar) wrote to Jamalzadah (from Paris to Berlin) to say that if he abandoned writing fiction (which the latter had threatened) in response

Iran 135

to fanatical denunciations of his book in Tehran, it would be tantamount to treason. Jamalzadah's *Yaki Bud, va Yaki Nabud, Once Upon a Time* was published in 1922. As a youth he had been steeped in the democratic traditions of the Constitutional Revolution, and was not unduly impressed by the (romantic) nationalism of the later period. His collection of short stories, written in simple, idiomatic Persian, combined his peculiar talent for story telling with social and (fewer) political criticisms, wrapped in a humorous and occasionally satirical garb. In *Farsi Shekar Ast (Persian Is Sweet)*, he pokes fun at the artificial Arabicism of the *mullah*, and the Franco–Persian babblings of the Europeanist alike, brilliantly exposing the contradictions of a society in a process of natural and unplanned transition, where the common man was at a loss how to communicate with either of those two *virtuosi* in plain simple Persian. There is also the narrator (the type who, in this century, lost out to the Europeanist and the traditionalist alike) who is modern, and has a good grasp of European culture, and yet he has a realistic understanding of his own society, and genuine sympathy for its people. And in the background there is the arbitrary political system in which each new governor releases the existing prisoners and jails another lot arrested at random. In *Rajul-i Siyasi* ('The Statesman') he brilliantly satirizes the grotesque and corrupt ways in which successful political leaders may emerge. It is a caricature for which there have been many real counterparts throughout this century. *Dusti-yi Khaleh Khirseh* ('The Friendship of Auntie Bear') relates the tragedy – though even in tragedy the author does not quite lose his sanguine spirit – of a chivalrous, but ordinary, young Iranian who is innocently executed by the treachery of a Russian soldier whom he has saved from certain death, so that the *saldat* can steal the money from his dead body. These are only some of the excellent short stories in the collection.

Once modernist forms had been developed, nationalist and modernist ideas, which included new and more Europeanized approaches to social criticism, put them to good use. In line with their political counterparts, the artistic and intellectual nationalist and modernist tendencies of the period were based on the following visions, sentiments and topics:

(i) A romantic and nostalgic vision of the ancient past, and the real and imagined achievements of pre-Islamic Persian empires; the lamentation for the loss of this glorious past, and a harking back to the Zoroastrian faith and customs (which in the case of a few, led to full conversion); and an earnest campaign to rid Persian of Arabic and Turkic, though not European, loan words.

(ii) The discovery of the 'historical enemy' in the Arab Conquest, who was held responsible for the destruction of the past glories (and perhaps even the present decline), and was thought to be an inferior nation and race.

136 *Modern literature in the Near and Middle East*

(iii) Islam – 'the Arab ideology' – everything about which was held to be cruel, backward, and ugly, especially as compared with (European) Christianity.

(iv) Turks, whose linguistic dialects were in fact spoken by more people in the country than was Persian, whose race had seldom ceased to invade Iran throughout the ages, and whose presumed brethren to the West in Turkey had been another historical enemy.

(v) Zest and zeal for full Europeanization in the shortest possible time (see Katouzian 1979).

Some of these sentiments had already been expressed in poetry, notably by Abu'l-Qasim 'Arif Qazvini, who had complained that 'ever since the Arab got a foothold in Iran, no word of happiness was heard from the land of Sassan'. When trouble broke out in the (Turkic-speaking) province of Azerbaijan, he implored them – in Zoroaster's name – not to 'extinguish fire by water' and not to forget 'the [Persian] tongue'. He was an incorrigible anti-*mullah*, and a naive republican who (persuaded by Reza Khan's campaign) believed that a republican system would necessarily bring social progress. In 1918 he even cried out for Lenin, when he must have known very little about him and his ideas, to come and 'load up all these donkeys' that is the ordinary Iranians ('Arif 1948). This is another important feature of the nationalism (and modernism) of the period: while it indulged in an abstract glorification of the past, and of the 'land-and-water' even in the present, it was contemptuous of the poor, traditional and ignorant Iranians who lived off the same 'land-and-water' (*Ab u Khak*).

Similar sentiments can be found in the poetry of Farrukhi, 'Ishqi and Lahuti, the first of whom was murdered in jail, the second assassinated, and the third driven into exile by the new nationalist state. Zabih Behruz's competent and amusing satires, which to this date have not yet been published, were loaded with abuse and invective almost exclusively against Islam and the Arabs. Like himself, the young scholars gathered around him (notably Muhammad Muqaddam) devoted a good deal of their time to ancient Persian studies, and to the task of proving that Islam itself had originated from Persian culture. Muqaddam was so advanced in this venture that he even interpreted his own name as having originally been *Mughdam,* alluding to the ancient *Mughan* or the Magi.

Of the romantic nationalist writers of the period (who also composed many realist and surrealistic works) Sadiq Hidayat stands out as the most prolific and the most persistent. In 1931, Hidayat together with Buzurg 'Alavi and 'Shin' (Shirazpur) Partaw published a collection of short stories, *Aniran* (*Un-Iranian*, or *Anti-Iranian*), which they dedicated to 'the learned scholar Zabih Behruz' (Hidayat *et al.* 1931). It consists of three short stories, one from each, on the three historic conquests of Iran: those by

Alexander, the Arabs, and the Mongols. Partaw's contribution on Alexander's conquest in *Shab-i Bad-masti* ('The Night of Inebria') reaches its climax in the middle of a most vulgar orgy which the author has faithfully described, when an inebriate Alexander is persuaded by a prostitute to set fire to Persepolis. The author concludes that as a result of this burning, human civilization was set back for several centuries. Buzurg 'Alavi's *Div, Div* ('Demon, Demon') describes the life of Iranians in Kufa and Hamadan after the Arab Conquest. The main characters are all modern Iranian nationalists. The simple and undeveloped plot seems to have been imposed on the narrative which is an horrific account of massacres, sadistic murders, and the kidnapping of women, by 'camel grazers' and 'lizard eaters', the Arab 'demon' with his 'dirty blood' who 'lies', and 'loots', unlike Iranians who are neither liars nor hypocrites! 'Alavi has recently reprinted this story perhaps partly because he is no longer a Communist (which he had become after those years), and partly because of the revival of such views and sentiments among modern Iranians in view of the events of the last ten years. Hidayat's *Sayeh-yi Mughul* ('Shadow of the Mongol') turns the attack to the Mongols and, for good measure, to the Arabs as well. A young man and his friends who were determined to destroy the Arabs and 'the semitic race' with the help of the invading Mongol hordes (at a time when the Arabs had hardly any presence in Iran), are disillusioned when the young man's fiancée is raped and killed before his eyes by a Mongol warrior. He vows for revenge, and they manage to kill a couple of Mongol warriors, but soon after he dies in an accident.

Since the publication of *Div, Div* romantic nationalism disappeared from 'Alavi's works, even before he became a Marxist. In *Chamidan* (*Portmanteau*, 1934) none of the short stories reflects romantic nationalist sentiments, or even tangible social criticism. There is, however, a strong level of Europeanism in two respects. One is his well-known application of Freudian psycho-analysis which was familiar from the European films of the time. This, however, varies from one story to another, and the short story *Sarbaz-i Surbi* ('Tin Soldier') is the most successful in this respect. The other somewhat neglected point is that especially in the case of *'Arus-i Hizar Damad* ('Everyman's Bride'), the atmosphere, values, and modes of behaviour are such that, with some editing, Berlin would be a more appropriate location for the story than Tehran; the story ends with a mad dance between a man and a woman in a night club, in a country where women were still obliged to wear *hijab* whenever they went outside the home. In 1937, 'Alavi was imprisoned as a member of the Fifty-Three Marxist group, only to be released by the 1941 general amnesty. Shin Partaw, a much less prominent writer than the other two, also rather changed his tune. He concentrated on writing romantic (i.e. unrealistic)

138 *Modern literature in the Near and Middle East*

fiction mainly about pre-Islamic Iran, which, although motivated by nationalist sentiments, involved little diatribe about other nations and races.

Hidayat's was a different case. He neither began his nationalistic fiction with *Aniran*, nor did he end it with that. His first romantic and nationalistic fiction, *Parvin Dukhtar-i Sassan* (*Parvin the Sassanian Girl*, 1930), was written in Paris. This historical drama unfolds in the ancient city of Rayy, as the Arab armies are approaching it. Parvin's fiancé is an army officer, and says farewell to her to go to fight in the city's defence. When 'the Arabs' come, she is taken to the commander's residence, and there she learns that her fiancé is dead. She refuses to convert, the commander makes sexual advances to her, and she kills herself with his dagger. The extensive narrative consists mainly of the most uncomplimentary remarks about Arabs, plus highly idealistic descriptions of the motherland.

In *Maziyar* (1933) Hidayat's literary romanticism and ideological nationalism reach their climax. These were times when Europe was swept by an aggressive Aryanism whose seeds were falling on fertile ground among Iranian officials and intellectuals alike. *Maziyar* is an historical play about Maziyar b. Qaran, the rebel Iranian prince who was eventually defeated and killed by the caliph, al-Mu'tasim. There is a long historical introduction, jointly written with (Mujtaba) Minuvi, which denigrates the 'semitic race', Arab and Jew alike. The play portrays Maziyar as a nationalist hero who loses in the end because of the treachery of his secretary 'Ali b. Rahn – apparently an historical figure – whose alleged Jewish ancestry is meant to be the cause of his treachery.[8] In a remarkable finale, the girl travels all alone from Northern Iran to Baghdad, and dies in the arms of Maziyar.

In its literary and historical characteristics, the short story *Akharin Labkhand* ('The Last Smile', 1933) is considerably more subtle than the previous plays. The Eastern Barmecides – who are secretly Buddhist – plan to rise and separate Khurasan from Arab rule. They are in contact with their Western cousins who are covertly disloyal to the 'Abbasids. But in the end the plot is discovered and they all perish. The reader might wonder whether all these noble nationalist efforts had not been doomed to failure by an unseen hand. *Isfahan Nisf-i Jahan* (*Half the World is Isfahan*, 1932) is an excellent travelogue in which Hidayat wonders if some of the city's designs had not been emulated by European cities like Berlin. When he visits the ruins of a Zoroastrian temple outside the city he has a vision of Zoroastrian priests in long white robes holding cups of wine. On one occasion when they stop to repair the car, he sees a lizard, and wonders whether the Arabs had not come to Iran in search of this.

Iran 139

Hidayat's interpretation of Khayyam's quatrains (in *Taraneh-ha-yi Khayyam*) is loaded with romantic, idealistic, and nationalistic views which are intermingled with his own particular philosophical and ontological reflections. In the introduction to that book there is less of Khayyam's ideas – which are, admittedly, open to a wide variety of interpretations – than of the various intellectual dimensions of the critic himself. The short story *Talab-i-Amurzish* ('Asking for Absolution', 1932) – one of Hidayat's best – is highly realistic and critical, and falls between the two categories of nationalism and social criticism because of its anti-Islamic overtones. In a caravan taking pilgrims to Karbala', a woman and her son meet another woman, and an old man. On reaching their destination, they decide to share a room. The young man's mother suddenly disappears, and is eventually discovered in the Imam's mausoleum, weeping, wailing, crying, and begging for absolution. It turns out that she had killed two of her husband's babies by his second wife, and then the woman herself who was the real mother of the young man. Her companions put her mind at rest by telling her that they too had killed, and that the 'moment the pilgrim decides to go on pilgrimage, all of his sins ... are washed away'. 'The Arabs' are briefly there, but the edge of criticism is directed at religious superstition, though it is doubtful if the author distinguished between superstition and religion. Polygamy is also in the background both as a religious institution and as a social reality.

Despite its strong nationalist and modernist currents, literature also played a significant role as a vehicle for social criticism in this period. Political criticism, although abundant, had no vehicle for public expression, and in literature it had to remain buried in unpublished works such as Bahar's *Karnameh-yi Zindan* (*Prison Record*). The publication of Parvin I'tisami's collected poems was quite an exception to this rule, because as a recluse, and young woman of thirty, she was not already in the secret police's bad books, and the mystic quality and abstract subtlety of her art was beyond their comprehension as 'subversive' material. The greatest Persian woman poet for a thousand years (i.e. since Rabi'ah bint Ka'ab) she was (at least intellectually) the most prominent mystic poet since Jami six centuries before. Hers was not just another version of traditional mysticism. It was an authentic and original conception which contained important elements of modern rationality and ethics, and emphasized social justice and morality, as opposed to the traditional preoccupations with ontological puzzles or methods of personal atonement. Indeed, her moral and intellectual profundity is now positively startling, and deeply moving:

140 *Modern literature in the Near and Middle East*

> An ignoramous read books, and thought he was wise;
> An idiot boarded a boat, and felt he was the captain.
> A king did once pass through a thoroughfare,
> amidst the oohs and ahs of the crowd;
> A wretched orphan was there, and asked:
> 'What's that lustre on the crown?...'
> A bent old woman went fore and said:
> 'This is a drop of my tears; a clot of your blood!
> He has duped us by posing as a shepherd.
> This wolf has long been with the flock...'

She died of tuberculosis at the age of thirty-five in 1941. None the less, even in much of Parvin' s poetry the criticism is less in the form of a direct political challenge, and more in the guise of wider moral and social discontent. Therefore, even broader, and almost apolitical, socio-cultural criticism was harmless enough not to provoke the wrath of the state.

Some of Hidayat's works of this period also fall into this category. *Dash Akul* (1932) is a chivalrous *luti* who falls desperately in love with his own ward, but is too proud, too dutiful and too modest to contemplate marriage with the late Haji's daughter. Instead, he arranges her wedding with another man, and loses his life, on the wedding night, in a fight with a rival *luti*. In *Muhallil* ('The Legaliser', 1932), two men meet in a traditional tea-house and discover that, many years before, one of them had acted as the temporary husband of the other man's wife. He had done this in order to legalize their re-marriage according to Islamic law, but had broken his word and kept the woman. Later, he himself had been abandoned by the woman, and left to wander around without cause and purpose. The woman is absent from the scene, and seems to exist only for the purpose of the plot. Yet, in a fairly subtle way, the finger of blame is pointed at her perhaps more than at either of the two men. The story ends with the two men wondering what other unfortunate man she was engaged in ruining at that time. *Murdeh-Khurha* ('The Ghouls', 1930) begins with an authentic description of the mournings of a dead man's two wives. Soon it becomes evident, however, that they are both hypocrites, having rushed to steal their husband's money and goods even before he was dead. There is also the character of the ghoulish *mullah* trying to secure his own share of the loot. The drama ends (or does it begin?) with the fright the dead man gives to his wives when he appears and explains that he had been wrongly certified as dead. *Alaviyeh Khanum* ('Mistress Alaviyah', 1933) opens with the scene of a pilgrims' caravan bound for Mashhad, in which – it turns out – almost everybody, man, woman and child, is sharing everybody else's bed. It is much less of an attack on religion than a

Iran 141

portrayal of the sheer wretchedness, hypocrisy and amorality of poor, ordinary mortals. A most distinct feature of the form of the story – although it is somewhat overdone – is the masterly use of folk-expressions of abuse, invective and obscenity.

Hidayat was considerably more successful as a realist and critic than as a nationalist and romantic. An outstanding feature of his socio-cultural criticisms is their almost complete objectivity as regards the lives of the ordinary people whom he depicts and describes. Unlike much that was written by others on similar themes, there is no moral undertone, no romantic glorification of the down-trodden, no explicit or implicit condemnation of society because of the poverty, ignorance and wretchedness of the common folk. On the contrary, their amorality and villainy turn out to be just as widespread as amongst the more fortunate members of society. In their own eyes as opposed to the view of middle class social critics who shed tears for their misery and deprivation, their lives are more valuable than would appear to the outside observer. They are poor and ignorant, but that does not turn them into saints, nor does it make their lives unworthy of living. This is Hidayat's greatest single achievement in the realm of literary social criticism. The period 1930–41 was his most prolific period of writing which included many outstanding pieces – such as his masterpiece, *The Blind Owl* – but almost all these belong to another category of Hidayat's works, and fall outside the present context.[9] The occasional claim that *The Blind Owl* is a symbolic description of life under Reza Shah's dictatorship is simply untenable and will not be further pursued here. Hidayat did write a short story, 'The Patriot' (1941), towards the end of this period which was – for the first time – a scathing attack on the political situation in the country.

One of the most (if not *the* most) prolific fiction writers of this century is Muhammad Hijazi, who was the most popular writer, especially among the upper and (modern) middle classes, under Reza Shah. As a writer Hijazi falls neither into the category of romantic nationalists nor into that of social critics, although elements of both do exist in some of his works. Instead, his most distinctive characteristic is consistent upper-class moralizing and idealism (though the morality is secular and modern) with occasional elements of Iranian mysticism in the background. The novel *Homa* (1927), apart from its structural shortcomings, is little other than a journey through pure, unmitigated, literary idealism. The voluminous novel *Ziba* (1931) – a much more successful novel, and probably the best he ever wrote – is in certain respects more convincing. Here, there are even traces of social criticism in his somewhat realistic portrayal of administrative corruption which he might have owed to his own experience as a senior civil servant. *Ayinah* (*Mirror*, 1932), the last

142 *Modern literature in the Near and Middle East*

volume published in this period, is a large collection of short stories, one of which, besides its merits in other respects, has an undertone of romantic nationalism. In *Shirin-Kula*, the author visits the landlord in a fictional village. A peasant girl is being wooed by two young men. The matter is put to the test of the bulls whereby the two men's bulls are put to fight each other and the winner's owner takes the girl. When one of the bulls defeats the other, there are cries of 'home', 'home' from the village crowd. It turns out that, contrary to the rules, the winning bull had made its place home by being put there long before the fight. And, as it was defending its home, it was bound to win. The girl marries the other man.

Muhammad Mas'ud, even more than Hijazi, falls outside the categories of nationalists or social critics. His *Tafrihat-i Shab* (*Night Diversions*, 1932) is an open statement of amorality, bitterness, and envy. If there is any social 'criticism' somehow implicit in this work, it is of a sort for which 'nihilism' would be too glorified a term, notwithstanding the fact that it shows obvious talent. The sequels to *Night Diversions, Dar Talash-i Ma'ash* (*Making a Living*, 1932) and *Ashraf-i Makhluqat* (*The Noblest of Creatures*, 1934) are, from a social as well as literary viewpoint, in much the same mould.

Jahangir Jalili's *Man Ham Giryeh Kardeh-am* (*I Too Have Cried*, 1933) represents a type of 'social criticism' – very popular for its time – which is distinct both from Hidayat's socio-cultural objectivity and Mas'ud's 'nihilistic' amorality. It is a type of (modern) middle-class moralizing, with emphasis on the familiar theme of the evils of prostitution which had had a few precursors among the writers of an earlier period. Jalili's later novel, *Az Daftar-i Khatirat* (*From The Notebook of Memoirs*, 1935) contains a greater degree of realism and a more sophisticated approach to social criticism. Had he not died young he might have been an important writer in the years to come.

THE DECADE OF SOCIAL CRITICISM: 1941–50

When the war broke out, most Iranians – as well as the Pahlavi state which they disliked – had pro-German sentiments; the war was viewed as the struggle between 'Aryans' and the British Empire which it looked as if the former were winning. The Allied occupation of Iran (1941), although not welcome in itself, began to modify this conception; their removal of Reza Shah was almost universally welcomed, and they began to succeed in the war. Instead, the old enemy, now the Soviet Union, rapidly emerged as the new liberator, not least because of its monumental victory at Stalingrad. Press and publications became free, and there was a publications explosion of both hitherto unpublished and unwritten

Iran 143

material; the focus of attention for some time was on the ills and illiberalities of the former regime. There was anger, frustration, and demands for retribution. The Tudeh (later, Communist) party was formed initially as a broad democratic front (even though its leadership was dominated by Marxists), and it became the centre of activity, or political sympathy, for many, if not most, educated Iranians below the age of forty.

Buzurg 'Alavi, 'Abdulhusain Nushin, Firaidun Tavallali, Jalal Al-i Ahmad, Nadir Nadirpur, Ahmad Shamlu, Mehdi Akhavan-i Salis, and many other younger or intellectually less prominent writers and poets, joined the new party, and an even greater number formed a band of party sympathizers. At the time, the party advocated freedom, democracy and progress, and its broad sympathies for the Soviet Union were an asset rather than a liability. These were the reasons why Sadiq Hidayat, the eternally non-ideological and non-organizational writer and intellectual of them all, became a party sympathizer, although despite later propaganda to the contrary, he never joined the Tudeh party, and, moreover, from 1946 onwards he completely lost sympathy with it, and turned hostile towards it and its leadership.[10] Many of the short stories in Hidayat's collection *Sag-i Vilgard* (*Stray Dog*, 1942) had been written before 1941, including *Mihan-parast* ('The Patriot'). A satire of sorts, this is the first time politics and literature are brought together by Hidayat in an outburst against Reza Shah and his intellectual clientèle. The minister of education sends an important intellectual (of the kind who were in the service of the regime) to India to campaign for the great cultural achievements of the Pahlavi state. When he dies on the boat to Bombay, his statue is posthumously erected, bearing the Pahlavi version of his Arabic name, and the title of 'the patriot'. Both the satire and the politics are mainly in the narrative, but the author is apparently oblivious of the fact that a good deal of the ridicule is directed against the official counterpart of his own nationalist sentiments.

Haji Aqa (1945) is the most famous work of fiction Hidayat wrote after 1941. An overtly political story, it was hailed then, and has been hailed recently (in response to the rise of Islamic politics in Iran) as an *engagé*, indeed ideological 'novel', to the extent that one author has called it Hidayat's masterpiece, better even than *The Blind Owl* (Keddie 1981). The choice of the title and personage Haji Aqa, and the use of some new-fangled political terms and concepts must surely have been due to the contemporary literature of radical politics. The rest, however, has nothing to do with a presumed Marxist analysis of 'the Iranian bourgeoisie', as is often implied. Although apparently in import-export trade, Haji Aqa, far from being a symbol of the Tehran bazaar merchants of the time, is no less than a powerful upper-class political potentate engaged in political manipulation and machination all day long. The critique of religion is in

144 Modern literature in the Near and Middle East

fact milder than some of Hidayat's previous treatments of the subject, and the poet's scathing address against the Haji represents the views of an upright and sophisticated upper-class intellectual, rather than a Marxist class analysis.

The short story *Farda* ('Tomorrow', 1945) is also somewhat misleading in its choice of title and subject-matter. A print-worker is killed (perhaps in a strike, the point is apparently deliberately obscure), and another reflects about him and his death. However, from the dead worker's reflections on life, the night before he is killed, it is clear that he is a selfless, honest, moody and depressed individual who is alienated from his fellow workers. He is not a (Tudeh) party member, and is critical of it, unlike the party activist amongst them who is shown in a bad light. It looks almost as if his death was an indirect suicide. Thinking about his death, his friend wonders whether the troops know exactly whom to shoot, which implies that party members are not meant to be shot.

Hidayat's *Tup-i Murvari* (*The Murvari Cannon*, 1947) is his last work of 'fiction' although it has never been openly published. Once again, in the country's present circumstances it has become highly popular (where barely ten years ago it would have been condemned by most people, intellectuals included) although, compared to his previous works, it contains little that can be called original. There is an attack on Reza Shah, and a longer one on religion. The only differences with the earlier works are, first, that in this story even other religions have not been spared; and secondly, that invective and obscenity abound in the text. The bitterness in this piece is a subtle indication of the mental torture which was to have tragic consequences for an exceptional Iranian writer of this century. In his last work, *Payam-i Kafka* (*The Message of Kafka*), he launches a merciless attack on Ihsan Tabari (then 'the Zhdanov', later, the ideologue of the Tudeh party) without naming him, describing 'them' as the upholders of the chain, the whip, and the gag, and as enemies of freedom. Hidayat took his own life in Paris, in 1951.

Buzurg 'Alavi joined the Tudeh party after his release from jail. His *Panjah-u-seh Nafar* (*The Fifty-Three*, 1942) is an account of the life and times of himself and his Marxist fellow prisoners, yet it can almost be read as a piece of social realist fiction, an idealistic glorification of all the inmates in whom political conflict, human weakness and disreputable behaviour are completely absent. More realistic accounts of the event have proved the contrary, but for many years 'Alavi's romantic story played an important role in determining the historical vision of the development of communism among Tudeh and non-Tudeh communists alike.[11] 'Alavi's only other work of fiction written in this period is *Varaq-Pareh-ha-yi Zindan* (*Prison Notes*, 1942) a collection of short stories apparently written on the back of cigarette

Iran 145

packets and other materials while he was in prison. In spite of the book's title, its contents are not the kind of political fiction which one would expect a communist writer to write secretly in jail, and publish in exceptionally free political circumstances. In fact this is a peculiarity of 'Alavi's which has seldom been recognized, and least of all by Iranian critics: there is hardly any visible attack in 'Alavi's works on Reza Shah or the political system; even in *The Fifty-Three* the tone is relatively moderate as far as the regime and the prison warders are concerned.

The short stories in *Prison Notes* are also mostly about arrest, imprisonment and life in jail. *Sitareh-yi Dunbaleh-dar* ('Halley's Comet') is about a man who is arrested on the eve of his marriage: here the author makes direct references to his own seven-year sentence, as if to emphasize that he is writing in jail. In *'Afv-i Umumi* ('General Amnesty'), the prisoner writes to his wife about his unhappiness and psychological torment in prison. *Raqs-i Marg* ('Danse Macabre'), the most well-known short story of the collection, is a long and involved love story which ends up with murder and imprisonment. Here, elements of 'Alavi's Europeanism are (even in the story's title) once again apparent. The social and political dimensions of these short stories are so broad as to be almost unnoticeable, the characters, their lives, and their psychology being the main focus of attention. 'Alavi's next collection of short stories, *Nameh-ha* (*Letters*) (and the novel *Chishmhayash, Her Eyes*) appeared in 1952. One short story, *Gileh Mard* ('Man from Gilan') deserves mention, even though it does not belong to our period, For this is 'Alavi's only political, almost ideological, short story about a captured rebel peasant who bribes a gendarme, overpowers another, and tries to make his way home when he is shot in the back by the first gendarme. It is a fine piece, more sophisticated and authentic than a mere social realist story, but the claim of a critic that it could be the best Persian short story written in this century probably owes less to literary criticism than it does to political sentiment (Kamshad 1966).

Jamalzadah, who had stopped writing fiction for the whole of the Reza Shah period, wrote four novels in the 1940s. His *Dar al-Majanin* (*Lunatic Asylum*, 1942) tells an amusing tale of two sophisticated, though not entirely normal, intellectuals who seek refuge from society in the lunatic asylum; one is the narrator, the other, his friend Hidayat 'Ali Khan, known as the Blind Owl. It is a touching as well as humorous story about the kind of people who find society too crude, too cruel and too dishonest to accommodate them; and an example of social criticism which runs deeper than the usual sociological comments. *Qultashan Divan* (*Mr Bully*, 1946), is a typical Jamalzadah tale of the exploitation of an innocent and naive individual by a self-seeking, crooked and anti-social bully. This has misled some critics into the view that the basic theme of the story is the familiar

146 *Modern literature in the Near and Middle East*

struggle between good and evil, ending with evil's victory, at least for 'the moment'. This is a fundamental misinterpretation which almost relegates two perfectly realistic Iranian characters to the realm of metaphysics. Far from it being a conflict between good and evil, the story is a realistic account (albeit with the usual simplifications to highlight the social significance of otherwise everyday characters and events) of how the exploitation of one man by another goes on as ever, without any obvious role played by the prevailing social ideology or political system. Indeed, if, untypically of modern Iranian writers, Jamalzadah had not been so unconcerned with European literature and its use in modern Persian prose and poetry, the critic might have been tempted to compare the moral and psychological fibre of his characters to that of Orgon and Tartuffe in Molière's famous play. Yet, *Qultashan Divan* is an even more familiar Iranian personage, perhaps, than his French counterpart three centuries before. At any rate it is this almost unsystemic conception of social injustice, apparently rooted more in persons than in politics, which sets the tone for this and many other of Jamalzadah's stories, including the excellent novel, *The Drain Story* (of which more below).

Sahray-i Mahshar (*The Plain of Resurrection*, 1947), is the author's somewhat light-hearted vision of the ultimate meeting between man and his Maker. Here though, unlike the previous novel, men and women come from different social groups and categories, and this would understandably seem to give the characters societal, as opposed to purely personal, significance. The high and the low – judges, politicians, philosophers, *mullahs* and prostitutes alike – are brought to account for their deeds, for once in perfect equality, before the Arbiter who recognizes no social class, rank or privilege. But this is precisely where the strong appearance of societal criticism melts away, and the personal distinction between the noble and the wicked comes into its own. For, despite the critics' common agreement, the *mullah* who is thrown into Hell is not necessarily a villain on account of his profession, just as the woman whom he heartlessly exploited does not go to Heaven because she happens to be a whore. In other words, it is primarily the individuals themselves (as opposed to their social status) who determine their own relative worth and virtue. His *Rah-ab Nameh* (*The Drain Story*, 1948) is a masterpiece, and probably the best of all that he has written. A student returns from Europe for his vacation, and naively gets involved in the repair of the main drain through which fresh water is distributed to the houses of the alley where they live. This apparently simple matter drags on for so long and creates so many complications that, in the end, the young man, having spent his money and over-stayed in Tehran, gives up his studies and gets a room in a far corner of the city. This novel would have to be read to be fully appreciated. The character description is masterly, and the account of hypocrisy, dishonesty, deviousness, and brazenness, of some of the characters is so brilliantly realistic that the (Iranian) reader might feel it has all happened to him.

Muhammad Mas'ud's *Guha'i keh dar Jahannam Miruyand (Flowers Which Grow in Hell*, 1942) and its follow-up, *Bahar-i 'Umr (The Spring of Life*, 1943), though far more mature than his earlier works, betray the same amorality, bitterness and cynicism as before, almost as if the author's real complaint is that he does not have the same privileges as the rich and mighty. The plot (whose real counterpart in the author's life was somewhat less glorious) is about the narrator and his Belgian wife, and why, because of the hellish conditions in Iran, he would have to abandon her. His incidental criticisms of Reza Shah's system are almost mandatory in the circumstances, especially since he was regarded as a radical journalist, who spared almost no one from invective and defamation in his newspaper *Mard-i Imruz (Daily Man*, or *Man of Today)*, but the description of the humble circumstances in which he grew up contains a good deal of biting realism and social criticism.

Of the younger men in Hidayat's circle of intellectual friends, Jalal Al-i Ahmad and Sadiq Chubak displayed early talent for writing fiction, the former emerging in the 1950s and 1960s as the most brilliant Iranian writer, social, political and literary critic, essayist and pamphleteer, as well as anthropological observer and reporter, before his premature death at the age of forty-six. He was an active, though critical, member of the Tudeh party, and became a leader and organizer of the famous 1948 Split from the party, led by Khalil Maleki, with whom he later cooperated in founding the Third Force party.[12] In this decade, he published three collections of short stories – *Did u Bazdid (Exchange of Visits*, 1945), *Az Ranji Keh Mibarim (From Our Suffering*, 1947) and *Seh-tar* (1949). In the first two books, which were written when Al-i Ahmad was still a member of the Tudeh party, the influence of direct politics is apparent: according to the author himself, *From Our Suffering* is a social realist work. Yet they cannot quite be described as *engagé*, in the ideological sense of this term. For example, *Basij-i Mellat* ('Mobilization of the People') in the *Exchange of Visits*, is an overtly political piece – a ridiculing of Reza Shah's empty response to the 1941 invasion – but there is nothing ideological about it, and in any case, it is far from a pure work of propaganda. A relatively neglected short story of this decade is *Bach-che-yi Mardum* ('The Other Husband's Child') which is a detached and unmelodramatic description of a mother who abandons her child from a previous marriage in the street in order to pacify her present husband. The hard objective realism, reminiscent of some of Hidayat's short stories discussed before, makes the story more effective than if the author had

148 *Modern literature in the Near and Middle East*

assigned a role to his own judgement. As it is, socio-cultural criticism implicit in the story is left to the reader to discover for himself. Not surprisingly, a major theme in the work of this decade is the author's critique of religious leaders and preachers, and religious cant and superstition: it was the fashion of the day, and Al-i Ahmad himself had rebelled against his own deeply religious family. He was to revise his views on this subject in the 1960s.

The established view that Sadeq Chubak is not a 'political', perhaps not even a social, critic is somewhat exaggerated in two respects: first, he was a Tudeh party sympathizer, but later, having changed his sympathies and style of life, and become a member of the social establishment, his implicit politics were of a different kind from those of Hidayat, Al-i Ahmad and their like; second, his social criticism in the works of the 1940s usually takes more subtle form of observation and description, once again, reminiscent of some of Hidayat's short stories – not to mention his overtly anti-religious views which find full expression in the 1960s.

In his works of the 1940s, the two collections of short stories, *Khaimeh Shab Bazi* (*Puppet Show*, 1945) and *Antari Keh Lutish Murdeh Bud* (*The Baboon Whose Buffoon Was Dead*, 1950), he writes mainly about the lives of the ordinary people, but with few comments of his own. In these works he seems to have taken one or two leaves from Hidayat's book, although his realism is somewhat coarser and more empirical, and this has led many critics to describe him as a 'naturalist'. In his first book, when both the political situation and his own personal circumstances still allowed it, there are a few scathing allusions to Reza Shah and his system. Curiously, however, the best two stories in the two books are about animals, in fear and distress. *'Adl* ('Justice') is a short piece about a cab-horse which has fallen in a large open gutter, with a broken hoof and knee, 'watching the people with wide, tearless eyes'. It is the description of the horse and the by-standers' comments which gives this piece its fine effect. 'The Baboon Whose Buffoon Was Dead' is meant to be more than a display of impressive insight into animal psychology, and of their fear of human cruelty. The death of the Buffoon at first gives the animal a sense of freedom, but in no time the dangers of insecurity begin to manifest themselves. The conflict between freedom and security is common-place; Chubak's originality is to make the point in the case of animals, and do it with a subtlety that has made it almost invisible to readers and critics alike.

POETRY IN THE 1940s

Bahar's last great *qasidah* was on the subject of peace, and was recited in the Iranian Peace Club shortly before his death (in 1950) which

Iran 149

pronounced the end of an era for Persian poetry. Leading poets were creeping in the direction of modernity and modernism. Nima, the founder of modernist poetry, entered the new era almost as little known as he had been before. His one-man revolution was so radical that time was still needed for it to be fully absorbed by poets and the public alike. Besides, he was a private, almost reclusive, individual, and had hardly published any of his works. Nevertheless, he began to attract the attention and admiration of young poets, nearly all of whom were members of the Tudeh party. Firaidun Tavallali was a leading (perhaps, *the* leading) member of this group who was to some extent influenced by Nima – he even called his first daughter after the master – but did not go too far with it: he was a modern but not a modernist poet. His poetry was strongly affected by his politics: he even went so far as to ridicule, in a poem, the Tudeh leadership for its mistakes in the Azerbaijan episode (Khameh'i 1983), both when he was a party member and when he joined the 1948 Split; he continued to do this afterwards when he joined the socialist Third Force party, led by Khalil Maleki. Tavallali's main contribution to the modernization of poetry was jointly achieved with Mehdi Hamidi, although the latter was probably first in introducing it. This was the 'four-verse' form whereby, with a single metre throughout, every four verses had separate rhymes in their second and fourth verses. Hamidi was a talented poet whose later crusade against Nima's modernism led to the undervaluation of his own poetry by younger generations. Although not a political activist, he wrote a considerable amount of poetry, in the 1940s, on social and political issues. His book *Sal-ha-yi Siyah* (*Dark Years*, 1943) contains, among other pieces, some few damning poems about Reza Shah and his rule:

> In peace time he was a formidable lion; he looked a man, but gave up on the day of danger.

Nadir Nadirpur, also a Tudeh member who later joined the 1948 Split, was, at the time, a follower of these two poets. His lyrical, tender, almost sweet language and vocabulary accounted for much of his popularity at the time, but his growing formalism and the declining social relevance of his poetry later made him more popular with older and more conservative generations. Parviz Khanlary, who was then a Tudeh party sympathizer, did not write social and political poetry, although his excellent *'Uqab* ('Eagle'), apparently an allegory about Sadiq Hidayat, does contain a faint undertone of social criticism.

Mehdi Akhavan-i Salis and Ahmad Shamlu were also party members who became disenchanted only after the 1953 *coup*. They are now the two most prominent Persian poets, but in the 1940s they were still in the early

150 *Modern literature in the Near and Middle East*

stages of their careers. Unlike the others, they stayed in the Tudeh party long enough for it to become an ideological Communist Party, and this had an impact on the content of their poetry, especially Shamlu's which has no obvious precedent in the works of earlier writers and poets. One of Shamlu's best-known poems of this period is his long and symbolic *Pariya* ('Angels') which, using folkloric themes and folk vocabulary, glorifies communism and the Soviet Union, condemns 'the city of captive slaves', and promises early victory for the 'masses':

Ever since the Tudeh rose; the City became the domain of the masses.

Akhavan and Shamlu both became devoted followers of Nima, and defenders of his revolution, but in their interpretation of the master they took two different, although not conflicting, routes. With his solid Khurasani base and background, Akhavan's is a more Persian interpretation of Nima's poetry, and, therefore, still a part of that continuity. Shamlu, on the other hand, seems to have a more European conception of the new paradigm. Which version of the two is more likely to survive? That question would take us far beyond the scope of this chapter.

CONCLUSION

The number of authors and titles which we have had to cover within this space may have made this chapter look like an overview of the subject. Overviews have their uses, but here the purpose was different, and we must now try to integrate the main strands of the argument into a coherent analytical framework. Literature is a means of social communication, but specific questions about the public and political utility, the ideological implications and sociological functions of literature are directly related to the corresponding, but uneven, developments in all the relevant variables which involve society, politics and culture. This question of unevenness is of special significance.

By far the largest factor in the socio-economic shake-up of Iran in the nineteenth century was the rise of industry and empire in Europe. At first, the political and (much less visible) economic impact was considerably greater than the literary and cultural. It was towards the end of the century that literature was discovered as a means of social criticism, political struggle and, occasionally, of outbursts of nationalistic anger and indignation. Literary forms had then to be adjusted to the new and popular uses of literature, and this took place gradually until it reached a certain degree of maturity during the Persian Revolution (1905–9). In spite of the limited achievements of the Persian Revolution, the frustration of the

Iran 151

ideals of revolutionary intellectuals in their struggles against absolute and arbitrary rule *(istibdad)* pushed aside the open and democratic spirit of the old Constitutionalists, and curiously but understandably, led to impatient cries for a utopia in a context in which it had proved difficult to establish a civil society. This explains the outburst of romantic nationalism in politics and literature, and among the modernists, right and left alike.

This romantic nationalism had several distinctive aspects to it, not all of which were necessarily represented by the same author (or political leader) at once, or with a similar degree of emphasis. Its three most important strands were Aryanism, anti-Islamism and Europeanism. While the connections between the first two and the last two strands are uncomplicated, Aryanism and Europeanism would appear to be inconsistent because, in a number of ways, the nostalgia for ancient Persia would seem to contradict the glorification of modern Europe. The solution to this problem lies in Aryanism itself, and the consequent belief that Iran's had been essentially a Europeanic race and culture which would have developed in the same way as Europe, had it not been for Islam, the Arabs, the Turks, the Mongols and, finally, the Europeans themselves. The most fundamental cause of the cultural and socio-psychological (hence, also political) conflict and disorder in modern Iran has been the apparent dichotomy between the pre-Islamic and post-Islamic national and personal self-awareness, which was a direct result of the rise and supremacy of modern Europe.

Hidayat's anachronistic portrayal of Maziyar as a modern European nationalist hero, perhaps a precursor of Bonaparte, contains all the main strands of romantic nationalism mentioned above, although his anger against the contemporary Iranian 'Bonaparte', whose personal rule was based on a nationalist ideology not too dissimilar to his own, would appear to be self-contradictory. Here, too, the problem is largely explained by the fact that Europe was both the source of romantic nationalism and the founder of modern liberalism, except that the conflict between these two ideologies and their different implications for the political system, were evidently lost to generations of modern Iranian intellectuals and political activists. Likewise, Buzurg 'Alavi's imputation of European *bourgeois* morals and values to Sassanid Iranians under the yoke of the Arab 'demon' carries, all at once, the three characteristics of this nationalism, Aryanist, Europeanist and anti-Islamist.

But although romantic nationalism dominated both politics and literature between the two world wars, this was not entirely at the expense of social and cultural criticism, which was due both to European influence and the prevailing conditions in society. This, too, had various aspects and strands to it, but, in total contrast to the 1940s, it excluded any but the

152 *Modern literature in the Near and Middle East*

faintest pronouncements on political ideas and issues. Not surprisingly, different writers had different views and priorities on social problems and how to cure them. One approach which was highly popular in its time was to put forward idealistic diagnoses and prescriptions for moral and social ills, and to try to contrast reality as perceived by the author to an 'ideal type' which was presumed to be the common goal of the society. This 'ideal type' took two main forms: the Perso-European code of private and public morality held by the middle and upper classes; and a similarly Perso-European attitude towards personal and social propriety, held by the rapidly growing, but nebulous, social class which was being formed by the movement 'upwards' of sections of the traditional middle classes. It was this mobile community which supplied the educated base for active nationalism, Tudeh communism, Musaddiq's Popular Movement, as well as the Islamist and Marxist–Leninist wings of the most recent Iranian revolution, although this apparently sweeping assertion would need to be justified elsewhere.

The first form of 'ideal type' was best represented in Hijazi's novels and short stories, and was more popular among the reading public. Here, description is flowery in form and picturesque in appearance, while prescription is nothing but moralizing and pontification – a soothing and optimistic reassurance that all would be well if we gave up our ignorant or wicked ways, and took a few leaves from the author's code-book for happy living. There was nothing new in this mellow approach to social and personal problems which has probably a rich historical source in Persian as well as European cultures. The novelty lay in the literary *genre*, the language and the specific social context to which it referred. As usual, it emanated from a social class whose members were free of anxiety about material needs and personal security, and more concerned with introspective problems and preoccupation. To call this approach idealistic complacency would be somewhat misleading; let us call it critical idealism.

The second trend of this idealistic social criticism shared many of the characteristics of the first by virtue of their common outlook and vision. But there was a marked difference in the issues selected, and solutions offered. Jahangir Jalili is the most successful example of this idealistic criticism which is meant to reduce the reader, as it apparently does the author, to tears over the gap between the moral aspirations of the mobile social community mentioned above, and the author's romantic portrayals of empirical reality. Here we have criticism in the popular sense of the term, that is, disapproval of what there is, and exhortation for its removal and replacement by what there ought to be. Hence the essential difference between Jalili's idealistic criticism and Hijazi's critical idealism which is

Iran 153

neither unduly disturbed by the facts, nor in much of a hurry for social reform. On the other hand, the realistic approaches to cultural analysis and social criticism run deeper and are more sophisticated both in content and in technique, though not necessarily in form, when we consider Hijazi's highly literate prose. But here, too, we observe at least two specific, and in some ways conflicting, tendencies. By analogy with the case of idealism we may call them, respectively, critical realism and realistic criticism. Realistic criticism is coarse, aggressive and sometimes based on purely personal grievance, while critical realism is subtle, descriptive, detached and void of any explicit judgement. Jamalzadah's early short stories were the first examples of fictional social criticism without the author himself looming large in every passage of the toil and trouble.

It was Hidayat who brought this critical realism to maturity, setting a clear framework for an art of cultural anatomy which, however, has had only a few imitations in some of the early works of Al-i Ahmad and Chubak among later writers. It is impressive as well as peculiar that the writer who put so much passion into his nationalist fiction and into his essentially non-societal, ontological, novels and short stories, could display such an empirical, almost scientific, coolness and detachment when he put his scalpel to use in social and cultural dissection. Once he chooses the plot and makes the related character selection and scene, he sits back and lets them do the rest of the work with little or no personal participation, comments or suggestions about saving the unfortunate creatures from themselves or social injustice. This would appear to be somewhat parallel to the Hijazi-type idealism in its end results. But the appearances are deceptive because, while Hijazi sees no obvious need for social engineering as long as the people learn the right modes of thought and behaviour, Hidayat remains silent and is apparently unaffected; he neither approves nor disapproves; hence, he offers no prescription of any kind. Apart from the overt display of personal involvement in his nationalist fiction, this author ends many of his stories, which are concerned with timeless metaphysical and ontological puzzles and problems, with the flight, madness, death or suicide of the Fallen Creature. In such examples he is at the peak of his achievement as a writer.

This apparent switch in the 1940s from this supremacy of romantic nationalism to the dominance of social criticism in Persian literature, much like its counterpart in politics, was determined by the forces of outside intervention. Furthermore, one does not have to be too imaginative to suppose that, had the country been occupied by the Axis powers in place of the Allies, romantic nationalism, which at the time had an even stronger hold on both the state and the society than before, would have come into its own, and captured the country as wholly and completely as

154 *Modern literature in the Near and Middle East*

the Holy Inquisition had once captured Spain. Most of those who filled the ranks of the Tudeh party would have packed the local Nazi meetings perhaps with even greater enthusiam, and many of its intellectuals, writers, poets and journalists would have supplied the apposite literature: Nur al-Din Kiyanuri who joined the Tudeh party at that time, and ended as its leader in years to come, was still a Nazi activist at the beginning of the Allied invasion. This is neither to pass judgement on the men, nor on the nation to which they belong, if only because the subject is familiar from other times and places. The fact is that the basic domestic issues beneath the radical changes in politics and literature after the arrival of the Allies, could easily have been adorned in quite another ideological cloak. These consisted of anti-imperialist sentiments, an Aryanist national self-consciousness, the old sense of shame about underdevelopment, and the zest for social involvement and participation (the urge to be subject rather than object, which at the time was the general perception of 'freedom'). All this would have been no less satisfied by a Nazi revolution. As it happened it was the Allies who came. The point of the argument is that in the 1940s there was not much change in the basic elements of romantic nationalism and social criticism as compared with the preceding period. But there was a radical change in appearances, that is in how ideas are expressed, which had its own independent impact on the form and content of literature. For example, the attack on Islam continued unabated, but this time it was more in the guise of radical progressive ideas and programmes rather than in the deep-seated form of nostalgic glorification of pre-Islamic Persia. Likewise, Europeanism became an even stronger outlook and sentiment than before, but the favoured model began to change from France to the Soviet Union. In the same vein – except in the case of Jamalzadah who was writing in Geneva largely unperturbed by these domestic Iranian developments – literary social criticism lost Hidayat's realistic detachment, and Hijazi's detached idealism, and became a vehicle for overt manifestations of political dissent.

Yet, much of this was carried out through literature in its broader sense, that is through essayism, journalism and pamphleteering, rather than in prose fiction and poetry. The freedom of expression and publication in the 1940s resulted in an explosion of published material – which largely concentrated on the sins of the defunct dictatorship – of which literature in its specific sense had but a small share. Buzurg 'Alavi's romantic epic about the fifty-three Marxists in Reza Shah's jail is one of the best, and considering the political atmosphere, most moderately-toned examples of that broader political literature. Whereas, in his collection of short stories, *Prison Notes* (which was published in the same year) much less can be attributed to any political, let alone ideological, commitment, in spite of

Iran 155

his Marxist professions and his membership of the leading *élite* of the Tudeh party. That, however, is a general peculiarity of 'Alavi and his works, with one or two exceptions, of which the short story 'Man from Gilan' (1952) is the outstanding example. Hidayat's *Haji Aqa*, on the other hand, is an attempt by a politically plain and uncalculating writer, with no claim to ideological commitment or political activity, who has been swept along by the tides of positive political currents. Consequently, and despite his use of a few well-known ideological terms and allusions, the work lacks ideological depth and authenticity. The Haji is far from being a genuine bazaar merchant: the scene at his home is a caricature of the then upper-class gatherings at the house of a powerful political manipulator; the peroration of the righteous poet, full, as it is, of admirations for Firdowsi and the Iranian nation, is more like the contemptuous reproach of a nobleman of subtle values to an uncouth scoundrel, than a revolutionary speech by a proletarian intellectual before the leader of the *bourgeoisie*. In fact, the only absolutely genuine political aspect of this novel – and one which is close to the author's own heart – is the abuse and invective which fills the air the minute Reza Shah's name is mentioned. This finds expression once again in his *Murvari Cannon* which, far from being a contribution to literary politics, is an explosion of combined anti-political, anti-religious, nationalistic as well as ontological anger and indignation – a synthesis of which there is no other example in his works.

This ideological literature was to develop gradually and largely to the exclusion of the old guard. It was the new generation – Tavallali, Al-i Ahmad, Shamlu, I'timadzadah, Tabari (as a literary critic), Akhavan, – who began to write prose, poetry and criticisms which increasingly began to resemble the ideological aspirations of the New Man. But even that had to take time, for, putting aside Tabari's direct borrowings from Soviet guide-books to literary criticism, there was still little in the new literature which was authentically Marxist–Leninist. Al-i Ahmad's *From Our Suffering* might be an exception to the rule, but, even in this case, the author's own later description of it as a social realist work is more indicative of a vague knowledge of the rules and requirements of the school. It was no sooner than the Tudeh party split of 1948, or its banning in the following year, that theoretical Soviet Marxism began to dominate its politics and literature, and the young modernist poets – Shamlu, Akhavan, Kasra'i, Ibtihaj – took to the field to sing hopeful hymns about the imminent recovery of the promised land, in the language and paradigm which they had been taught by Nima. That is also when Bahar died, Hidayat took his own life, 'Alavi left the country and wrote no more fiction, Jamalzadah was carrying on in Europe in his own timeless fashion, Chubak went to the Oil Company and did not write fiction for a long time

156 Modern literature in the Near and Middle East

to come, Khanlary gave up poetry altogether, and Al-i Ahmad was still a promising writer of hazy prospects. This was the context in which Persian poetry – in its modernist, 'Nimaesque' form, reasserted itself strongly as a major literary channel for social criticism and political struggle in the next three decades until the 1980s.

NOTES

1 See Yahya Aryanpur (1971) for an extensive descriptive account of the early historical novels, and novelists, as well as later writers of the end of the century. Aryanpur's account, however, although highly competent for its own purposes, suffers from a certain lack of analytical depth.

2 These issues have been extensively discussed in Homa Katouzian, (1981b: chapters 3 and 4), and 1982.

3 Fath 'Ali Akhundov was so perfect a forerunner of the romantic nationalism of the 1920s and 1930s that, by hindsight, his romantic, anti-traditionalist, anti-religious, nationalist ideas amount to no less than an historical prophecy. At the time, however, his ideas did not find many converts, although such ideas – in less extreme forms – did spread further among a small number of intellectuals, for example, Mirza Aqa Khan Kirmani. It is interesting that almost none of the mainstream modern intellectual leaders of the Revolution, e.g. Taqizadah, Sur-Israfil, Dehkhuda, Bahar, Khiyabani, would fall into this category.

4 See further, Homa Katouzian (1981b: chapter 3) and (1982). The subject has been more fully discussed in a forthcoming paper, 'Iranianism and Romantic Nationalism in Iran'.

5 Yahya Aryanpur (1961) has reprinted a statement signed by a number of Iranian students in Europe (several of whom were to become functionaries in the Pahlavi state) who speak about the Europeanization of Iran almost in so many words. See further, Homa Katouzian, (1981b) for a discussion of the concepts of modernity, modernism and pseudo-modernism in this context.

6. Iraj, *Kulliyat,* mocks the idea in a verse: 'I shall launch a literary revolution; I shall turn Persian into Arabic'. Sadiq Sarmad – an average poet of his time – wrote a letter in verse to Bahar imploring him to give the lead for a revolution in poetry, but, in his reply, the master would not be drawn. See, M. T. Bahar, (1957).

7 To this writer's knowledge the term *Shi'r-i naw* (modernist poetry) occurs for the first time in a verse by Bahar, in his lament for 'Ishqi's violent death: 'he was a modernist, and his poetry modern; the modernist poet died, and modernist poetry vanished'. This is surprising, especially as it is normally thought that the term came into use in the late 1930s and 1940s. See M.T. Bahar (1956).

8 There followed an interesting controversy between Jamalzadah (in Berlin) and the two authors (in Tehran) both about the romantic nationalism of this story, and (specifically) over the ancestry of 'Ali b. Rahn. (The arguments and counter-arguments were all written in the margins of Jamalzadah's copy which is currently in this author's possession.)

Iran 157

9 See Homa Katouzian (1977) for a classification of the different categories of Hidayat's works.
10 In January 1947 he wrote to Tavallali (from Tehran to Shiraz) that – in the Azerbaijan episode – 'the betrayal had many sides to it: the Tudeh are rubbing shit on themselves in the hope of covering up the basic truth. In any case, we have to eat our own shit spoon by spoon, and say how nice it is too.' See Homa Katouzian (1981a).
11 For the accounts of other members of the fifty-three, see Anvar Khameh'i (1982); Homa Katouzian (1981a) and Iraj Iskandari (1986).
12 See his own extremely interesting account and analysis of the 1948 Split in Al-i Ahmad (1978).

PART III

THE AGE OF IDEOLOGY AND POLARIZATION SINCE 1950

11 The age of ideology and polarization

David Pool

The Middle East has undergone great social and political change since 1950, and much of it has been violent. Events of the 1970s have been particularly dramatic: the 1973 Arab–Israeli war; the Camp David Agreements and the Egypt–Israel peace treaty; the civil war in Lebanon and the Syrian and Israeli invasions. The earlier decades have also had their dramatic moments: the overthrow of the monarchies in Egypt, Iraq and Libya; the 1956 Suez invasions and independence in North Africa bringing an end to European colonial power; and the 1967 Arab–Israeli war bringing in its wake the occupation of the West Bank, Gaza, Sinai and the Golan Heights. Even the more stable states like Turkey and Israel have exhibited sharp discontinuities, with three military interventions in Turkey and the rise of the nationalist and religious Right in Israel.

Because the Middle East is an area defined by geographical contiguity and the strategic interests of the Great Powers rather than by any homogeneity of social structure or historical background, it is difficult to find themes which unify the political experience of states as different as Libya and Israel, Tunisia and Iran, and Lebanon and Turkey. Even where states have cultural, social and historical characteristics in common (like those of the ex-Ottoman Arab states of the Fertile Crescent) there have been very different patterns of politics. The monarchy was overthrown in Iraq but has survived in neighbouring Jordan, and although Syrian regimes have achieved an authoritarian stability over a religiously divided society, Lebanon has disintegrated. A few general points can be made.

(i) The decades after the Second World War have been the era of the state and the struggle for its consolidation against both internal and external forces. In most instances this process has reproduced repressive authoritarian regimes.

(ii) Because the majority of states in the region are either ethnically or religiously heterogeneous there has been a complicated interplay between state and nation. Arab nationalism in its Pan-Arabist version has stood

162 *Modern literature in the Near and Middle East*

counter to the existence of separate Arab states. The Zionist project of establishing a Jewish state was successful in creating Israel but the majority of Jews remain outside it, Israel has a significant Arab minority and, since 1967, has ruled Jews and tens of thousands of Arabs outside its legally recognized borders. The relationship between Jews, Judaism, Israeli citizenship and the sovereignty of the Israeli state is not a straightforward one. Ideologies of nationalism which incorporate secular ideas of the state run foul of both Islamic populist and fundamentalist conceptions of government and law, as Islamic fundamentalist conceptions of the *umma* (the Muslim nation) collide not only with an entrenched secularism but with the interests of non-Muslim minorities. At different times secularizing policies in Turkey, and the implementation of Islamic law in Egypt and the Sudan have led to political conflict. Thus, as Middle Eastern states have attempted to expand their authority over their societies, ideologies of legitimation, be they of modernization, nationalism, socialism or religious authenticity, have brought in their wake movements and ideologies with very different conceptions of the political community.

(iii) Linked to our second point, the nature of the relationship between class and local community (ethnic and sectarian solidarities) and between these social categories and the state and its institutions has played an increasingly important role in the domestic politics of the Middle East. In some cases (like the 'Alawis in Syria) minority groups have achieved a political position out of all proportion to their numbers, status and wealth, whereas in other cases (the Shi'a in Lebanon, the Arabs in Israel and the Kurds in Turkey) life has been one of deprivation and discrimination. Lebanon is a tragic example of the complex relationship between social position and sectarianism and its political repercussions.

(iv) The nature of contemporary Middle Eastern politics has been profoundly affected by regional conflicts and international tensions. Strategic position and oil resources have made the area an arena of superpower competition which has both facilitated and encouraged inter-state tensions. In the immediate post-war period, France sought to maintain its colonies in North Africa and Britain, its influence through military bases and client governments in the Middle East. In the 1950s, in an effort to contain communism the West attempted to incorporate the area into an alliance system which the Soviet Union confronted by providing assistance to nationalist governments and movements. Arms have been poured into the Middle East and have fuelled the Arab–Israeli conflict during the process of which the struggle for a Palestinian state has been marginalized.

Of the contemporary Middle Eastern states Turkey was the only one

The age of ideology and polarization 163

which inherited anything approaching a state tradition, which was both indigenous and strongly articulated, and a dominant ideology in the form of Atatürkism. This latter incorporated secularism, statism, republicanism and Westernism and had social and institutional support from army, bureaucracy and intellectuals. When, in 1946, the single party system was opened up, liberal democratic multi-partyism (with some restrictions) became an additional component. The contemporary history of Turkey is the history of the attenuation of Atatürkism and its core support.

The introduction of party politics, one of the hallmarks of westernism for the Turkish political élite, brought with it a contradiction: competition for electoral support was sought from an electorate which was by no means persuaded of the value of the dominant ideology. Officers, bureaucrats and intellectuals, guardians of the system, were confronted by a coalition of national politicians and local notables who were able to get out the rural vote through a conservative, populist and moderately anti-secularist appeal. After the 1950 elections the anti-Atatürkist Democratic party formed a government and introduced policies which favoured the market rather than statism and a populist Islam rather than secularism. In 1960 the military intervened in defence of Atatürkism. (It was the first of three military interventions.) The return to electoral politics brought with it a greater convergence of Atatürkist and anti-Atatürkist parties in pursuit of the popular vote, as the electorate changed significantly through industrialization, migration into the towns, greater commercialization in the rural areas and an expansion of capitalist agriculture.

In the 1970s these social changes, combined with economic crisis, produced conflict between right and left, Kurdish nationalists and radicals and the authorities, trade unionists and employers and between the Shi'i 'Alavis and Sunni Muslims. Bureaucrats and intellectuals, no longer above the fray, became increasingly politicized as an unprecedented violence was unleashed. Liberal democratic Turkey took on a politics more typical of the former Ottoman Arab states as ethnicity and sectarianism became entwined with social conflict. In 1980 the army intervened for the third time and established military rule, imprisoning politicians and trade unionists and introducing martial law over large parts of the country. In some respects it was the return to an Atatürkist authoritarianism but in a very different social and international context. First, even if the majority of Turks favoured the crack-down on 'terrorists', prolonged military rule and the abrogation of civil liberties were not acceptable. Secondly, the logic of policies of Westernism and capitalist economic development had led Turkey's rulers to seek membership of the EEC, a prospect unlikely to succeed with a continuation of censorship, the banning of trade unionists and the imprisonment of politicians.

164 *Modern literature in the Near and Middle East*

Iran, like Turkey, succeeded to an imperial tradition and, in the inter-war period, underwent reform directed by Reza Khan, a former cossack officer. Whereas Atatürk broke with the Ottoman past and established a republic, Reza Khan proclaimed himself Shah. Deposed by the British in 1941, his legacy to his son, Shah Mohammad Reza, was a new dynastic autocracy shorn of any ideological or institutional support and lacking historical roots. After an early challenge to the monarchy by nationalists and communists (the Shah fled and was restored with the direct assistance of the CIA) the history of the Pahlavi monarchy was the history of the parallel expansion of the power of the state and the Shah's despotism, both of which were supported by the United States. The ideological legitimation of the Shah's rule was 'modernization' but equal weight was given to the undermining of the autonomy of groups, institutions and political movements and creating a systemic web of authority and power with the Shah at the centre. Oil revenues were the motor for the Shah's development of Iran into a 'Great Civilization', and royal patronage and Savak (the internal security apparatus) repression the twin instruments for rewarding friends and persecuting enemies.

The impact of oil revenues and the Shah's development programme unintentionally succeeded in creating the preconditions for the political mobilization of Iranians against the Shah and his regime. The Shah's autocracy and his grip on the instruments of state made him the focus of an opposition which drew support from almost all Iranian social strata. The land reform of the early 1960s, rather than solving the problem of peasant poverty, expanded commercial agriculture and, combined with the oil-fuelled construction boom in the cities, brought a large-scale peasant migration. Uprooted from their conservative *milieu* and living in shanty town conditions, these urban migrants were integrated into urban life through the mosque. The traditional bazaar merchants, competing with state sponsored and foreign business (like the migrants and the clergy), found the secularism and Western consumerism, both of which were symbolized by the extravagant Western lifestyle of the palace, repugnant and un-Islamic. Groups which had prospered through the oil bonanza were alienated by the absence of basic political freedoms and the corruption and venality of those closest to the Shah and his family. Students, workers and the Western-educated middle class were denied any form of political participation or organization and suffered censorship, harassment, arbitrary imprisonment and the almost paranoid atmosphere of suspicion and dread induced by the activities of Savak and its large network of informants.

An additional source of opposition to the Shah was Iranian nationalism. Iranian foreign policy and the involvement of foreign business interests

The age of ideology and polarization 165

and advisers in Iran's economic development unified the diverse political tendencies which were otherwise antagonistic to each other. Islamic socialists and fundamentalists, liberals, radicals and Marxist–Leninists opposed the Iranian role as one of the 'Twin Pillars' of the United States' Gulf policy, the billion dollar purchases of US arms, the extra-territorial legal position of the 20,000 US advisers and the alliance with Israel. Although European and Japanese companies were involved in joint ventures in Iran it was the role of US companies which aroused most ire because of US links with the Shah. In 1953 the CIA had restored the Shah and the FBI 'modernized' Savak and trained their personnel. The 'Great Satan' was as real a demon for the Iranian opposition as the Savak, and that slogan was a mark of the political acumen of Ayatollah Khomeini whose exile by and subsequent steadfast opposition to the Shah and all his works enabled him to convert a symbolic leadership into a real one. At the root of Khomeini's personal success was the way in which Shi'i Islam had retained a high degree of autonomy from the predatory Pahlavi state and possessed independent financial support, a network of graduates from the religious colleges spread through the villages and towns in Iran, and a clergy which had incorporated to some extent an Islamic modernism. Despite the popularity of Khomeini, the consolidation of a republic under the guidance of Islam and the mullahs had to confront a wide range of secular and Islamic political movements and spasmodic uprisings of Kurds, Azerbaijanis and Turks. The Islamic fundamentalist wing of the clergy resorted to force rather than Islamic legitimacy to quell opposition, and it took the Iraqi external threat to generate a broader Iranian nationalism.

The most significant change in the immediate post-war Arab world was the overthrow of the Egyptian monarchy in 1952 and the emergence of Jamal 'Abd al-Nasir (Nasser) as head of state. Because Egypt was the most populous and advanced of the Arab states the changes which took place under the new regime set a pattern to either emulate or oppose. The challenge to Western interests by its emphasis on national independence and neutralism, the establishment of a republic and the first reform of a landownership system, which benefited a handful of families, launched Nasser, Nasserism and Egypt onto centre stage. Refused Western finance for the Aswan dam, Nasser nationalized the Suez canal and turned to the Eastern bloc for finance and for arms supplies. Nasser's popularity was further enhanced by the Israeli, British and French attack on Egypt in 1956 and the Egyptian regime's stress on Arab nationalism to combat imperialism and colonialism. The Nasserist mixture of populism, reform and Arab nationalism (backed by a vigilant internal security system), proved a powerful mobilizing agent for a younger generation of

166 *Modern literature in the Near and Middle East*

nationalists against Arab governments which were, generally, formed from pro-Western landowners.

The high tide of Nasserism came in the late 1950s. In 1958 Egypt and Syria joined to form the United Arab Republic (UAR), Arab nationalists threatened to topple the governments of Jordan and Lebanon and the Iraqi monarchy was overthrown by reformist officers. Radical reforming Arab nationalism seemed to be sweeping all before it. In the event, the Nasserist tide ebbed. The popular appeal of Arab unity could not overcome the practical problem of incorporating the interests of the particular Arab states with their different social and ethnic problems. In addition, the emphasis on Arab solidarity and the alignment with the Soviet Union brought the radical nationalist states into a direct collision with Israel and brought US backing for Israel and pro-Western Arab states. Divided on multiple axes, the Arab states drifted into the disasterous 1967 war on a wave of rhetoric. The destruction of the Arab armies in six days proved a humiliating turning point for Arabism and for Nasser. Israel swept into Sinai, took the Gaza Strip and established positions along the Suez canal, and occupied Syria's Golan Heights and the West Bank, including the old city of Jerusalem.

1967 was a particular tragedy for the Palestinians. Having played no part in starting the war, they saw those parts of the Palestine mandate which had remained under Arab control taken by Israel. It was ironic that this should have taken place just after the emergence of independent Palestinian nationalist groups dissatisfied with Arab inaction on the Palestine question. It was a further irony that after the 1967 war the most militarily powerful of the Arab states, Egypt and Syria, placed far greater priority on the return of their occupied territories than on the return of a Palestinian homeland and thus the pursuit of independent Palestinian goals became submerged in a set of bilateral Arab–Israeli conflicts.

The Arab defeat of 1967 led to a fundamental re-alignment in the Middle East, although another war in 1973 was required to realize it fully. Egypt again was the prime mover and the Palestinians the major losers. Anwar Sadat, the successor to Nasser in 1970, viewed the USA as the key to the recovery of Sinai, the re-opening of the Suez canal and the economic resurgence of Egypt. Egypt fought a limited war in 1973, the main purpose of which was to re-engage the attention of the United States in the Arab–Israeli conflict. The US involvement in arranging the cease-fire led eventually to a total rupture in USSR–Egyptian relations, the Camp David Agreements and the Egyptian–Israeli Peace Treaty. Sadat opened the domestic economy to private investment and gave a much greater role to private capital and the market. All of this was in marked contrast to the core of Nasserism. After thirty years of war the most powerful of the Arab

The age of ideology and polarization 167

states settled with Israel and stuck to the settlement despite Israel's subsequent invasions of Lebanon, the attack on Iraq and the destruction of the Palestinian fighting force in Beirut. The failure of the Arab states to isolate Egypt symbolized the demise of Arab unity, as the lack of Arab response to the Israeli attack on the PLO symbolized the death of the Palestinian issue as a touchstone of Arab solidarity.

While the fading glory of Arabism and Nasserism removed an external challenge to the legitimacy of the Arab states of the Fertile Crescent, they faced problems which derived from sub-state loyalties. Iraqi governments were threatened by the Kurdish nationalist movement; post-1966 Syrian governments, drawing their key military and political personnel from the 10 per cent minority 'Alawi sect, were confronted by the Muslim Brothers who recruited support from the urban Sunni Muslim community; and the Jordanian army faced an armed uprising from its Palestinian population. Whereas all of these states survived these upheavals, Lebanon disintegrated into civil war as warring militias based on the geographic heartlands of the sects established independent armed enclaves supported by most states in the area. Lebanon became a theatre of war not only for the contending Lebanese parties but for most of the conflicts in the region: Arab–Israeli, intra-Palestinian and Iraqi–Iranian. As the shift in Egypt had marked the demise of radical Arab nationalism, so the ferocity and barbarism unleashed in Lebanon marked the demise of an individualistic free-market capitalism there. Once again it was the Palestinian cause which bore the brunt of this maelstrom of Arab division and conflict. Seeking freedom of action in the weaker states, the PLO was pushed from Jordan in 1970, pulled into the civil war in Lebanon in 1975, and between 1976 and 1982 was caught between the Syrian anvil and the Israeli hammer. After being dispersed around the Arab world after the expulsion from Lebanon, the torch of Palestinian nationalism was transferred to the occupied territories of Gaza and the West Bank.

One of the major beneficiaries and promoters of Arab division has been Israel. The embattled state of 1948 has emerged as the most powerful in the Middle East. Such dominance, however, has brought with it problems which have threatened to undermine the rationale for the establishment of the state. The vision of the pioneer Zionists was of a haven for Jews, Jewishness and the practice of Judaism in a social-democratic, egalitarian and co-operative society. The uneasy compromise between the secular founders of the state and religious orthodoxy, between the problem of an Arab minority and a largely poor immigrant population from the Middle East and North Africa which did not share the ideology of the founders, was masked in the early years of independence. Again, 1967 was a turning point. In that year Israel occupied the West Bank and Gaza and introduced

168 *Modern literature in the Near and Middle East*

into Israeli politics an issue which had remained buried since 1948: the territorial limits of the Jewish state. Right wing nationalists, politically marginal in the early decades of independence, and religious parties found common ground in the historic claim to Judaea and Samaria, as they called the West Bank. At the same time, the Labour party's claim to historic leadership of the *Yishuv* (the Jewish community in Palestine) had been undermined by its machine-type politics, its patronizing direction of Oriental Jews and the shrinking role of the socialist sector symbolized in the kibbutz movement. The 1977 election was an earthquake. Labour was swept from power by the religious right, drawing on the votes of disgruntled Orientals, in combination with a middle class vote disenchanted by Labour's lack of vision. Successive governments were dominated by a militant right wing nationalism committed to large-scale Jewish settlement in the West Bank. Liberal and leftist Zionists were more sensitive to the effects on Israel of incorporating and ruling by force one and a half million additional Palestinians, but even in these circles there was little or no sympathy for the Palestinian demand for an independent state. For many Israelis, core values were brought into question: how could Israel continue as a Jewish state when half the subjects were non-Jews? How could Israel function as a democracy when half the population were under military rule?

The varying intensity of French rule was the most crucial factor shaping post-war political development in North Africa as the intensity of the struggle for independence and decolonization varied with the length and depth of colonial rule. Early colonization (1830 in Algeria, 1881 in Tunisia) was accompanied by settler colonialism and policies of cultural assimilation. Later colonialism (Morocco in 1912) involved economic penetration of the modern sector of the economy but left traditional social and political structures relatively intact. Independence for Algeria came in 1962 after a protracted guerrilla war convinced the French government to abandon the notion that Algeria was part of France. The war had a devastating effect on the Algerian economy and society: it caused a massive dislocation of rural life, a large-scale migration of Algerians to France and the flight of almost a million French settlers who had operated the modern sectors of the economy. The vision of constructing a socialist society and the pursuit of economic, political and cultural independence was confounded by a dependence on France for technical aid, capital, and export markets, and the power of an entrenched centralized bureaucracy. The struggle for cultural authenticity faced all the contradictions inherent in a reaction against French assimilation led by a secular and essentially francophone élite.

The paths of Tunisia and Morocco to independence were less violent

The age of ideology and polarization 169

than Algeria's and their post-independence politics shared a common feature: a continuity of personalized rule. In Tunisia, Habib Bourguiba, the leader of the nationalist struggle, dominated political life. In contrast to King Hassan of Morocco who operated through traditional court patronage, Bourguiba utilized the nationalist party, the Néo-Destour, as an instrument of rule. Despite Bourguiba's flirtation with socialist policies in the late 1960s, both Tunisia and Morocco remained within the Western orbit looking towards the United States rather than to France as an alternative source of assistance. Although the political unity of the Maghrib has been floated at various times, state sovereignty has never been threatened in the way that Arab unity threatened the Arab Mashriq states. Neither have sub-state loyalties caused the same level of internal turmoil, although Algerian governments have faced and tried to conceal a 'Berber problem'.

We mentioned at the beginning of this review of political developments since 1950 the high incidence of violence in politics. In part, this has been a function of large-scale social change and an inability of governments to establish new political frameworks, institutional or ideological, to cope with the strains of such change, the form of which has been frequently shaped by external economic forces. The nationalist search for economic and political independence at the beginning of the period has ended with states more dependent and more closely linked to Western economies. Although the oil-producing states benefited from the reversal of their formerly inert relationship with the oil multinationals, in the longer run, they have found themselves passive victims of the vagaries of Western economies and dependent for imports, skills and weaponry. Other states in the region, like Egypt, Turkey and Tunisia, have faced severe financial problems as a result of oil price increases and a consequent increase in internal social tensions.

Dominant ideologies, frequently linked to the policies and personalities of particular political leaders, did not survive into the 1970s. Although Atatürkism, Nasserism and Bourguibism provided a degree of legitimation for an earlier authoritarianism, by the 1970s these had given way to a more pragmatic kind of authoritarian rule increasingly challenged by a range of movements thrown up by the social changes of earlier decades. Regimes based on pragmatic authoritarianism, limited popular support and the defence of new privileged groups and classes have created political orders which stumble from crisis to crisis and, lacking any broadly acceptable vision of the future, they react by reaching for the gun and the gaoler's key. Writers with a critical perspective are forced to work in an intimidating context of elaborate security networks, censorship, arbitrary arrest and imprisonment.

12 Turkey

Cevat Çapan

About suffering they were never wrong,
The Old Masters: how well they understood
Its human position, how it takes place
While someone else is eating or opening a window
or just walking dully along...

(Auden n.d.: 3)

I take these lines by Auden as my starting point in this brief account of Turkish literature from 1950 to the present day, because I believe that the new literary masters of that period were also concerned about suffering and its human position in Turkish society; that this period is full of drastic and dramatic changes and that these changes that were the cause of great pain and suffering is now a commonplace. What needs elucidating here is the way these changes affected the literature of the period.

The most notable change following the Second World War was the liberalization of political life. This 'bloodless transition in Turkey from a single-party authoritarian regime to a multi-party democratic structure based on contested, free elections' was carried out under the responsible leadership of İsmet İnönü, the President of the Turkish Republic and the Chairman of the ruling Republican People's Party. Other factors inducing the change included:

(i)   increasing popular demand for greater participation in government by a growing middle class,

(ii)   Turkey's signing of the Charter of the United Nations,

(iii)   the Soviet threat and the authoritarian nature of the Soviet regime,

(iv)   the Turkish need for Western aid and support,

(v)   the victory of the more liberal nations over the more authoritarian in the Second World War, and

(vi)   the obvious growth of corruption within the single-party state and İnönü's personal reaction to this state of affairs.

Turkey 171

Only by the existence of a strong, vigorous opposition, could İnönü gain effective control over his own party, which by 1950 had become strongly tainted with corruption and oppression (Robinson 1963: 142–3).

The political struggle that brought the newly founded Democrat Party into power in 1950 created an atmosphere of optimism especially among the rural population and enabled them to identify with the politicians who were the new masters of the country. The dynamism of the first four or five years of Democrat rule, enhanced by the rapid economic growth, caused an uncontrollable flow of rural workers to the big cities. In fact, not only the flow of people moving from the villages to the cities, but the growing problems of inflation, undemocratic laws, student unrest, the demands of labour, and religious reactions all contributed to the crisis which brought the army directly into the political arena in 1960.

The military *coup* of 27 May 1960 and the Constitution of 1961 opened a new phase in the development of Turkish society. The following decade was a period of moderation and coalition governments. The new Constitution paved the way for a pluralist democracy. The labour law of 1963 made strikes legal, and with the workers taking part more actively in politics through the Turkish Workers' Party and the Confederation of Reformist Workers' Union, socialism ceased to be a dirty word – at least in legal terms. Another important turning point in Turkish political life was the memorandum presented by the chief of staff and the senior military commanders calling for the resignation of the government on 12 March 1971. The right wing Demirel administration which came to power in 1969 proved to be incapable of dealing with the political and economic crisis which threatened law and order in Turkey. So the new decade was again a period of coalitions, constitutional amendments, political and economic crisis, and growing violence. According to the majority of people living under these circumstances, the country was on the verge of a civil war. The military *coup* of 1980 was the inevitable step taken to stop terrorism and the escalating antagonism between the right and the left. A National Security Council under the leadership of General Evren took over all government responsibilities, dissolved the Parliament, political parties, and trade unions. The constitution was once more suspended and martial law was imposed in all the provinces.

Since 1982 Turkey has had a new constitution which had the approval of a great majority of the nation in a referendum. And in 1983 power was transferred to an elected parliament. For the time being, things look much calmer and in spite of the high rate of inflation and other socio-economic problems, Turkey is trying her best to be part of the European Community. This is, of course, a very sketchy account of the important events in Turkey during the last forty years. And it is against this background that I propose to deal with the literature of that period.

172 *Modern literature in the Near and Middle East*

As Raymond Williams points out:

> the relations between literature and society can be seen to vary considerably, in changing historical situations. As a society changes, its literature changes, though often in unexpected ways, for it is a part of social growth and not simply its reflections. At times, a rising social group will create new institutions which, as it were, release its own writers. At other times, writers from new social groups will simply make their way into existing institutions, and work largely within their terms.
>
> (Williams 1961: 243)

The rising social class at the beginning of the 1950s cared very little for poetry. What the new *bourgeoisie* expected from art was pure entertainment. There was a serious erosion of cultural and artistic values. The revolution of taste carried out by Orhan Veli and the 'Strange' movement had a shock effect in the early 1940s, but was soon tamed by its second-rate imitators. Even Oktay Rifat (b. 1914) and Melih Cevdet Anday (b. 1915) who were originally poets of the same movement and Metin Eloğlu (1927–85) whose first book of poems *Düdüklü Tencere* (*Pressure Cooker*) seemed to be an off-shoot of the 'Strange' school, veered away to create a more personal and elaborate style in their later development. The time was ripe to create a more contemporary poetic language that would express the complexity of the socio-economic change.

As Nermin Menemencioğlu writes in her introduction to *The Penguin Book of Turkish Verse*,

> the reaction to the brevity and simplicity of the 'Strange' school came with the 'Second New Movement' of the 'fifties, the members of which described themselves as writers of 'abstract' or sometimes of 'meaningless' poetry.
>
> (Menemencioğlu 1978: 54)

The influential left wing critics and old-guard poets immediately accused the members of this movement of being escapists or *bourgeois* opportunists. In spite of this hostile atmosphere poets like Cemal Süreya (b. 1931), Turgut Uyar (1927–85), Edip Cansever (1928–86), Ece Ayhan (b. 1931) and Ülkü Tamer (b. 1937) explored the possibilities of creating new rhythms and a more modern imagery. These poets were trying to recover the poetic qualities of the language which were banished by the 'Strange' movement in the name of a more popular aesthetics. This does not mean that the 'Second New Movement' was by any means 'élitist' or anti-popular. It was rather a bridge between the democratic approach of the 'Strange' school and the mystic and imagist poetry of Fazıl Hüsnü

Turkey 173

Dağlarca. But more than that it tried to depict the experiences of the alienated individual in the great metropoles. It was therefore more psychological, more metaphysical, and more esoteric at the same time.

Cemal Süreya managed to be the most popular of the group with his original imagery, subtlety, irony and wit. He also broadened the boundaries of poetic diction by introducing unconventional elements to his poetry. His first book *Üvercinka* (1958) won him many admirers even among his harshest critics. 'At First' is an example from that collection translated by Nermin Menemencioğlu:

> At first only your hands came between me and loneliness
> Then of a sudden the doors were opened wide
> Then your face and then your eyes and then your lips
> Then everything came
>
> A king of fearlessness surrounded us
> You took off your shame and hung it on the wall
> I placed the rules of decorum on the table
> That is how everything happened at first.

In the 1960s Süreya edited a monthly review, *Papirüs*, which published the most interesting creative and critical works of his contemporaries.

Turgut Uyar wrote his poems in long prosaic lines and tried to express the irrational, the 'dark gods' in man. He was never a perfectionist. Although he was interested in formal experiments he achieved his poetic intensity through the tragic content of his works. 'Triad of Sea-Blues Reduced to One', again in Nermin Menemencioğlu's version, is a poem that reminds one of the agonized energy of Cesar Vallejo:

> On a day of deceit and subterfuge, vile, not properly lived
> A day eyeless, earless, handless, footless, truncated
> All my deficiencies, blanks, confusions, piled high on high
> Adventures that have befallen me, these many thousand years
> The systems, the people, the deaths piled on high
> So many suns, so many water-snakes, so many plans
> Of a sudden the blue reminds me of someone
> Of a sudden I think of the mouth of a fish
> And I feel cool
>
> I have thought of three places for you and me
> One by the sunflowers, one at thirty and one – do not ask
> Do not ask me now I may tell you myself someday
> When I am braver more of a craftsman then I might tell you
> First let us brighten a little this angry darkness

174 *Modern literature in the Near and Middle East*

Let us build cities resembling the ones of today
Let us start anew the sesame seeds the loaves of bread
The going overseas the falling in love
Let us go and return
Perhaps that sound that drop those soft beds that green perhaps
I can break rocks I can mix mortar I can pave roads
We may be happy let us go and return
I will not yield I can crush stones mix mortar
And you have hair like a waterfall no matter what

Edip Cansever is also more interested in content rather than form. His subject-matter is the alienated man in a shabby genteel urban setting. Out of this non-communicative world he occasionally escapes to nature. The sea always attracts him as it does many other Mediterranean poets. He makes no effort to condense or intensify his meaning. He is content to wander in the semi-darkness of Bohemia murmuring to himself. Here is one of his earlier poems, 'The Gravitational Carnation,' translated by Feyyaz Kayacan:

Do you know you live in me bit by bit
Yet there is such a thing as being lovely with you
For instance we drink *rakı* and it is
As if a carnation is engulfing us.
Beside us a tree works with precision
Mind and belly lose sense and sway.

You are bent on that carnation, I take it
And give it to you. You then pass it on
To someone else. And a greater beauty is reached.
Do you know, that someone else forwards it again
And lo the carnation quickens from hand to hand.

As you can see we augment this love,
With warmth I dwell upon you, but that is not it,
Look how like seven colours into white translated
Each into each silently we cast our unison.

The most controversial and the most obscure poet of the 'Second New Movement' is Ece Ayhan. He owes this reputation of obscurity not to his first book, *Kınar Hanımın Denizleri*, which was full of nostalgic allusions to pre-First World War Istanbul, but to the prose poems in his second and third book. Ayhan is an avid reader of rare history books out of which he digs fables and legends of a forgotten past. He is also interested in the present day underworld. In his fourth book, *Devlet ve Tabiat (State and*

Nature) he shows that he can be a ruthless critic of his times without sacrificing his idiosyncratic style. 'Master's Work' is translated by Murat Nemet-Nejat:

I.
The poor bird never forgets, it was the year of the burning of books
From forty gates at once we saw penetrate in state
The headless horse and its pale, preened rider inside
Death smashed to bits, according to Holy Books, was returning from the East
For it a town was divided into three by bitter waters

II.
The poor bird never forgets, boys with dead masters
Combed each other's hair coming out of the water
Oh the ripe youth inside the watermelon, my Istanbul,
You hide your heart in shame and smell of rotting flowers
On this broken slate of a city, black pigeons go flying

III.
The poor bird never forgets, this golden dialectics in history
So many, such princes carried their horses on their backs without knowing
There, on their coffins, masterful odes are carved.

Sezai Karakoç (b. 1933) was also a member of the 'Second New Movement' who was inspired by Islam and who eventually expressed his mystic outlook in more traditional forms. Kemal Özer (b. 1935), on the other hand, began his poetic career as a meticulous formalist member of the 'Second New Movement', then after a considerable silence, reappeared as a politically committed poet in the Brecht tradition.

In the liberal atmosphere created by the Constitution of 1961 the Turkish reading public enjoyed something like a golden age of enlightenment. Hundreds of political and philosophical foreign works that were considered to be subversive in the past were now translated into Turkish, and Nazım Hikmet's poems were reprinted for the younger generations and provided them with the revolutionary fervour they were looking for. Most of the younger poets were also politicized and began to be naively critical of anyone who did not write political tracts in verse. Another poet who influenced the young poets of the 1960s was Ahmed Arif (b. 1926). When his single book of poems *Hasretinden Prangalar Eskittim* (*Fetters Worn By Longing*) came out in 1968 the smuggiers and the mountain bandits he wrote about were identified as romantic revolutionaries by the young readers. Ataol Behramoğlu, Süreyya Berfe,

176 *Modern literature in the Near and Middle East*

Özkan Mert and İsmet Özel, who began to publish their poems in the 1960s, started a joint action against *bourgeois* writers under the banner of 'Revolutionary Young Poets'. This solidarity, however, did not last after the 12 March 1971 Memorandum which dealt a hard blow not only to the left wing activists but also to some of the progressive journalists and university teachers. But some of them joined other groups in such literary reviews as *The Friends of the People, The Future* and *The Militant* and continued to accuse almost all the poets except Nazım Hikmet, Ceyhun Atuf Kansu and Ahmed Arif of being reactionary, opportunistic and derivative. Their own poetry, on the other hand, was not marred by the accusatory tone of their polemics. In fact, A. Behramoğlu purified his poetry by leaving out crude propaganda and naive didacticism. İsmet Özel, who was the most talented of the group, turned to Islam for inspiration, but preserved the revolutionary bravura of his Marxist days. Süreyya Berfe identified with the under-privileged by absorbing the rhythms of folk songs and popular language. Egemen Berköz (b. 1941) and Refik Durbaş (b. 1944), who did not belong to the same group, but who began to publish in the 1960s, continue to produce interesting works of great subtlety and sincerity.

Of the generation of poets who are now in their sixties, Attila İlhan (b. 1925) produced his best work in the 1950s and 1960s, combining the elements of classical and folk poetry. His exotic imagery and romantic approach to life made him very popular among the younger generations. His growing narcissism and sentimentalism in his recent poetry are signs of his loss of touch with his public. Can Yücel (b. 1926), on the other hand, goes on being the subtle ironist as well as the sensitive lyricist at the same time. His fearless tackling of both political and sexual matters in a good natured manner, his mastery of Ottoman and folk expressions, and his love of pun, make him one of the most sought-after poets in public readings.

There are other poets such as İlhan Berk, Necati Cumalı, Cahit Külebi and Hasan Hüseyin who enriched Turkish poetry in one way or another. But the four masters who dominated the last thirty years are Oktay Rifat, Melih Cevdet Anday, Fazıl Hüsnü Dağlarca, and Behçet Necatigil. The first three of these poets were mentioned by Dr. Geoffrey Lewis (see pp. 103–5). But they went on writing poetry and both Rifat and Anday in their mature years achieved an extraordinarily subtle poise, while Dağlarca became a more socially and politically committed poet. Necatigil had always been a poet of the 'heartbreak house'. In his later years he came out of his house and shared the plight of the anonymous urban multitudes caught in the wheels of perpetual struggle (Menemencioğlu 1978: 54).

All these poets mentioned here tried to create a personal style. There were among them those who expressed conflicting viewpoints. But one common characteristic shared by all was the spoken Turkish which provided them with a wealth of expressions and nuances. There is also a common theme shared by almost all these poets and that is the problem of underdevelopment. Oktay Rifat defines it in poetic terms:

To fall behind, in science, in art, leafless
Unflowering in the spring; an aching star
Imprinted on the forehead.
To fall behind, doomed to the wooden plough
When you could cut through steel like paper
Vanquished by time.
To fall behind; sand in the caves of dogma
Hand to your flanks and starved, against the torrent
Against the others.
To fall behind; fear men as one fears jackals
Where one could live in brotherhood, to grasp
At snakes instead.
To fall behind; ignorant and louse-ridden
Taut as a bow within a sombre gorge;
To break loose with that impetus!

To break loose with that impetus from the vicious circle of underdevelopment was also the preoccupation of the Turkish novelists of the 1950s and 1960s. Some of these novelists and short story writers were graduates of the 'village institutes' founded by the Republican People's Party in the 1940s. When these writers joined the social realist movement in the 1950s, an extremely popular *genre* called the 'village novel' emerged as the mainstream of modern Turkish fiction. The novels of Fakir Baykurt and Talip Apaydın, and Mahmut Makal's documentary collection of notes and letters, *Bizim Köy (A Village in Anatolia)*, received an enthusiastic response from the reading public. But Yaşar Kemal, Orhan Kemal and Kamal Tahir, who also wrote about the poverty and hardships of village life, transcended the limitations of the 'village novel' by treating these problems in a more universal context.

Yaşar Kemal writes about Çukurova, the vast plain surrounded by the Taurus mountains in the province of Adana. Within this natural environment he creates a fictional world where myth and reality merge and convey the spirit of the Anatolian people. Yaşar Kemal is not content to document the difficulties of the rural poor, but takes every opportunity to give a complete picture of this world in as many details as his unique *genre* of narrative allows. So we become familiar not only with the geographic setting and the historical background, but also with the

178 *Modern literature in the Near and Middle East*

traditions, beliefs, psychology, crafts, working conditions and philosophies of these people.

Kemal Tahir presented the Anatolian peasant from a completely different point of view. In his novels depicting the peasants and prisoners of central Anatolia, there was nothing to glorify or idealize. His cynical account of the sexual perversion and the bureaucratic corruption among the peasants and the government officials was considered to be a more realistic rendering of social life in Turkey during the 1940s. Kemal Tahir was even more idiosyncratic in his approach to the process of Westernization in general and in his evaluation of traditional institutions in particular. By rejecting a mainstream or orthodox Marxist analysis of Turkish society, he provoked an interesting discussion among the social scientists and the literary critics on the Asiatic mode of production as a determining factor for an understanding of Turkish sensibility. Most of his urban novels are marred by his nagging preoccupation with sociological and historical analysis. *Esir Şehrin İnsanlar, Esir Şehrin Mahpusu* and *Yorgun Savaşçı* are, however, successful dramatizations of events that anticipated the liberation of an occupied country.

The conflict of oriental and occidental values was also at the core of the novels of Ahmet Hamdi Tanpınar, who approached the problem from a more aesthetic point of view. As a matter of fact, his masterpiece, *Huzur*, is a Proustian reconstruction of Istanbul, both as one of the protagonists and also as an artistic background against which the characters attempt to achieve a synthesis of East and West. Oğuz Atay's *Tutunamayanlar* (1970) was still another example of the same trend written in a more satirical vein. Atay was trying to write a *bildungsroman* that depicted the sentimental education of a generation of Turkish intellectuals, as well as their tragi-comic adventures in the pursuit of solving social and economic problems. Atay's posthumous reputation as a cult figure among the young generations can be explained by his fearless confrontation with important themes and his formal experimentalism.

One of the remarkable developments in the Turkish literature of the last thirty years was the emergence of a group of women writers such as Nezihe Meriç, Leyla Erbil, Sevim Burak, Adalet Ağaoğlu, Sevgi Soysal, Füruzan, Tomris Uyar, Aysel Özakın, Pınar Kür, Nazlı Eray, Nursel Duruel and Latife Tekin. What makes them important and interesting as creative artists has nothing to do with the trendy entrenchment of feminist ideology which one encounters in so many Western countries. They are important and interesting because each has created a personal style that can effectively express an individual sensibility.

In drama, we also observe a parallel development. In the 1950s, the village plays dealing with rural problems became extremely common.

Cahit Atay, Necati Cumalı and Hidayet Sayın dominated the scene. The two playwrights that emerged in the 1960s, Güngör Dilmen and Turan Oflazoğlu, took as their models the Greek tragic poets and Shakespeare respectively. But the really original contributions to the dramatic literature of the period were Sermet Çağan's *Ayak Bacak Fabrikası* (1965), Sevim Burak's *Sahibinin Sesi* (1970) and Oğuz Atay's *Oyunlarla Yaşayanlar* (1975). All three of these playwrights wrote their plays in a period of Brechtian and absurdist influences. Yet their works show how Turkish themes and traditional forms could transcend such influences by assimilating some of the innovating techniques of these modern movements.

The last thirty years of Turkish literature reflect a society of dramatic change. The polarization of the past and the present, the East and the West, the right and the left, was the inevitable result of this change. But the ideological conflict can be detected not so much between the conservative and progressive writers, as between the writers of the extreme left and the representatives of a social democratic tendency.

13 The Mashriq

Edwar al-Kharrat

A fair assessment of the period since 1950 will have to take stock, however briefly, of the impact left by the 1940s, as no hard and fast boundaries exist between successive decades. The 1940s were a curious and insidiously seminal decade in Arabic literature; they carried a portent of things to come, yet apparently came to an end without a trace. It is then that we can detect, for the first time, the precursory elements of both the socialist–realist trend that was briefly to dominate the Arab literary scene during the 1950s, and the modernist trend that would constitute a major shift of the literary sensibility as well as a major challenge to established literary norms and conventions. Factors such as the social unrest, the dislocation of class relations ensuing upon the Second World War, the growing demands of a nationalist movement that was intermittently violent and never quite abated against European imperialism, the appalling conditions under which the poor, illiterate masses laboured, all undoubtedly contributed to the emergence of both these trends in Arab literature; but some inherent necessity within the cultural enterprise itself, and some inner urge for growth must also have played their part.

For some time before the 1940s in Egypt, Salama Musa, a controversial figure, essayist, translator, journalist and editor, an atheist Copt and a rebellious eccentric, had been crying in a cultural wilderness for modernism in many various fields: he wished to strip Arabic diction of its age-old excrescences of ornate rhetoric and embellishments, and went as far as advocating the use of the colloquial 'language' as he actually called it. In a similar vein, Taha Husayn, Lewis 'Awad, Husayn Fawzi and others were calling for a frankly 'Mediterranean' Western-oriented culture for Egypt, having taken for granted its Arab heritage in the first place. In the late 1930s and early 1940s such 'little' magazines as *al-Majalla al-Jadida* edited by Salama Musa and *al-Tatawwur* edited by Anwar Kamil, Ramsis Yunan and others, laid the seeds of modernity and *avant-garde* literature, a role that continued to be valiantly played by similar 'little' magazines

The Mashriq 181

such as *al-Bashir* edited by Badr al-Dib and others, *Fusul* edited by Fathi Ghanim, and *Gallery 68* in whose editing the present author participated. In the 1970s such publications were practically the only outlet left for young writers of any genuine talent and vision.

By the mid-1940s a wave of emerging awareness and pressing needs on the national, social and cultural levels was sweeping over Egypt. In 1946 the patriotic movement was violently demanding the evacuation of the British occupation troops. Both Marxist and Muslim fundamentalist groups emerged powerfully on the political scene, and the first clearly attributable socialist–realist trends and experimental, *avant-garde* modernist trends made their appearance in Egyptian literature. Even Taha Husayn, who gave us his exquisite piece of autobiography in *al-Ayyam*, dabbled in fiction writing with near-revolutionary intent, in his *al-Mu'adhdhabun fi'l-Ard* (1949). A heavy-handed, sometimes sententious story-teller (his lasting contribution to Arab culture lies elsewhere), he was almost swept off his feet by that upsurge of social awareness and unrest. The book was originally banned and was a resounding call for social justice, however utopian and abstract it might have been. Comparable situations prevailed in the other Arab countries of the Mashriq, with the Levant struggling for the end of the French protectorate and Iraq seething against a semi-feudal regime subservient to the British.

It is quite remarkable how influential and widespread the 'socialist–realist' trend in Egyptian literature came to be in the 1950s. One plausible explanation may lie in the historical, troubled (and probably fatal) *entente* that was made between the main Marxist groups and the Nasserite regime, after the 1955 Bandung Conference and the 1956 Israeli–British–French invasion of Egypt. The regime certainly patronized this trend. 'Social realism' or 'critical realism' had made its appearance in Egyptian literature much earlier, for some of the early work of Mahmud Taymur and Mahmud Tahir Lashin can certainly come under this category. But it was only in the late 1940s and 1950s that the *genre* became self-conscious and some writers dubbed themselves 'realists' with the general implication that they were political progressives. 'Socialist–realism', or 'realism', *tout court*, in fiction, poetry and criticism, came to mean a genuine concern for the vast poverty-stricken inarticulate mass of the people: it was inspired directly by Marxist ideology, however vague or utopian it might have been. Young and gifted writers who were sensitive to the untold sufferings of their people tried their hand at this vein of the creative mine which was at that time largely unexplored. In the Levant and in Iraq there were similar ventures along lines which matured in the late 1950s and the 1960s, inspired and abetted by the ideologies of communist, Ba'athist and nationalist parties in these countries.

182 *Modern literature in the Near and Middle East*

However, what was curious was the inflated, inordinate importance and influence which this trend came to assume during the 1950s. In fact, the sway that this trend came to hold, particularly in the media, was in direct contrast to the neglect that the establishment right-wing writers felt or rather claimed, was allotted to them. Writers such as 'Abd al-Halim 'Abdalla, Amin Yusuf Ghurab, 'Abd al-Hamid Guda al-Sahhar, let alone Yusuf al-Siba'i, were competent and capable in their own small way. It is, however, interesting to trace in their writings the preoccupations, worries, frustrations and anxieties of the little men they portrayed. Mostly both the writers and their protagonists were of peasant stock, raised and educated in provincial towns. They were prototypes of the peasant lower-middle class, putting an absolute faith in the virtues – material and otherwise – of higher education, as most Egyptians used, until recently, to do. They continued to grapple with the vague vestiges of hot-house romanticism bred by the previous generation of writers, such as al-Manfaluti or Mahmud Kamil, and with the rigorous *petit bourgeois* morality and customs still jealously guarded by their own families. They aspired, vainly in most cases, to advance up the social ladder, and to gain the status their education had earned them at the cost of sacrifice and deprivation to themselves and their parents. They were rudely shocked and frustrated by the dire economic and social facts of a community in crisis. These or similar themes were treated with regard to the same class in the Capital, by the earlier Naguib Mahfuz. This group of writers muddled along with their fiction for some time, gaining a fairly wide reputation under Nasser, yet always publicly complaining that they were excluded by the 'leftists' who held, they claimed, the reins of the media. In actual fact they themselves constituted a predominant wing of the literary establishment; they were ensured fat sinecures in ministries and public service concerns, and were published as never before.

Yet works of talent and distinction were, in fact, written by young authors who called themselves 'realists' and who made their mark. In this context, *al-Ard* of 'Abd al-Rahman al-Sharqawi and *Arkhas Layali* of Yusuf Idris, come readily to mind, both published in 1954. In the same year three books that come under the heading of socialist–realism and whose significance now is mainly historical and documentary were published: *al-Hayy al-Latini*, a novel by the Lebanese Suhail Idris, *al-Masabih al-Zurq*, a novel by the Syrian Hanna Mina, and *Hasid al-Raha*, a book of short stories by the Iraqi Gha'ib Tu'ma Farman; all three writers came to be widely known either for their later fiction or for their contribution to the general field of culture. In 1953, the Iraqi Badr Shakir al-Sayyab wrote his famous 'Ode to the Rain' in Kuwait, and around this time the Egyptian Salah 'Abd al-Sabur wrote his 'new' poetry, published

The Mashriq 183

in 1957, in his collection *al-Nas fi Biladi*. In 1954, the Lebanese Yusuf al-Khal published his second book of poetry, a play in verse, *Herodia,* in New York; his first book of verse *al-Hurriya* had been published in Beirut a decade earlier, in 1944. In 1957, the Syrian Adunis ('Ali Ahmad Sa'id) published his *Qasa'id Ula*. In short, this was a remarkable moment of Arab literary history, full of promise and daring. The seemingly endless wide vistas of hope and national resolve were opened by the outbreak of the 1952 revolution, not only for Egypt but for the entire Arab 'homeland'. The profound and vast social changes that took place in Egypt and other Arab countries after 1954, a fateful year, need only be cursorily mentioned. In March 1954, the abortive resistance against the military rule which was put up by the variegated political forces of the time, from the extreme right to the extreme left, was defeated, and the bid for a western-type 'liberal' democracy was frustrated. The dramatic and fast-moving scenario of historic events that ensued left its imprint, inevitably, on the literary scene.

It seems plausible to claim, at this point, that a certain measure of correspondence existed between the turn of events in Egypt (and elsewhere in the Arab countries), towards the assertion of a national ego, based on broad claims of 'socialist', 'Arab' pretensions, and the growing swell of pompous works of literature that dubbed themselves 'socialist' and 'realist', yet which in fact were crudely rhetorical. In such works people – who should by rights be alive and therefore self-contradictory and many-faceted – were reduced to mere stereotypes of the positive forthright optimistic and activist mould. Characters in these fictional works, portrayed as 'popular' or working-class, were mostly given curious nomenclatures, supposedly because the poor had to have odd-sounding names as a hallmark of proletarian honour. In fact most of these characters were effigies, stunted and made to design. In their own 'glorious' way, they were simply string-drawn, mere agents or tools of the 'dialectical process of history'. Examples of these writings can be found in the work of Muhammad Sidqi, with his limited talent and poor literary equipment, who, unfairly to him, was called sometimes the 'Gorky of Egypt', simply because of his class origin; or in the work of Mahmud al-Sa'adani, a light-weight lampoonist and satirist who subsequently published his first collection of short stories, *al-Sam'a al-Sawda'*: had it not been for the heavy-handed and fatuously optimistic allusions to glorious perspectives (as ordained by crude samples of this *genre*), his short stories could have been pieces of scathing black humour!

The swelling wave of socialist–realist writing in the 1950s was accompanied and abetted by a virtual crusade of literary criticism, codification and consecration (with its attendant excommunication!), all produced in a

184 *Modern literature in the Near and Middle East*

forthright, orthodox outdated Marxist tradition which derived from the European left of the 1930s. The crusade was led by Mahmud Amin al-'Alim, ex-phenomenologist and ex-existentialist, and 'Abd al-'Azim Anis, a mathematician and a physicist. Both of them were young Marxist lecturers who became publicists, both were of considerable intellectual integrity, and had a *penchant* for theoretical speculation. Historically speaking, the book which they wrote jointly, *Fi Mustaqbal al-Thaqafa al-Misriyya* enjoyed great popularity for a decade or so and is still remembered with nostalgic appreciation. In their wake emerged a school of either diligent or brilliant young critics, such as Amir Iskandar, Sabri Hafez, Sami Khashaba, Ibrahim Fathi, 'Abd al-Rahman Abu 'Uf and Sayyid al-Bahrawi. They followed their own different ways and developed their own different lines, but still shared one common legacy, that of the social realism of the 1950s.

Very early in the 1920s, dialogue in the colloquial was introduced in fiction and was a welcome device to most fiction writers. Quite a few writers did not, and still do not, have recourse to this device; purists adamantly refused to recognize it. Taha Husayn always rejected as invalid any fictional work 'adulterated' by the colloquial, although he had to make an exception of the play written and acted on stage in the dialect. As far as I know Naguib Mahfuz has never allowed his characters to speak in their own daily tongue, though he was such an accomplished craftsman you would hardly notice the fact. During the 1950s, and very much connected with the socialist–realist school, appeared a curious collection of short stories, *Messa'el Kheir ya Ged'an* (1956) by Badr Nash'at, written entirely in the colloquial, with both the narrator and the characters speaking in vernacular Egyptian Arabic. It was followed in 1962 by a second and last collection *Holm Leilat Ta'ab*. The venture did not make any further headway. A few works were published in the vernacular both earlier and later: apart from Bairam al-Tunisi's notorious *El-Sayyed we Merato fi Bareez*, there was a *novella* and a few short stories *Antaret elli Kafar* and *Hazayan* respectively in the 1940s and the 1960s. Lewis 'Awad once vowed publicly never to write except in that 'language' but he did not keep his vow. He published, nevertheless, *Mozzakerat Taleb Ba'asa* (1965) allegedly written in the late 1930s and early 1940s, entirely in the colloquial. Some other valiant attempts, such as the two novels *Rehla fi'l-Nil* (1965) and *Beit Sirri* (1982) by 'Uthman Sabri, all went virtually unheeded. These ventures, nevertheless, are diametrically opposed to what happened at the hands of Sa'id 'Aql or Yusuf al-Khal who both advocated and wrote poetry in the Lebanese colloquial, work that was inspired by a sense of acute patriotism as opposed to the ideology of Pan-Arabism prevalent in the 1950s. Again the poetry of Muzzaffar al-Nawwab, an *émigré* Iraqi communist poet, is written in an entirely different vein, more akin to the socialist–realism of the 1950s, but tinged with a sense of loss and frustrated hopes. On the other hand, the poetry written in the colloquial by the Egyptian Salah Jahine, published in the early 1950s, was inspired by the Nasserite venture all along and stems directly from the aspirations and the stirrings of the national soul evoked by Nasser. When the defeat of 1967 shattered these aspirations Salah Jahine's poetry verged on the near-philosophical searchings of a broken heart.

It may be relevant, in the context of the socialist–realism of the 1950s, to go deeper into its *rapport* with the language issue. Most of the works written in this vein leaned heavily on the vernacular, which was taken as a sacrosanct hallmark of the working people, not only in rendering dialogue, but also in the fabric of narration. But these writers look with a condescending eye at 'language' as the artist's tool; what mattered to them, naively, was not the 'form' but absolute priority was given to the 'content'. This meant, in most cases, that we had disjointed and rather feeble-muscled works, deadened and not revived by the unfortunate cross-breeding of dictions. Conversely, some exponents of socialist–realism, especially in poetry, had nothing to offer but the declamatory, bombastic, sonorous *fusha* of slogans, devoid of genuine spirit and directly related to the current ideological jargon of the day. Obviously, none of this applies to the sensitive ear and the accomplished talent of 'Abd al-Rahman al-Sharqawi, well versed in, and delicately tuned to, the colloquial of the Delta peasantry; or again to the masterly craftsmanship of Yahya Haqqi, who can insinuate the occasional incomparable vernacular word or turn of phrase that has no counterpart in the *fusha*, in such a well-balanced, closely knit manner that no jolt is perceptible. On the contrary he creates a precise music, seemingly and cunningly spontaneous.

The 1960s were years of specific and distinctive characteristics: this was the decade of great expectations and tragic failures, of national achievements and frustrations, of glories and sufferings both unprece-dented in the recent history of the area. The profound transformations of social relations, the widespread nationalizations, the decline of the European Empires, the rise of Pan-Arabism, as well as the charismatic figure of 'Abd al-Nasser himself, all lent a prestigious status to Egypt and the Arab 'Homeland'. Yet because of all this, the power wielded by the regime in Egypt came to be almost unchallenged and absolute, and a total imposed absence of legal opposition meant the smothering of democracy. The course of events finally led to the *débâcle* of the 1967 defeat and the occupation by Israel of sizeable portions of the same Arab 'Homeland' which had been so arrogantly confident of superiority, and which was shocked into a sense of bitter recrimination and tearing apart of the

186 Modern literature in the Near and Middle East

national ego. Indeed an almost masochistic bout of self-doubt and self-questioning was indulged in. The decade ended with the agonies of Black September and the near suicidal death of 'Abd al-Nasser. Against this background, however sketchily indicated above, the modern modes in Arabic literature came into their own.

All throughout this tumultuous decade, a slow but sure affirmation of the modern sensibility in Arabic literature was felt; the shocks and fluctuations only helped to lend it a richness and a density it had never gained before. Admittedly, as early as the late 1940s, the first precursors of this modern mode made their appearance either in print, in such small magazines as *al-Bashir*, or in manuscripts circulated among a select group of connoisseurs. During that period the present writer wrote the bulk of his book of short stories *Hitan 'Aliya* which was not published until as late as 1959, when it immediately, as it were, made literary history but was relegated to critical silence for almost a decade. The poetry of Badr al-Dib written during the same period was never printed, although it was constantly circulated. By the late 1960s a group of young writers who solicited and immediately got all the help I could give, published the magazine *Gallery 68* of which only eight issues appeared over two years, but which proved to be the first genuine platform of the modern sensibility in Egypt; the venture was briefly duplicated in Iraq and Morocco. The 'generation of the 1960s', as it came to be known, proved itself in spite of an almost complete silence on the part of the literary establishment.

With the advent of the 1970s, the Sadat decade, Egypt and other Arab countries knew an almost diametrical reversal of fortunes. A sharp dual polarization set in, with a dubiously partial, yet definite, victory of the Egyptian army over Israel in 1973, the first of its kind. What immediately ensued can be referred to only briefly: the Camp David talks and the 'Peace' Treaty with Israel; the qualified recuperation of Sinai; the severance of Egypt's diplomatic relations with almost all the other Arab countries; the open-door policy of Sadat; the growing ascendancy of consumerist 'values' and the attendant recession of 'socialist' ideologies and practices alike; the 'brain drain' and the intellectuals' emigration; the occasional outbreaks of communal violence and the re-affirmation of Islamic fundamentalism; the rampant monetary inflation, and the decline of both moral and material resources. This period saw the first decade of the protracted Lebanese fratricidal civil war, the second exodus of the Palestinians after the Israeli invasion of Lebanon, the continued occupation by Israel of what remained of the old Palestine, the supremacy of the oil countries, the floundering discrepancy of the Arab States' policies, the national rifts and ethnic conflicts in Morocco, Iraq and Sudan, and the almost total eclipse of Pan-Arabist ideology. With this rapid and tumultuous course of events, the very precept of reality came to be questioned in Arabic literature.

The old established mode was frankly mimetic. It took for granted, in whatever philosophical order it was conceived, that it was possible and even desirable to portray, or reflect, that is to represent, *the* reality in literature. A work of art, it claimed, derived validity, indeed, its very *raison d'être* from that established reality, even on the assumption that it set out to help to change it. Therefore, an essential reciprocal *rapport* was pre-assumed, between established literature and established reality, to such an extent that it has come to be almost a *cliché* of the Arab literary mind, a norm of literary production and criticism. With the crude shattering of the established national and social reality, it was only to be expected that modernist trends in literature would supplant the now older, almost anachronistic mode of realism. It is the contention of the present writer that modernity has, in fact, a definite affinity with a whole legacy of Arab culture. My claim is that the Arab literary mind was nurtured on the epic, the frankly phantasmagorial, the communal and the non-realist, ranging from ancient self-renovating folklore, to the tales of one thousand and one nights; from the august challenge of mere mundane reality, in temples, churches and mosques that deliberately broke the human-scale perspective rules, to the abstract, non-figurative calligraphic and ornamental designs – infinite by their very nature, and only in decadence merely ornate; from the old *maqama*, as purist, formalist and abstract a work of art as any, to the mystical incantations of al-Niffari, Ibn 'Arabi and others, near-inarticulate but immensely communicative. The modernist Arab fiction-writer or poet, therefore, draws on a rich heritage of his own, while dubiously reaping the benefits of the modernist achievements of the West.

If modernist creative writing in Arabic literature is in continuity with an old valid legacy, it is at the same time certainly a break-away from the conformism of the realist mode, a constant questioning with no pretence to ready answers, a leap in the dark by neither a complacent nor a complaisant literary enterprise. Contrary to the old mode, the techniques of the modern sensibility in Arabic literature vary from the breaking of the pre-ordained order of narration to the dismantling of the classical plot; from the plunge into the interiority of the character to the interpolation of self-contradictory terms in the time sequence; from the assault on the hallowed structures of language to the widening of the scope of 'reality' so as to incorporate or re-incorporate dreams, legends and implicit poetry; from the questioning of the established social form to the demolition of the consecrated language contexts; from the penetration into the limbo of the sub-conscious to the use of the ego as a formula, not of sentimental soliloquy nor of an assumed objective entity, but of self-doubt and a

188 *Modern literature in the Near and Middle East*

passionate quest for inter-subjective communciation. These are techniques that are not, simply, a formal overthrow of the old regime of literary power, but are intrinsically linked, indeed fused, with a vision and a mode of perception.

In poetry, it was during the early 1950s that the school of 'New Poetry' emerged, with such forerunners as Badr Shakir al-Sayyab, Nazik al-Mala'ika, and later 'Abd al-Wahhab al-Bayyati, all from Iraq, and in Egypt Salah 'Abd al-Sabur. Earlier, in 1947, Lewis 'Awad published his new experimental *Plutoland and other Poems* in Cairo; these were rebellious poems written between 1938 and 1940 in Cambridge, England. The same stresses of the late 1940s and early 1950s and the same urge for social and cultural change that underlay the birth of socialist–realism in fiction, were plausibly behind the emergence of this school. Though the traditional conventions of Arab verse, with its established equi-balanced metrical values and its strict monorhyme, were challenged as early as the 1930s, yet the progressive course of rejecting this tradition continued through the 1950s. It reached its extreme in the poetry of later modernists such as the distinguished Syrian *émigré* Adunis who is now the father-figure of modernism in Arabic poetry, as well as in the works of the Lebanese Yusuf al-Khal, Unsi al-Haj and Khalil Hawi, the Syrian Muhammad al-Maghut, the Iraqis 'Abd al-Wahhab al-Bayyati and Sa'di Yusuf, and the Bahraini Qasim Haddad, to cite only a few well-known names. By the turn of the 1960s the school of 'New Poetry', timorously innovative as compared to later modernity, had considerable influence on younger poets such as Amal Dunqal in Egypt, and a host of other poets all over the Arab countries. It was only in the 1970s that the characteristically modernist poem emerged, finally shedding all semblance of adhering, in whatever flimsy way, to the sacrosanct metres of traditional Arab verse, frankly espousing daring innovations both in form and content. The twilight of traditional sensibility set in, and a new stage in Arabic poetry definitely dawned, inspired by the work of Adunis and the school of the magazine *Sh'ir* whose first issue was published in Beirut in 1957. A host of poets everywhere in the Arab countries began to write of a fragmented shattered state of reality, inner and outer, sublime and trite alike. Gone were the days of Higazi, Bayyati and other naively optimistic missionaries of a bright future, the self-appointed advocates of triumphant nationalism and glowing aspirations who proved to have built on both literary and political quick-sand. Even poets who understandably and quite legitimately started as outspokenly committed militants, such as the Palestinians Mahmud Darwish and Samih al-Qasim, have come to write poetry with a markedly modernist tinge. Darwish reverts in places to prose-poetry, but remains obviously and deeply committed to the cause of his people.

With the advent of a modernist mode, the mythical in poetry was intertwined with the daily. Hallowed legends were stripped of their symbolic halo and reduced to the level of mere documentation. Modernist poets were not after depicting reality but sought to compose their own poetic reality. They claimed that no mechanical *rapport* between reality and poetry was possible, that a positive, optimistic tone was not always the criterion for a good poem. Correspondingly, they sought to invent their own metrical non-standardized and unconventional rhythms, while prose found its place in their poems, either as a component among others or solely as prose-poetry. The diction was expectedly as novel as the subject-matter, and the colloquial was extensively used. A surprising syntax could be derived freely from various disciplines, while drama, narrative, documentary devices and factual down-to-earth language could be readily adopted. Surrealistic and phantasmagorial interplay was often resorted to. The modernist poem was no more a communication of choice but an invitation to questioning. It usually raised a problem and no longer advocated a cause. Certainly it was not a poem of emotional identification between reader and poet but a poem of estrangement and crisis. Muhammad 'Afifi Matar in Egypt was a pioneer along this road, while a host of younger poets gathered around the small magazine *Ida'a 77* and the group *Aswat* are still pursuing this hazardous quest. A legion of young poets in all Arab countries keep them company. Poetry written in the colloquial did not lag far behind: after 'Abd al Rahman al-Abnudi and Sayyid Higab and many others in Egypt there came the 'generation of the 1970s' with poets like Magid Yusuf who deals subtly with themes and images of considerable sophistication for a dialect that is only beginning to explore its own possibilities. But although colloquial Egyptian Arabic can be understood and partially appreciated in other Arab countries, the same does not yet apply to the dialects of these other countries at the moment.

Modern sensibility in Arabic literature is obviously not a rigorously monolithic uni-dimensional 'school' of thought or of creative enterprise. We can discern certain subsidiary polarizations within this overall modernist context. It is possible to detect in fiction-writing, broad currents that centre around at least four poles, under the umbrella of what we call modern sensibility. Obviously these are not water-tight compartments hermetically sealed off, but they intermingle and overlap with each other. Yet the main characteristics of each current are identifiable as follows:

(i) The internal, organic, current of inner-vision is, by definition, self-explanatory. Here it is not only the inner eye that is involved but it is the entire inner life that is evoked, both at the sensual or even the visceral level, or in the ephemeral dream-like fields of vision and perception. Man,

190 *Modern literature in the Near and Middle East*

and indeed his *milieu*, is conceived as a fluctuating pulse, an ever-moving mass of sensations and notions, a plastic amalgam organized only through the device of art. Works of this trend probe, sometimes painstakingly and sometimes in spontaneous spurts, some primal hidden reality of man. Obviously, therefore, it is temporal as well as transcendental; normal time ceases to count, and a fleeting moment or 'lasting forever' would hardly be differentiated, as the time category simply does not apply. Scanty dialogue or a thin plot, amongst other devices, help to remove barriers between dream and wakefulness, ambiguity and sharp-edged lucidity, inner and outer, reality and illusion. The concrete and tangible are liquefied, a viscous consistency sets in, sometimes dense and luscious, at other times smooth and transparent. Surrealistic imagery and diction seem to have a natural place here. Obviously all that entails a plunge away from 'reality' towards another 'reality', the better to come to grips with both. The diction here has to be, necessarily, poetic, sensitive, tenuous or dense as the case may be, packed with energy and explosive potential. The syntax has to be fragmented, or else endlessly protracted. Works within this current seem to retreat from social problems and give in to psychological or emotional stress, but they are certainly involved in the very same issues they seem to avoid, and are inordinately preoccupied with questions of 'truth', 'being' and so forth. The Syrian *émigré* novelist Haidar Haidar falls readily under this rubric, as well as the Egyptian writers and novelists Muhammad Hafez Ragab, Muhammad Mabruk and Mahmud 'Awad 'Abd al-'Aal. The present writer, since the late 1940s and up to the present time, has made what contribution he could to this vein.

(ii) The second trend is, conversely, the external-oriented, things-in-themselves mode of writing. Its preoccupation with the minute, neutral depiction of outer reality takes it away, paradoxically, from 'reality' towards the mere semblance of it. The alienation, or the estrangement of man, here seems to reach its ultimate end. Objects, characters and scenes are conjured up – or more appropriately pin-pointed as in photographic stills – in a cold light, with an eye completely void of interest, let alone passion. The emphatic stress is never there, but rather the tone is nonchalant though never carefree. The diction is so bare, so stripped of emotive connotations, that it has a barren colourless quality. This is an austere – almost monastic – endeavour. There is, here, a basic rejection of reality, yet I would claim that here we only have a simulated rejection, as it stems indeed from an inverted, frustrated, passionate, completely repressed love for life. In fact, it is a denunciation of the arbitrary waste of beauty and compassion, inflicted ruthlessly on people and on communities by the powers that be, a denunciation that almost comes to be a renunciation, but in fact never is. On the contrary, it rests on the assumption that life, in all its vehemence and gusto, though inscrutable, is always extremely lovable. What we can grasp is only its façade. The diction, therefore, is compact and polished, by design or by inspiration alike: little, brittle pellets or words that fall in with a monotonous click. To all intents and purposes they are sollipsistic, contained in themselves, rounded off, having almost no reference except to themselves. They are things, inanimate, that stand in a state of stark denudation. Apparently light-weight, stories and *novellas* (pertinently never full-length novels) written in this vein are imbued with almost incurable pessimism. They concede implicitly the *credo* that communication is unattainable. Yet the underlying quest here is again for a world freed from alienation and repression, where love (whatever that be) and communication, or simple sympathy, are possible. In the 1960s, the then young Ibrahim Aslan in *Buhairat al-Masa'*, and Baha' Tahir in *al-Khutuba* were the pioneers of this style. In later works the trend seems to have come to a dead-end, significantly, since a number of social and cultural changes have taken place. Yet Mahmud al-Wardani, a writer of a later decade, has embarked on a similar type of fiction in works that deal with the aftermath of the October war. Earlier work by 'Abdu Gubair would also fall under this rubric. Some of the work done by the Lebanese writer and critic Ilyas Khuri could be classified within this current, though his experimental and versatile moods make him difficult to categorize.

(iii) The most complex trend, richest in promise and achievement, is what may be called, for want of better terms, the contemporary–mythical current, which resorts to legend, fantasy, folk-tale and every-day themes, scenes and characters, whether in a contemporary or in a historical setting. This and the two currents previously indicated are clearly non-representational, non-figurative work. They do not assume that 'reality', a finished product, is there to portray or to try to change. They are 'modern' by virtue of trying to create (or re-create as the case may be) their own parallel reality, by setting out to grasp the various modes of reality. Some works done in this third trend of fiction-writing have no difficulty in communicating with a large audience, as is often the case with the two previous trends. The pattern is easily grasped and a large measure of entertainment is present. Therefore it is an enterprise fraught with artistic danger. It may be facile and can easily lead nowhere. The blending of myth and contemporary theme, if not done in lucid and at least competent terms, can create a permanent and irremediable fissure in both structure and vision. Almost the whole of the later work of Yahya al-Tahir 'Abdulla, written shortly before his untimely death, is a consummate achievement in this vein. Some of Gamal al-Ghitani's earlier work, fairly gifted and evocative, can fall under this heading. Recently he has turned to

192 *Modern literature in the Near and Middle East*

the blending of a mystical diction, reminiscent of and sometimes directly lifted from Ibn 'Arabi, with a passionate or documentary-like treatment of actual, autobiographical or political events A host of writers have done work in this general category, with varying success and different idiosyncratic approaches: Muhammad Mustagab, Nabil Na'um Gorgi, Sa'id al-Kafrawi, Muhsin Yunis, Yusif Abu Rayya, 'Abdu Gubair, the inimitable 'Abd al-Hakim Qasim, the young Khayri 'Abd al-Gawad and Ibrahim Fahmi. The present writer in his novels *Ramah and the Dragon* and *The Other Time* has delved deeply into this general style. The Iraqi Muhammad Khudair has dabbled in this trend and the Sudanese al-Tayyib Salih, in his exquisite two volume *Bandar Shah,* is a master-craftsman in the field. It is always futile to classify creative writings but some of the work of the two *émigré* Syrians Haidar Haidar and Zakariya Tamir may be fitted into this category. All throughout these years, established writers continued to work in their old established fashions as a matter of course, with Naguib Mahfuz as their dean hacking away at his annual novels which declined appreciably from year to year. Hanna Mina in Syria, Fu'ad al-Takarli and 'Abd al-Majid al-Rabi'i in Iraq, 'Abd al-Rahman Munif, an *émigré* Saudi writer now living in Paris, Emile Habibi and Sahar Khalifa, both Palestinians living in Israel, and many others all published to feed the steady stream of Arab fiction, with different measures of talent and competence.

(iv) What I would reluctantly term the 'neo-realist' current may be seen as bordering on modern sensibility yet not quite embracing all its tenets. What differentiates them from the older realists is a questioning of social relationships that goes deeper than has been done ever before, to the point of posing a challenge to the established order of values. At the level of form, though the diction, devices and terms of reference may appear to have much in common with those of the old realists, yet there is here a rigour, a precision, and a sharp edge that make them qualitatively different. The cynical, sophisticated bitterness of Sun'alla Ibrahim, the techniques of direct political verbiage and political involvement of Yusif al-Qa'id, the delicate and cunning craftsmanship of Gamil 'Atiyya Ibrahim, the terse, luminous, subtle and stark short fiction of Muhammad al-Makhzangi, and the work of many others, show promise and daring, and demonstrate that reality is, in fact, inexhaustible.

14 The Maghrib

Ahmed al-Madini

IDEOLOGY AND MODERNITY IN MAGHRIBI LITERATURE

If the question of method is an obvious aspect of any form of rigorous research which seeks to obtain valid conclusions, it takes on a particular importance in the context of the subject of this chapter, i.e. 'Ideology and Polarization in the Modern Arabic Literature of the Maghrib Countries': this is because of the very nature of the subject and of the particular problems that it raises at a preliminary stage, before we can embark on it properly. Thus we need to know whether it is in fact possible to begin our study from a particular date: in other words, is the year 1950 really a reliable point of departure from which one can study modern North African literature and on which one can erect the bases of its ideological context? A second question comes immediately to mind: to what extent is it possible to treat together the literature of three countries (Algeria, Morocco and Tunisia) because they belong to the same geographical region, or because of the existence of factors which we must study to see if they have contributed towards the creation of a common vision, or a vision which might become common on the basis of a group of themes or values?

These questions are closely linked to the problem of how to deal with the subject as a whole, in the sense that it is not evident *a priori* whether we are to be concerned with literary history or whether our analysis will be guided by literary theory: in the former case, historical periods become important and the various elements proper to this domain can be treated in the classical academic manner, an approach which is not without interest in the context of Maghribi literature. In the latter case our task would be doubly complex, because on the one hand, literary theory has been elaborated on the basis of Western texts, albeit giving rise to numerous generalizations which could be applied to the literatures of different peoples; on the other hand there does not yet exist a specific theory of literature, a theory of aesthetics or of reception, or any other type of similar approach, based essentially on Arabic

194 *Modern literature in the Near and Middle East*

creative texts. In either case, to deal with the subject according to a given concept of the theory of literature would lead to results very different from those which we would obtain if the subject were examined in the light of literary history as practised by Gustave Lanson (1858–1934). In the same context, the choice of method is closely related to the essence of our subject: its title in fact leads us directly to the field of the sociology of literature, a field of literary study well known for its theories and approaches (it has been expressed through four trends in French literary criticism, represented by Lucien Goldmann, Pierre Zima, Jacques Dubois and Robert Escarpit. To these one might add a fifth trend concerned with the problem of 'reception' as worked out by Jacques Leenhardt and Pierre Josza). There is no doubt, at least in our opinion, of the interest which this approach to literature holds, in spite of the extent to which it has been devalued in recent years in works of structuralism and semiotics.

In our opinion, the basic problem in the application of a sociological approach to the study of Arabic creative texts lies in the fact that the modern literary *genres* in this context have not yet been clearly categorized or verified. When we examine Western literature in the light of the sociological approach, we know that we are dealing with coherent, generic spheres, which are subject to precise schemes and classifications based on epistemological and aesthetic typologies which are clearly defined in the teaching of Western literary criticism. This is not at all the case in Arabic criticism where the same approach runs the risk of reducing the literary text to the level of a simple element amongst the various mechanisms and means of social expression: this would be to underestimate the specific nature of the elaboration of modern Arabic *genres* and their development in relation to the ideology (or ideologies) which has created polarization, which has conditioned and modelled creative literature, which has classified its themes and marked its artistic rhythm.

We can now establish the initial lines of our study, and we find ourselves immediately face to face with the problem of Maghribi literature written in French, and considered by some as an integral part of the creative work of this region, and therefore something which ought to be included in the overall study of its literature. In our own case, we have no doubt that this literature written in French (and particularly that produced in Algeria) is a genuine expression of feelings and situations both individual and collective, and that it is an account of the decisive turning points in the lives and struggles of the peoples of the region. We are convinced that these peoples were, and still are, imbued with the nationalist spirits and the historical aspirations of their countries during the periods of colonial occupation and post-independence. Nevertheless we think that in spite of its fundamental significance, this recognition is not enough to convince us

The Maghrib 195

to include this material within the limits of our study. We hold the view that the literature of a people is written in their mother tongue; it is linked inextricably to their beliefs and their heritage, and is indicative of their belonging to a common social and cultural sphere. When it is expressed in a foreign language, it then depends on the foreign cultural space and on its basic values. When it demonstrates particularly fertile artistic features, it is merely enriching the language in which it is written, its aesthetics and its rhetoric. We do not have the space here to pursue this argument in greater depth, at the risk of seeming to adopt an arbitrary position. However, any such arbitrary tendency becomes less serious when one notes that Maghribi literature written in French is radically different in structure, theme and artistic context from the special preoccupations of the Arab literature of the Maghrib, which is an Arabic literature by definition and not simply a literature written in the Arabic language.

An indispensable point of departure for us is to specify some of the preoccupations of literature in the Maghrib countries – those which will allow us to establish a unified typology or which at least have common elements. If we also raise the theme of ideology in the context of this literature, then we have to consider the following points:

The idea of literature

This concerns the way in which literature and literary experience were perceived during the 1940s and 1950s in cultural environments possessed of a considerable literary heritage and linked organically to classical Arabic literature, which exercised a quasi-total domination over *genres,* themes and rhetoric. One needs to know precisely whether these environments had detached themselves from traditionalism and the imitation of the classical modes of literary expression, or whether they were still attracted by the traditional text and therefore by the systems of thought and ideologies which surround it and form part of it. Or given the fact that these environments found themselves in a new historical era which made its own demands, we need to know whether they tended towards new types of creativity and thought with a view to entering into the spirit of the age and rising to its challenges (essentially the challenge of Western thought).

Modernization

One can say with certainty that during the 1940s and 1950s, cultural and literary society in the Maghrib adhered progressively to the idea of establishing the bases of modernization, of which literary expression was

196 *Modern literature in the Near and Middle East*

one of the most notable. However, behind this desire for renewal there was no real intention to cut oneself off from the past, since the form of this renewal was not understood as having necessarily to express a new vision of life and reality. In other words, reformism rather than change was the order of the day, a reformism which tended to compromise between the old and the new, in spite of its reservations and doubts about the 'dangers' of renewal. Two phenomena thereby appear: on the one hand there is the presence of a traditional cultural *milieu* which allows these reformers to group themselves around it, for even if they opt for a new façade, that which lies behind remains the same; on the other hand there is the fact that it is this traditional *milieu* itself which undertakes the function of renewal.

The meaning of modernity in literature

In essence this is to borrow the artistic form of literary *genres* which are foreign to medieval Arabic literature, and to try thereby to produce a new type of writing, above all in prose, because poetry only begins to change from the 1960s onwards. We will not enumerate here the various characteristics of these transitions in prose style. Nevertheless we must point out the fact that the precursors of renewal already had the sense, however confused, that experimentation with a new literary form was part of the overall mission of an intelligentsia who aspired towards a process of change which was more vast and went beyond the limits imposed by their own time.

The first signs of modernity

This occurred in prose and not in poetry which modernity was not yet able to affect – even though the Arab poets of the Mashriq had already shaken its classical foundations and structure. But modernity did not appear in all prose, or rather in all its themes. The discourses of religion and patriotism retained until recently their traditional stamp because this form enabled them fully to carry out their functions. The writers themselves were engaged in the search for new forms of expression in order to perform the functions assigned to them by a society on the verge of a new historical phase which demanded the participation of literature. These writers preferred the short story as a vehicle for literary modernity and for the description of a society subject to colonial occupation. The same choice was made in all three of the Maghrib countries where this type of literature appeared at more or less the same time – generally towards the end of the 1930s – and showed similar characteristics. But it was only during the 1960s that it achieved higher levels of activity in each of these countries.

The ideology of modernity

Modern literature in the Maghrib was born in the climate of a general social and cultural reformist movement; it became adapted to it and conditioned by its logic and its discourse. The course of this literature from the beginning was surrounded by the ideologies which emerged at the beginning of this century and which were to see a significant expansion in scope. Reformist movements which promoted the new *Salafiyya* ideology (an offshoot of the *Salafiyya* movement in the Mashriq led by Muhammad 'Abduh and Jamal al-Din al-Afghani, but adapted to the specific Maghribi context) then set about the task of re-assessing the spiritual, ethical and social orientations of the Maghribi societies which were in open conflict with the foreign occupiers. These movements had taken upon themselves the task of defending the authenticity of belief, of preserving the links with the heritage, of consolidating the Arab–Muslim personality through safeguarding the Arabic language and defending the specific aspects of national identity in order to protect it from Westernization and alienation in the face of invasion by a foreign culture. They had also mobilized forces against foreign occupation and finally they were prepared to assume the destinies of the countries concerned at the dawn of independence. The struggle to spread and to establish these values was at the centre of the idea of modernity, in spite of the archaic nature of certain of the values in question. In fact modernity ought not to be understood in the light of the ideology (or ideologies) of Western culture. As far as the Maghrib countries are concerned, modernity must be seen in a strictly national context. This is why the famous debate of modern Arab thought known as 'The Question of Authenticity and Modernity' *(ishkaliyyat al-asala wa'l-mu'asara)* did not arise in the Maghrib in the same form as in the Mashriq: in the former it appeared in the 1940s and 1950s in terms of the 'Modernization of Authenticity and the Authenticity of Modernization'. Thus we can see how the Maghribi writer was able to borrow modern literary *genres* (in particular the short story and the novel), while at the same time preserving a content which often did not fit such *genres*. This is one of the problematical features of the literature of this region.

The polarization of modernity through ideology

The reader will have doubtless noticed that we have not bothered to explore the meaning of the term 'ideology' or indeed the various meanings that are assigned to it, for that would lead us into a theoretical and fastidious debate which will be of little or no help, in so far as it is clear that we mean by this term the totality of the values which surround

198 *Modern literature in the Near and Middle East*

thought and society within a certain period of time. We should add that we also mean by it the influence exerted by ideology and its various manifestations on the content of the literary experience, as well as the means by which it makes artistic form an extension of its field of activity and its discourse. There is no doubt that the link between any work of literature and its ideological context is an extremely fertile theme which is difficult for us to treat comprehensively within the limits of this study, for we must at the same time give a general descriptive account of Maghribi literature. Even so, at this stage of our presentation we can indicate three essential elements of this theme: the first is that modern experience in Maghribi literature has been subject, either partially or totally in terms of the contents of its works, to the ideology of the reformist movements in the 1940s and 1950s; then in the 1960s and 1970s (i.e. after independence) it was subject to the ideologies which sought to build the nation state, demanding structural changes at the social, political and economic levels, and denouncing the exploitation practised by the ruling classes. The course followed by literature which was 'ideologized' in this way shows clearly – and this is our second element – how literature assumed the responsibility of commitment and of consecrating itself to reality, in such a way that commitment to society, its problems and aspirations, became the guiding principle of literary activity which controlled its visions. This principle took on two fundamental dimensions, one of which was linked to the general status of literature, and the other to the norms for the evaluation of this literature – that is to say the criteria by which it could be accepted or rejected. The third element in this context concerns the general content of literary experience in the Maghrib (and this is the area in which the polarization of ideology was at its strongest), a literary experience which was tied to its overall vision, namely the vision of realism.

THE QUESTION OF LITERARY *GENRES* IN THE SPHERE OF IDEOLOGY

Whoever does research on Maghribi literature, and on modern Arabic literature in general, inevitably comes face to face with the complex problem of the constitution of this literature, unless he or she follows the simple path of the historical descriptive 'method'. Apart from the literary heritage itself, and the influences from the Mashriq and the West which both played an important role in encouraging writers in North Africa towards literary innovation, the fundamental aspect of innovation lay in the progressive adoption of previously unknown literary *genres*, notably the play, the short story, and the novel. It is well known that these three *genres* have their origin in Western literature; they were transposed into Arabic

The Maghrib 199

literature under the effect of different forms of acculturation which appeared in the Arab World since the end of the last century. The sociology of literary *genres* (developed notably by Erich Köhler) tells us that social and economic mutations which affected the psychology and the behaviour of the individual in Europe, were amongst the major factors behind the emergence of these *genres*. This emergence took place through the adaptation of classical prose to the romantic universe and the grouping together in the space of the novel, according to fixed narrative types, of disparate social, economic and psychological structures at a time when they were undergoing a phase of conflict and qualitative transformation. Later, the same pattern applies to the emergence of the short story, with the mutations in this case giving rise to contrasting and conflicting human situations, and to states of mind which were brief and intense and which only this literary *genre* could assimilate and articulate. On the other hand, we see that in the case of modern Maghribi literature – and to some extent in the literature of the Mashriq – the joint opposition of social and cultural structures (and their surrounding ideology) against occupation and foreign influence, was to a large extent at the origin of the *genres* mentioned above and of their particular vision. In these circumstances, the constitution of modern Maghribi literature, or rather its place in the context of the modern literary *genres,* is essentially subject to a previous point of reference, namely to an extra-textual dimension made up of a collection of values, themes and ideologies. The result of this situation is that the themes explored and the general process of ideological polarization only reveal their true value within the literary *genre* as a result of the artistic techniques through which they have been treated. As for the meaning that we can draw from this literature, we do not wish to consider it solely as a source of documentation. Of course it is a form of documentation, but it is so by virtue of its literary nature which must lay stress upon its literary quality. Therein lies one of the most important problems surrounding this literature, one which requires particular study, and which we must keep constantly in mind as we read it.

We now come to the second phase of our study where we will examine in turn the literature of each of the Maghrib countries, having considered the principal issues underlying the questions relative to ideology and polarization, taking for granted that there are other issues of considerable importance which we prefer to treat in the detailed case studies. As far as the case studies are concerned, we draw attention to the fact that these have been condensed to conform to the limits of this chapter. Nevertheless it is hoped to give as complete a picture as possible of the literatures of these countries. Therefore we shall restrict our treatment to the major movements and the most representative authors of the literatures in question, being well aware of the risks of such an approach. Two points must first be made:

200 *Modern literature in the Near and Middle East*

(i) There is a relative disproportion, which is at times considerable, between the preoccupations of these literatures, their visions and their artistic techniques. Thus, as we have already indicated, there are certain dangers in treating them all in the same context. Tunisian literature, for example, followed its own particular theoretical and abstract path. The comparative youth of modern Algerian literature implies a clear distance in artistic value compared with Moroccan and Tunisian literature. This emphasizes the arbitrary nature of considering them all together.

(ii) Our second point is concerned with the themes and the literary *genres* best able to demonstrate the significance of ideology and polarization in Maghribi literature. As we have already indicated, the prose *genres* of the short story and the novel provide the most appropriate solutions to this problem. It is preferable for us to base most of our material on these as they have appeared in considerable numbers in recent years and were the first to introduce modernity. Nevertheless we will not neglect entirely other types of literary expression to which we shall refer whenever they can help to clarify our case.

MODERN TUNISIAN LITERATURE

Most Tunisian scholars agree that the history of modern literature in their country falls into four periods: that prior to the struggle against French colonialism; the period of struggle for national emancipation; the post-independence period; and the period of the construction of the future. At first sight this classification according to historical periods is based upon the themes and the content of the literature concerned. The approach of these scholars (we refer to those who contributed to the book *Mukhtarat min al-Adab al-Tunisi 'l-Mu'asir* [*Anthology of Modern Tunisian Literature*, 2 Vols., 1985, *al-Dar al-Tunisiyya li'l-Nashr*, under the direction of the Ministry of Culture]) is made clear by the fact that in their opinion almost all modern Tunisian literature revolves around one common denominator: mankind *(al-insan)*. This underlines the theoretical aspect of this literature referred to previously. The contents with which the texts are concerned are derived from this 'essential basis' *(al-asas al-jawhar)*, and they coincide with the historical periods referred to previously. In the words of al-Bashir b. Salama, these periods divide according to the following four axes:

(i) Mankind and the various aspects of the relations between men and women.
(ii) Mankind and the struggle for liberty.
(iii) Mankind and the struggle for social justice.
(iv) Mankind and the struggle to create a better society.

The Maghrib 201

The purely thematic nature of this typology which takes no cognizance of the artistic nature of the writing, or which puts this into second place, is thus clearly confirmed. With one or two exceptions, from the 1940s to the 1960s modern Tunisian literature did in fact develop around the four axes quoted above. From the 1970s onwards, it underwent a qualitative transformation through a process of experimentation in writing at the level of vocabulary and syntax, thus affirming the influence of the intellect over writing. But although the new style seeks deliberately to dislocate and break up the themes which it treats, nevertheless it continues to be haunted by a certain idea of mankind which is still situated in a fixed referential context, either in the vision of the writer or in the manner in which the characters are represented in the text.

The article *(al-maqala)* was one of the first means to which the Tunisian writer had recourse to express his preoccupations and to elaborate the concepts and values relative to his context and to his ideological and cultural perspectives. He did this to adopt an ethical attitude towards history, the present and the future. From the 1930s until shortly after independence (1955), the literary article came to grips with the Arab, Islamic and human dimensions of the Tunisian personality. 'Abd al-Salam Lamsaddi stresses (in the anthology quoted above) that these dimensions were treated in the context of a group of conflicting relationships, the clearest of which were those concerning identity and time. The former appears in the attitude of the 'self' *vis à vis* others, and the latter is concerned with the predicament of the Arab–Islamic personality between the past and the present. The literary article has also sought to explore the themes of the Arabic language in its historical dimension, and as a mark of authenticity and a symbol of the Arab personality. On the one hand this forms part of the context of a reformist ideology and a modernizing trend, both of which sought to preserve national identity in the face of foreign challenges; on the other hand it is a sign of the particular usage of linguistic and syntactic experimentation which was to appear later in innovative Tunisian literature.

Narrative writing, the short story in particular, gives an account of the ideological elements which surrounded Tunisian literature in the different stages of its development. The rise of the prose *genres* in the 1930s is, according to Tawfiq al-Bakkar, linked inextricably to 'the general movement seeking to modernize the country under colonial domination, and also the structures, systems, values and concepts of society'. Indeed if the rise of the prose *genres* was closely connected to the movement of awakening and reform, it soon proved to be a medium for the preoccupations of this movement, supporting its ideas and working for the new awareness which it tried to inspire in society. Thus we can see in the

202 *Modern literature in the Near and Middle East*

short stories a call for emotional liberation and for love; an attack on the traditional family system; an attempt to undermine paternal authority which was strongly rooted in traditional society, and so forth. Seen in the light of its simple, basic early stages, and of the themes which predominated, the short story proclaimed the first signs of social change. Its primary objective was to transmit a message, and therefore the dominant tone was generally didactic. The structure of its style depended more on discursive pronouncements than on narrative writing.

During the 1940s, Tunisian prose, still at an elementary stage, became involved in theoretical questions concerning the perplexity of some intellectuals – the meaning of existence, the predicament of a human being torn between instincts and morality, the meaning of desire, and so forth. At a later stage after the abstract approach, narrative writing became deeply involved in social issues, and gave precise images of these through descriptions of caricature, filled with bitterness and acerbic criticism. At the same time, it made progress towards greater artistic mastery and equipped itself with narrative techniques which allowed it to deal with external reality, to reformulate it and represent it with a specific texture. 'Ali al-Du'aji (1909–49) was an original writer for his time, and one who had the merit of taking Tunisian prose in this direction. The following is his opinion on his own art:

> In fact fiction is the true painting of an anomalous image ... (and the art) of the writer is to expose raw reality in terms that are clear and unambiguous; to refrain from all superfluous comment, from showing his own feelings and from ponderous preaching.

Al-Du'aji described marginal individuals, the harshness of their lives, the exploitation to which they were subject, and their sense of deprivation. We should point out that this author was one of the first Arab writers to treat the theme of the relations between the 'self' (= the Arab world) and the 'other' (= the West). With him, the problem of acculturation takes on special artistic significance in his story entitled *Jawla hawla Hanat al-Bahr al-Mutawassit* ('Tour round the Bars of the Mediterranean', Tunis 1935).

During the 1950s, the common people were to be consecrated as the heroes of prose fiction. This is confirmed through the works of al-Bashir Khrayyif, Tayyib Triki and Rashad Hamzawi, where the dialectal language is the means used to transmit the writers' message. In the works of Faraj Shadli, al-'Arusi al-Matwi, Mukhtar Janat and others, the message is devoted to the struggle against the colonizer and the glorification of the resistance. With the onset of independence, social polarization in literature was to continue and move towards themes related to contemporary issues. It continued to follow a type of duality and conflicting relationships,

The Maghrib 203

which appeared clearly in numerous short stories treating the hunger of the poor and the surfeit of the rich, expressing in commonplace form the opposition between poverty and wealth. Clearly this stance forms part of the fundamental structure which controls the duality of good and evil according to an idealistic, philosophical conception. In fact the writers who dealt with this subject were only partly successful in demonstrating that inherent contrast in conflicting situations which is indispensable in order to transcend them and to create the work of art. Their representations of reality were designed to convey misery or to express disapproval, because they were governed by a general ideology, that which goes with any national movement in the early years of independence and which looks for the creation of justice and the abolition of iniquity. All this is in total harmony with the ideal moral attitude of the religious system and with the world view of the national *bourgeoisie*. Among the representatives of this line we can quote Mustafa al-Farsi, al-Madani b. Salih, and al-Hadi b. Salih. In a constant context of duality of relationships, fiction (the short story and the novel) concentrated on the theme of migration from the country to the city in search of better living conditions, the theme of abandoning the land, and deception in the city of mirages (see the novel *Nasibi min al-Ufuq, My Share of Horizon*, 1970, by 'Abd al-Qadir b. Shaykh). Two tendencies are discernible in this type of narrative: the first expresses the shock of confrontation between two environments and two mentalities, and the other illustrates the collapse of an ideal (the land) and the brutal victory of the city. The subject is treated either via the psychological approach or in terms of social class. The narrative remains essentially a tributary of a moral attitude; it affirms abstract values and these are extra-textual rather than deriving from the social condition or everyday space which narrative writing ought to reproduce according to its own vision and special techniques.

From the 1970s until the present, one can detect new directions in short story writing or in what one supposes to be a narrative text. This trend, which describes itself as *avant-garde*, experimented from the beginning with new forms of writing, calling into question the traditional or inherited structure of Arabic syntax by overturning the links between words and logic in the use of verb tenses. At times this trend indulges in verbal acrobatics in order to deprive the linguistic heritage of its sacred character. 'Izz al-Din al-Madani provided a theory for this trend in his book *al-Adab al-Tajribi* (*Experimental Literature*, 1972), after having illustrated it himself through a series of narrative texts entitled *al-Insan al-Sifr* (*Man Zero*, published between 1967 and 1971). He was followed by numerous writers who produced variations on his theme, or who were inspired by his initial approach. The manipulation of language was both the subject and

204 *Modern literature in the Near and Middle East*

the object of this writing. This importance given to language was equally clear in the theoretical research in modern linguistics which Tunisian university scholars were the first in the Arab world to undertake (Muhammad Rashad Hamzawi, Salih Garmadi, both of whom were linguistics specialists and novelists). It is important to note that this trend in research and in writing was initially established in the atmosphere of a political and social experiment conducted by the ruling Destour Socialist Party which called for 'Tunisification' *(al-tawnasa);* its purpose was to emphasize the specificity of national identity at all levels, in an attempt to set it apart in relation both to the West and to the Mashriq (which has often underestimated the cultural and literary contributions of the Maghrib countries). Experimentation with the language of the literary text in the narrative mode continued into the 1980s with Tunisian writers indulging in stylistic exercises to the extent that the world of prose disappears and the hero vanishes and is transformed into 'linguistic matter'.

This type of transformation sought in fact to stem the flow of sentimentality and the tones of moralizing ideology which had previously dominated prose forms, in order to allow the literary nature of the text to prevail – in our opinion, only Samir al-'Ayyadi has been able to produce work in which this type of experimentation is not incompatible with genuine artistic creation and a quest for real meaning. We think that although such a transformation was due to the desire to promote the evolution of writing, and although it was influenced by Western literature – most Tunisian writers are bi-lingual – and wanted to set itself apart from the literature of the Mashriq, it was also nevertheless subject to external factors. The most crucial of these was, on the one hand, the collapse of the ideology of the nation state which over the years had transformed itself into a means of repression and class domination; on the other hand, there was the darkening of the perspectives of social change and the subsequent deceptions. The writer had no other place than the text itself in which to carry out an almost masochistic process of experimentation (or change).

MODERN MOROCCAN LITERATURE

Scholars in this field (including ourselves) can see that modern Moroccan literature begins (in terms of its semantic elements, its discourse and its aesthetics) within an ideological context and social points of reference which pre-date its existence. These have conditioned it since the 1940s (the period which saw the first attempts to write in the modern *genres,* in particular the short story), and they have continued to affect it until the 1960s when this literature achieved maturity.

The new Moroccan *Salafi* movement, known as *Salafi* Nationalism, which called for reform and renewal of identity, bore the message of renewal in Moroccan society which had been colonized since 1912. This movement had prepared the ground for the birth of Moroccan political nationalism and subsequently was incorporated entirely within it. Moroccan nationalism had appeared from 1933 onwards through a series of demands for reform at the social, economic and administrative levels, and had made its presence felt particularly from 1944 onwards when the *Istiqlal* (Independence) party was founded as a national movement which included all the patriotic forces. In this context, the Moroccan writer became involved in the process of defending his country's national and cultural values, devoting himself to the description of the changes in society which affected habits, behaviour and the way of life. We should emphasize at the outset that, through his writing, the author did not see himself as the creator of an independent artistic universe which would reflect his own vision of things, but he was a part of the dominant ideology and the social ambiance. Furthermore, his choice of the short story follows inevitably the path of this polarization, very much in the manner of the Tunisian writers. The history of the rise and development of Moroccan prose *genres* (which we have studied in detail in a number of works) shows the close links between the structure of the work of art on the one hand, and the development of the ideological context and the various details and aspects of its discourse on the other. This went on through various historical stages until the beginning of the 1980s.

From the beginning of the 1940s until the beginning of the 1950s, the first attempts at narrative writing revolve around three principal axes: society, history and the nationalist spirit. All three of these co-exist in the same sphere, namely the Moroccan personality which needs re-generation and which needs a discourse corresponding to its new identity at the crossroads between the past (the heritage), the present (the colonial challenge and the regaining of sovereignty) and the future (programmes of the National Movement for post-independence). In terms of formal creation, these axes were not expressed with equal quality as can be seen at the structural level of the short story. At the beginning of its development, it was closely related to the article and propaganda speeches, and dominated by didactic tones. The story, plot and characters were treated only superficially and in order to transmit a given message (see, for example, the works of al-Madani Hamrawi, Khadir al-Risuni and Muhammad Binnani). Towards the end of the 1940s, and the beginning of the 1950s, the idea of fiction means the description of images of society, sometimes in a documentary style and sometimes in a full and traditional style, the ultimate object being to promote a moral point of view. Towards the end of the 1950s in the period preceding and immediately following

206 *Modern literature in the Near and Middle East*

the country's independence, the short story evolves more and more towards artistic maturity. It is built around the idea of the three unities, and gradually casts off distracting elements such as didacticism, the demonstrative style, absence of action, and so forth.

In the 1970s, modern Moroccan literature reaches genuine maturity, and not merely as a result of historical evolution, for a number of objective factors had prepared the way and their increasing impact on literature allowed it to pursue its quest for modernity until the present time:

(i) The tendency for the social and cultural structures which had grown up during the first years of independence to seek more appropriate means of expression.

(ii) The desire of the writer to give a particular tone to his own voice in the general concert of social expression.

(iii) The gradual mastery of the laws of literary fiction, due to careful reading of experiments in prose writing, in particular those in the Mashriq.

(iv) The breakdown in the mid-60s of socio-political space which lost its previous homogeneity and became a theatre of intermingled contrasts and conflicts, with the short story being the most appropriate *genre* to relate them.

The conflicts and contradictions referred to in (iv) were rapidly contained by the prevailing ideology which was that of the middle classes: after they had progressively built themselves up they asserted themselves via a clear political path which was directly opposed to the ruling power and which at the same time carried on an ideological struggle against the national *bourgeoisie*. The latter decided that it had fulfilled its historic role at the moment of gaining independence and since then it concentrated on the accumulation of its material interests and on the propagation of opportunistic principles of social and cultural compromise. In this context, the short story began to describe social injustice, to reveal the deprivations of the disinherited classes and the social contrasts of independent Morocco, as well as the state of tension of the individual, suffering from the dislocation between his ambitions and the pathetic possibilities available to him. The most significant areas of prose literature were polarized by a so-called progressive ideology, which could not envisage the writer's role outside commitment to pressing social problems. So the Moroccan writer had not yet achieved his independence. He only existed in so far as through his literature he played a role in the gamble for change and the creation of the conditions of a better society. Naturally this situation affected the criteria of literary criticism which at the time granted primary importance to the content and stated objective of the work, giving short shrift to the artistic and stylistic values of the literary text and to the importance of the narrative art. Furthermore, literary criticism saw the

The Maghrib 207

individual as a mere cog in a large machine. Thus any individual expression, any vision which diverged from that imposed by a rigid concept of realism, made up the exception. The institutionalization of writing also influenced, if not to say contaminated, the idea of narrative (literary fiction was not understood first and foremost as an imaginary universe presenting reality in the form of the possible and the probable) and this held back the evolution of the modern *genres*. The authors whose works showed these characteristics in the 1960s are Muhammad Ibrahim Abu 'Allu, Muhammad Bidi, Mubarak Rabi', 'Abd al-Jabbar Shimi, 'Abd al-Karim Ghallab, Muhammad Zifzaf and Idris al-Khuri. Most of them, and others, continued the evolution of prose writing throughout the 1970s, where it remained generally conditioned by the realistic vision polarized around the 'progressive' ideological discourse and the increasing social contradictions. Nevertheless, this vision was soon to broaden and diversify. It no longer limited itself to social issues and gradually moved away from the preconceived notion of commitment. The resultant writing increases in complexity and submits individual and social relations to the laws of the universe of creative prose. The novel *par excellence* was the first area of this evolution, and it is possible from the 1970s onwards to speak of various modes of realism rather than of a single realism. Modern Moroccan literature, in all its forms of expression, henceforth takes on the signs of maturity and literary legitimacy. We are now far from the simple discourse which is monopolized first and foremost by external referential contexts. Authors such as Muhammad Zifzaf, Muhammad al-Harradi, 'Abdallah Laroui, Mubarak Rabi', Muhammad 'Izz al-Din al-Tazi (and also the author of this chapter) have brought about the qualitative transition of the short story and the novel in Morocco, by introducing fundamental changes in the levels of narrative structure; the diversification of the modes of narrative; recourse to poetic language and to the interior monologue and stream of consciousness techniques; the introduction of the fantastic; interaction between the situations of the narrator and the characters, and so forth. The totality of these elements as well as certain others, helped to make the idea of narrative writing truly synonymous with fiction, thus winning the day against the concept of naturalistic, documentary realism.

All in all this evolution added up to a sort of counter-reaction to a closed experience which was lived in political and ideological circles fighting amongst themselves and producing only increasing frustration. Since the end of the 1970s, the ideology of the ruling circles and their material structures have consolidated their position and forced the so-called progressive opposition forces into gradual marginalization, even while allowing them to play the game and giving them access to

208 *Modern literature in the Near and Middle East*

democratic institutions. At the same time they disseminate far and wide their technocratic, pseudo-liberal message which, to date, has not been able to produce any genuine literature which is devoted to it, for – and there is no doubt about this – the whole of modern Moroccan literature since independence consists of members of the middle class who have embraced left-wing ideology or who are in sympathy with it. Equally since the end of the 1970s, the 'progressive' discourse, having lost the means of direct action, has turned more towards what it calls the deepening of mass consciousness, and the intensification of the ideological struggle. At the strictly cultural level this debate has gone on in areas of civil society where the cultural question had become the central point of conflict and polarization amongst the different sections of the Moroccan intelligentsia.

As far as literature itself is concerned, two points must be made at the end of our study of the Moroccan situation. First, contrary to the previous situation of literary criticism which concentrated on questions of commitment and the social relevance of literature, recent years have seen a trend which favours the formalist style, and relies essentially on methods inspired by linguistics and semiology. Obviously such a trend fits in well with the attempts at a new literary experiment the importance of which we cannot yet assess. Moreover our second point must be made in connection with this new experiment. It concerns the path of literary creativity in the course of the present decade towards a profound exploration of the subjective and towards the representation of society via an optic which is both interactive and disjointed, instead of the old conventional unambiguous vision. To conclude these two points, modern Moroccan literature seems to assert its modernity according to the extent to which it detaches itself from any direct ideological polarization. Yet the impact of ideology does not disappear completely but is transformed into a process which infiltrates the deep structure of the creative work and its literary nature.

MODERN ALGERIAN LITERATURE

All the authorities on modern Algerian literature (in particular Abu'l-Qasim Karru, Muhammad Musayif and 'Abdallah Rakibi) tend to trace its origins to the 1930s, as part of the same trend as the reformist movement represented by the Association of Algerian *'Ulama'* (1931) which was *Salafi* in outlook and espoused the doctrine of renewing the bases of the Algerian personality primarily through the Arabic language and Islam. The traditionalism of this movement left its traces on this emerging modern literature. Thus the short story in its early stages reflects the reformist tendency in the manner in which, for example, it treats the position of women, or avoids the theme of love, because as Rakibi (1968) says:

The Maghrib 209

most of the writers belonged to the reformist movement and to deal with love and women could have a severe effect on their reputation and social status.

In its second stage, Algerian literature developed within the ideological context of the national liberation movement, and particularly after the rise of the National Liberation Front in 1954 (F.L.N.), it concerned itself with questions relating to everyday reality in the national struggle. It is noticeable that writers stressed the new links which had been forged in society through confrontation with the occupation, and this happened in a style in which the rhetorical tone of the 1940s was starting to diminish, without, however, developing an adequate narrative style: the essential objective remained to describe reality (see 'Abd al-Majid al-Shafi'i in his short story entitled *Qissa min Samim al-Waqi'* – 'A Story from the Heart of Reality', 1955). This reality and realism sought at the same time to describe the hero/individual in ordinary situations, rejecting any abstract or idealistic concept of man.

Nevertheless, whether we are concerned with the first or the second stage of this narrative writing, as was the case with Tunisian and Moroccan literature, the moral message which sought to mobilize people took precedence over the artistic structural nature of the *genre*. We must remember that this was because of the fact that the origins of this literary fiction and its evolution were conditioned by the ideological and social referential context. In fact Algerian literature continues even today to operate within this general scheme and to develop according to its demands. This at least is the conclusion we have reached after reading a number of Algerian short stories and other Algerian prose texts. This enables us to state that literary fiction in the 1960s (the beginning of independence) and in the 1970s revolves around two fundamental axes:

The past

Here the ambiance of the war of liberation and the basic values of that period form the centre of interest in the narrative. The short stories written around this axis reproduce the memory of the past which sustains the present through being its heroic dimension. Indeed the reproduction of the past was part of a general process of reconstruction of the Algerian state which was historical, ethical and ideological. The F.L.N. promoted this through various institutions and political and cultural instances, literature being one of the intermediaries to carry out this task. The hegemony of the F.L.N. as a unique party, responsible for the ideological orientation of culture, the means of information and outlets of publication, 'adapted'

210 *Modern literature in the Near and Middle East*

literary creation to its propaganda, indeed to its instructions, which explains in these circumstances the prizes awarded by the Directorate of Information to books which followed the party line. The consecration of the past in narrative literature is also explained by the relative youth of modern Algerian literature, which was not yet ready to express the new reality of independence which was coming into being. Literature was thus constrained to dip into the well of the recent past which was still omnipresent in the collective memory. Furthermore, people have always needed myths and ideals to sustain their profound spiritual desires. The cultural heritage of the Algerian people is one of considerable richness, but more than 130 years of colonization (1830–1962) nevertheless created a chasm between the distant past (the heritage) and the present. To dedicate oneself to the celebration of the exploits of the national struggle and the commemoration of the heroic episodes in the life of the nation is a striking expression of the urgent need to create new myths in a wave of triumphant nationalism. One should stress that the dominant ideology brought up the new generation with the key idea that the spirit of the Revolution had to be kept alive, in other words that the Revolution had not been accomplished simply through independence (1962). Subsequent years have merely confirmed this by the succession of a series of 'revolutions' (cultural, agrarian, industrial) preached both by the party and the language of power.

The present interacting with the past

Here prose literature is concerned with the following themes: the situation of the individual in the city; the uprooted individual in an environment which is not his own; the opportunistic values of the new rising social classes; perplexity in the face of a society in the process of decomposition and reconstruction. In all these themes, the memory of the *Mujahidin* (the fighters) is omnipresent. Sometimes this appears like the mirror in which daily reality is reflected and thanks to which it takes on its true dimension. Thus we can say that the vision of the past (surrounded and sustained by reformist ideology on the one hand and by national liberation ideology on the other) underlies almost the whole of modern Algerian literature. Furthermore in view of the *dirigisme* exercised by the cultural pressures from the F.L.N. on literature, the prose literature which revolves around the second axis is characterized by a total dependence on the different slogans and doctrines of the state. Thus it is possible to categorize modern Algerian literature from 1965 in the light of the following phases:

The Maghrib 211

The industrial revolution

This led to a number of narrative, poetic and other texts which stress the importance of the event and describe – in the short story in particular – the multiple changes in society and in social relations.

The agrarian revolution

In this context literature echoes the political discourse on the justice achieved for the *fellah*, it denounces feudalism, and sings the praises of socialism which saved the citizen from exploitation and submission. Yet in spite of the fact that the agrarian revolution followed the period of colonialism, literature concentrates on this period, and above all on the exploitation of the peasants and the expropriation of their land. This is proof of the predominance of the past over actual lived experience. The following novels illustrate this: *Huna Tahtariq al-Akwakh* (*Here the Huts Burn* by Muhammad Ztily, 1977); *al-Shams Tushriq 'ala'l-Jami'* (*The Sun Rises over Everyone* by Isma'il Ghamuqat, 1978); *Huna Yubar'im al-Rafd* (*Here Flowers Rejection* by Idris Boudhiba, 1978). The latter in particular writes in the introduction to his novel:

> While writing it, I confess to having known moments of anguish and melancholy for I was torn between two contradictory poles, the real and the imaginary. In spite of the attraction exercised over me by the latter, it was the real which dominated my work, forbidding any possibility of going beyond it.

This confession shows the extent to which a certain idea of reality had taken root in Algerian writers: it was reality as conceived by the decrees and slogans of the regime, and not the inner reality of daily life. As a result, the concept of realism which is explored in prose literature identifies itself from a technical point of view more with documentary reporting than with artistic realism. The confession is also indicative of the gap between the true nature of prose literature and a fiction which is based primarily on the notion of verifiable reality.

In effect the ideology of the F.L.N. completely conditioned and indeed strictly canalized the evolutionary possibilities of modern Algerian literature, making it subordinate to the rhythm of the state's achievements and to its social and economic planning. In this regard it is hardly an exaggeration to say that Algerian writers were, and perhaps still are, considered as servants or employees of one of the 'public sector enterprises' of the state, whose task is to represent in prose the progress and achievements of the Revolution. It is quite significant that no short

212 *Modern literature in the Near and Middle East*

story writer or novelist has been able to go beyond the naive propagandist stage of realism. Tahar Wattar at one moment in his literary career showed definite talent (see his novel *al-Zilzal – The Earthquake*), but he soon reverted to the prevalent norms with the novel *al-Laz*.

In the 1980s, a new generation of writers, short story writers in particular, is moving towards a literary experiment in which the individual voice seeks emancipation while continuing to cope with the contradictions of a reality which is more and more complex and no longer lends itself to facile, systematic, ideological polarization. It is still too early to evaluate the importance of this experiment, but as is the case in Tunisia and Morocco, the new generation of Algerian writers seems convinced that the mission of modernity can be promoted and deepened only through a personal quest which is open and free of the constraints of a discourse which is both *dirigiste* and mono-dimensional.

15 Israel

Leon I. Yudkin

INTRODUCTION

In spite of the radical alteration of circumstances, Israeli literature, the Hebrew literature of the state of Israel, derives much of its original postures, vocabulary, syntax and overall consciousness from early modern Hebrew literature. That this originated in the modest attempt at Hebrew reconstruction in the Germany of the mid-eighteenth century is largely accepted.[1] Moreover, in spite of historical discontinuity and geographical dispersal, there is a coherent tradition of Hebrew writing from that period to the present day. With hindsight, modern Hebrew literature, stemming from the circle of the Berlin *Maskil,* Rabbi and philosopher, Moses Mendelssohn (1729–86), was a breakaway attempt to set up a Hebrew equivalent of the sort of literary forum represented by the English *Tatler* and *Spectator* and their German equivalents. The aim was to offer a new readership translations of European poetry into Hebrew, moralistic essays and correspondence, Biblical-toned original Hebrew poetry and notices of current literature. It is the miniscule and abortive journal *qohelet musar* (mid-1750s) and its successor *Ha-Meassef* (1780s), from which modern Hebrew literature is derived, rather than medieval literature or even the Italian Renaissance tradition (see Yudkin 1986–7).

This was a movement which in Germany died out for lack of fertile soil. The Jewish community was small and rapidly assimilating culturally. Within a few generations, it had become German speaking and 'enlightened' beyond Hebraism, and had on occasion become Christian too. It took the very different environment of Eastern Europe, with its much larger culturally, religiously and linguistically separate communities to nurture a substantial literature in Hebrew, paralleling and also rivalling the new Yiddish literature. It was in the Galicia and Lithuania of the mid-nineteenth century that the *genre* of the novel was first developed in Hebrew, thus preparing the ground through satire (the epistolatory novel)

214 *Modern literature in the Near and Middle East*

and romanticism (Mapu's first novel, *ahavat tziyon* of 1853 was set in the Biblical Palestine of Isaiah's time) for something approaching 'Realism'.[2] This 'Realism' must be qualified by inverted commas, as it is a necessarily qualified phenomenon. The very language of the representation was vastly distanced both from the putative reader and from the given setting of the work. Hebrew was not a spoken language. The first fictionist to contrive a convincing language of speech and description, Mendeli Mocher Sforim (1836–1917), succeeded by deploying all layers of Hebrew (Biblical, Rabbinic and medieval) and Jewish Aramaic in a construct which was supposed to stand for the Yiddish vernacular. It is an 'as if' language that seeks to sound authentic within the unavoidable confines of a language which is limited in register and not spoken.[3]

Nevertheless, in the late eighteenth century, particularly following the rise of a proto-Zionist national consciousness in the 1880s and the first modern wave of emigration to Palestine in the wake of the pogroms, a vital Hebrew literature was created. It was in the vanguard of European experimentation, using symbolism and free verse in poetry, new forms of fiction writing and representation of reality, including stream of consciousness. A profusion of radical notions, including those challenging the Jewish *status quo* in every respect, was introduced into belletristics, fictional and discursive. The literature was undoubtedly in a peculiar situation, without national roots, and without a substantial or stable readership. The authors of this literature were likewise unrooted, between two worlds, moving out of a Judaic environment, often represented as disintegrating,[4] and yet not finding a natural home in the host societies. The very language used is an expression of this alienation, and the prominent themes and subjects project the difficulties of the heroes (universally anti-heroes). The world was to change. Empires were to be broken down into national units after the First World War, with each political unit characterized by its majority language and people. The Jews would eventually have to assimilate into the environment, in East or West Europe, compulsorily or voluntarily. The only possible source of native cultural and linguistic expression was to be Palestine, which, under the British Mandate, was to adopt Hebrew as an official language. The adoption of Hebrew constituted a significant element in the building up of a 'Jewish Homeland'.

So, from Germany to Austria and Eastern Europe, then through to Palestine with its developing *yishuv*, composed of three major waves of immigration between 1881 and 1924, the path of modern Hebrew literature was set out. The leading exponents of Hebrew literature were mainly of European origin, writers who were dressing European techniques and experiences in Hebrew garb, expressionists and futurists

Israel 215

possessed not only by the horrors of universal catalogues and apocalyptic vision, but also by a sense of possibility in the new–old land with its own specific function. Hebrew literature had for some decades now been preoccupied with the future 'return home', to a place where Hebrew had not only a right but a duty to flourish.

The decisive turning point for the focus of Hebrew writing came in the 1920s. It was during this decade that Europe was to be fragmented into nation-states with their separate national interests and cultures, tending more and more towards exclusivist chauvinism in an increasingly dangerous world. This was the case in the xenophobic Soviet Union under Stalin (from 1924 onwards), in renascent nationalist Poland and, of course, in Germany and the German-speaking world too. Hebrew was banned in the Soviet Union and marginalized in the USA. When most of the leading Hebrew writers settled in Palestine (e.g. U. Z. Greenberg and H. N. Bialik arrived in 1924), this confirmed the *yishuv* as the most exclusive centre of Hebrew culture. Now diaspora activity was indisputedly peripheral. The implications though had to be understood. Palestine had to become a subject and Hebrew had to offer a total register capable of expressing the totality of life, feeling and activity. Whereas the Hebrew writer hitherto had expressed Jewish man in his partial capacity, separate from his secular non-Jewish concerns in a 'special' language, the tendency of the new Palestinian settlement was to integrate Jewishness into a Hebrew Palestinianism that would become statehood. H. N. Bialik (1873–1934), U. Z. Greenberg (1896–1983) and even S. Y. Agnon (1888–1970) were rooted in Europe and observed this new environment with foreign eyes, relating to it as from Europe and diaspora Judaism, albeit a Judaism secularized and Zionized.

PALESTINE

For the generation born in the land whose reality was bounded by this local experience and territory as expressed primarily in Hebrew, this older Hebrew literature, even if written by contemporaries, was itself foreign. There was a perceptible need for local literary representation by writers at home in the territory, otherwise there could not exist a literature of the land of Israel with its own colour, landscape and nuances. This does much to explain both the sense of estrangement between 'here' and 'there' and the search for Palestinian–Hebrew roots. The origins of pre-Israeli Palestinian Hebrew writing⁵ are generally located in those Palestinian-born writers such as Esther Raab (1894–1981) and S. Yizhar (b. 1916), whose primary subject and locale was the Land and who did not have to strain to adopt new postures and attitudes in any pretence at naturalization. The

216 *Modern literature in the Near and Middle East*

decade of the 20s was still dominated in literary terms by the writers of the third *aliyah* (1919–24), young immigrants bearing a message of Jewish Europe, of Russian Futurism, of Yiddish or German Expressionism, now applied to a secularized Messianism in a resurgent future Israel. These writers may have been retiring to their spiritual home, but a major subject still had to be the difficulty and the rejection of the exilic past and diaspora present. Raab and Yizhar knew no other reality. So in the former's poems and the latter's stories, Palestine is naturally the primary subject, not contrived or induced.

Literary historians have to find a method of describing the process of literary performance that makes two things clear:

(i) that literature is the product of interaction with society; it is read by readers in a social and economic context.

(ii) that literature is literature, however, and not politics, philosophy, economics and social comment.

As the Russian formalists insisted, the object of scrutiny for the literary historian/critic is not just any printed material, but literature, so that in order to discover this object a definition of literariness has to be propounded (see Lemon and Reis 1965: 99–139), i.e. of what constitutes literature as a discrete entity, of what makes it special and worthy of study. I will assume just that interaction between society and literature posited by Zohar Shavit,[6] in her attempt to characterize the literature of the *yishuv* as accurately as possible. Y. H. Brenner (1881–1921), novelist, essayist and would-be pioneer, who settled in Palestine in 1909, found it difficult to welcome the Palestinian *genre* as such (see Yudkin 1985). He found the *yishuv* either dull, in so far as it was a continuation of the past, or uncrystallized, if new. In his own material he perceived the need of norms and historical continuity. Yet he himself, in his last decade, was the leading exponent of the new Palestinian–Hebrew literature. But his Palestine was the Palestine of the problem, and the figure within the narrator or bearer of narrative focus experienced difficulties of absorption and reconciliation with reality. He is the suffering individual and Brenner always regards himself as a conveyor of the sense of the individual. I. Y. Lamdan (1900–54), in more exclamatory vein through his best known poem, *Masada* (see Yudkin 1971), treats the symbolic Masada, standing for the fortress Palestine, as the object of a spiritual enterprise, as an unattained peak rather than as an already assimilated reality. The poet A. Shlonsky (1900–73), also endowed the pioneering enterprise with secularized, messianic character, and the expressionist poet, U. Z. Greenberg, who had hitherto written mostly in Yiddish, turned to Hebrew for his first collection in 1924, comparing his own function to the Biblical Ezekiel's, returning from exile with his people. Agnon's main chosen setting in his early stories is either contemporary Europe or a more distant, Hasidic past. Raab and Yizhar, more than Brenner, M. Smilansky (1874–1953, Yizhar's uncle, an early immigrant) and the poets of the third *aliyah*, heralded a genuinely native tendency. This tendency had to express wholeness, where language and subject were integrated, each part of a whole, belonging to one society, albeit immature and unformed.

ISRAEL

That there is a peculiarly Israeli Hebrew literature, a subdivision of modern Hebrew literature, is undeniable. Needless to say, it is not precisely co-terminous with the history of the Israeli state. It would, indeed, be surprising if in May 1948 there had emerged at one moment a new collective voice. It was rather a process of re-adjustment to the developing reality, a recently crystallized focus. Various are the attempts made to characterize the literary voice (see Miron 1962 and Shaked 1983). Inevitably, this attempt is doomed to generalization and abstraction and must be open to challenge. There can be no one point of abrupt re-orientation in the way that a political event is tied down to a date. In the course of the 20s, several things had become clear. On the one hand, alternative channels of Hebrew expression had been cut off, and, on the other, following the Balfour Declaration and the assumption of the British mandate to execute its directives, the three waves of immigration had established the basic framework that was also to serve the emergent state. Now, although Palestine was still not a massive community,[7] it became (as we have seen), the sole source of Hebrew literature. At some point, writers, who were either born locally or who had received their formative background there, began to publish and became influential in the literary life of the country. It is not surprising that there is a dispute about which point may be taken as a starting point for the process. Indeed there is no one point. Evan Raab's early poems in the 20s or Yizhar's first story in 1938 would be an arbitrary anchor. The immigrant poets had heralded the tendency by attempting to be reborn like Y. Karni (1884-1949), who immigrated in 1921, but then opted for a totally Palestinian identity. This was an extreme position but characteristic in general tendency.

Nevertheless even such an abstract notion as Israelism was expressed indirectly in literature. Yizhar's concentration on the *flora* and *fauna* of the Land, on its local inhabitants, on its colonists, on the army, observed from within rather than expounded from without is one example. The author could only draw contrasts with earlier and diaspora Jewish history by implication and on the limited basis of what he observed. He was faced though with the enormous task of providing and sometimes even creating

218 *Modern literature in the Near and Middle East*

an adequate language. Hebrew had functioned in a restricted register only and only for certain types of literature. In reading Yizhar we are aware of the effort of linguistic creation and of the delight the author took in *virtuoso* use of language. He extended the vocabulary of literary Hebrew and produced a complex syntax in convoluted sentences, intended to bear the complexity of his subject, which was the wavering consciousness of individuals projected at critical junctions. Whether the overt subject was dissatisfaction with kibbutz work, indecision about whether to release a prisoner in conformity with his own inclination rather than submit to the group pressure of his army colleagues, or indecision on the part of a horse in the story 'The Runaway' (*In sipurey mishor*, 1964), the theme is always the effort of resolution within the mind (see Yudkin 1974: 71–89 and 1984: 54–67). Representation of individual thought and feeling, with its movement through internal monologue, is difficult linguistically, in both syntactic and lexical terms. Yizhar's language is the most complex yet in Hebrew writing, with the widest lexical range, in spite of the very limited span of action in the story and its limited development. The Yizhar story, including that of his single enormous novel, *yemey tziglag* (1958), proceeds through the indecision of a character or characters, who are subject to alternative pressures around a specific issue. The character does not change significantly or develop and there is no great range of external action, but he does consider the options and he does immerse himself in the moods deriving from those possibilities. He seems to represent the weight of conscience, that is, of conscientious decision, but he has to face the mass (the kibbutz, the army, the horse's captors) and, by implication, submits to greater power. The third force in the Yizhar story is Nature, specified and various, but neutral, conveyed in all its range. As the Yizhar plot does not develop, neither do the characters, each one being a brilliant variant on the others. And, in fact, he has produced no fiction in the last twenty years. The stories have said what they have to say.

Yizhar's was a striking Israeli voice, hailed by critics as the most original and quintessentially Israeli of the new Hebrew fictionists. Not many tried to imitate these tones and there were other directions for Israeli prose. Moshe Shamir (b. 1921) was one of the more orthodox voices of current *Sabra* tendencies, whose novels started to appear just about the time of the State,[8] and whose action revolves around the momentous Israeli events of the period, and whose heroes are the native-born young Israelis fighting in the *Palmach* and the Israeli army, rather like the author himself (see Yudkin 1984: 39–53). The Shamir range is much broader than Yizhar's, there is more action and more plot development. Although the linguistic issue is paramount, the language is not as innovative and dominant as with Yizhar. Characteristic is the portrait of the *Sabra*, strong,

Israel 219

unreflective, always contrasted with the diaspora figure, uncertain, introspective, bearing the impression of other times and places. A new ideology was emerging, creating amongst the young Hebrew what came to be known, somewhat pejoratively, as Canaanism. This ideology stressed the difference of interest between the Jews of Israel and those abroad, and the supreme Israeli is the *Sabra*, the very embodiment of the distinction, with a different perspective, fate and language. In a sense, this is an absurd notion, as the Israeli is the product of this external situation which was, and is, still in force. The Israeli is where he is because of Jewish history, he derives his meaning and purpose from Jewish existence and his support from the Jewish people. But the 'Canaanite' cast doubt on this reality. Certainly the *Sabras* of Shamir's early novels exemplified the populist outlook. Shamir developed differently from Yizhar, moving at a later stage to treatments of Israelite historical themes, then to existential considerations of the contemporary Israeli situation in the 60s, then to political ideology (moving away from his early Marxist orientation to an ultra-nationalist position) and autobiography. He has tried to adapt to changing circumstances, personal and general, and to write in various manners and *genres*.

Poetry, too, both responded to and created a version of Israelism. The tradition of modern Hebrew poetry had been rhetorical and prophetic, deploying the exalted tones of the Bible even in undermining the Biblical message, as Bialik had done in such a poem as 'davar', with its anti-theistic thrust. The poetry of the third *aliyah* was indeed revolutionary, challenging, apocalyptic, expressionistic and shocking. But it derived its effect from its exploitation of traditional materials, assumptions and language, and was constantly referring to its own history. What young Israeli poetry brought to Hebrew verse was the introduction of the Hebrew vernacular and the capturing of the patterns of normal speech. The poetry of such writers as Amichai, Zach, Gilboa, Dor, Sivan and Bernstein was anti-rhetorical and generally laconic, not only relating to Israeli reality from within but doing so colloquially, puncturing the rhetoric of early generations in the sobering light of the contemporary situation, apparently the apotheosis of Zionist achievement.[9] It is true that such as Bialik had already broken away from metrical verse in the late nineteenth century, but free verse had become the norm rather than the exception. The preference now was for understatement, as the enthusiasm of the pioneers and the pre-pioneers could now be tested in the crucible of the fulfilment of an earlier period's aspiration. What had looked like a messianic hope became for the so-called *Palmach* generation[10] an everyday, common-place, even a rather grey reality. This is now a reality compounded of the inner space of the writer bound by the rhythms of external events, particularly by the unending war.

220 *Modern literature in the Near and Middle East*

THE 1960s ONWARDS

Each action creates a reaction and each reaction invokes further reaction. So it is with Hebrew literature. Just as unrooted intellectualism was rejected by the notion of return to the Land and to a specific Land, so that return seemed to contain the seeds of its own discomfiture. Not only could the concerns of the *Sabra* hero be seen as limited and parochial but he could also be dismissed by later commentators as raucous and provincial, with less achieved human potential than his forbears. The first phase of Israeli literature proper, in the wake of Israeli statehood, had been marked by a sense of collectivism, by a sense that the Israeli, of whatever political or ideological hue, should be conscious of his obligations to that collective. The individual was operating within a national context. But soon voices were to be heard protesting against the pressure, the pressure by the government, the army and their agencies, by the constant talk of peoplehood and nation. P. Sadeh (b. 1929), for example, had deliberately cultivated his own garden, and his first novel *hahayim kemashal* (*Life as a Parable*, 1958), like his later prose and poetry, is autobiographical and lyrical in character. He tells of the pressure of 1948, of his army conscription and of his subsequent desertion. From that point on, he chose to see things in terms of their wider symbolic and mystical significance and to reject a this-worldly approach. His concern now would be with the ultimate reality beyond the transient *trivia* of the everyday, the concerns of this world and specific territory. He specifically rejects mainstream Judaism, because it is only interested in social redemption rather than in individual salvation. He argues that every individual genius has had to go beyond the boundaries of Judaism, and he casts aside local patriotism by declaring: 'This national war had no meaning for me, and I could see nothing to fight for. My real enemies were lying in wait in another place in the dark recesses of the soul'. So public, political life is considered inferior in significance and status to the private life of the spirit.

This kind of disassociation from predominant public concerns made itself felt in the fiction of the 1960s with great regularity. It proceeded through Y. Kaniuk's *hayored lemaalah* (*The Acrophile*, 1960), where the first-person narrator finds himself totally detached from his environment in New York (although there, thankfully, he did not have to be a pioneer), and A. Megged's *hahay al hamet* (*Living on the Dead*, 1965), where the narrator cannot fulfil his contract to write a book about a great Israeli leader, to M. Shamir's own *hagvul* (*The Border*, 1966), where another first-person narrator is also preoccupied by a restless search for freedom. In all these works the theme of the 'flight of the hero' recurs (see Yudkin 1974: 90–103). This is the flight from the encroachment of the public into the private sphere and from the imposition of collective values on the individual.

Israel 221

This does not mean that the public realm was ignored. The two most prominent fictionists of a later generation, A. B. Yehoshua (b. 1937) and Amos Oz (b. 1939) in their stories and novels from the mid-1960s onwards attempted to interweave public concerns and national interests into private symbol and allegory. Thus, in Yehoshua's 'Facing the Forests'(Mul Hayearot, 1968), the forest clearly stands for Israel, where the tree is a symbol of Zionism burying the submerged Arab village. The wars of the crusaders being researched by the hero of the story reflect the Arab–Jewish struggle in the Land, and his relationship with the dumb Arab servant has an overtly symbolic function. But this political drama is framed by a setting in which the focusing agent of the story (unnamed) is described with all his personal and psychological baggage. It is clear that his imperfect eyesight and his own difficulties of relationship have created his own circumstances. So the political element is borne on a personal impulse; psychology and politics are totally intertwined. His novels too, *hameahev* (*The Lover*, 1977) and *gerushim meuharim* (*A Late Divorce*, 1982), combine allegorical structure with personal and particularly family relationships. Oz makes the bearer of his stories an unreliable narrator. *Mikhael sheli* ('My Michael', 1968) is recounted by the depressive Hannah, who lives in a world of fantasy, and moves close to the precipice in being unable to distinguish reality from her own imaginative life. In his later work, there is a sense of danger encroaching on the integrity of the personality and on the stability of society (see Yudkin 1984: 135–48). It would seem that in the work of Yehoshua and Oz there has been a return to local concerns. But they are local concerns as seen through the lens of the individual (not the author's but the fictional narrator's as created by the author). The stories and novels of A. Kahana-Carmon, from the mid-1960s onwards, are entirely focused on the individual and her (always her) relationships, and sometimes tend to the hermetic. A. Appelfeld (b. 1932) sets his fiction, also published in the 1960s, in a non-Israeli context, either in a pre-Holocaust Europe, implying the future outcome known to the reader, or in a post-war setting, with the characters immobilized by their war experiences. All this is a far cry from the initial stages of Israeli literature.

THE CURRENT SCENE

No survey, however brief, would be adequate without some consideration of Israeli drama. For obvious reasons this long remained the Cinderella of the *genres*. Drama, unless within a ritual context, has to be limited to the spoken language of the environment. And originally, Hebrew drama, for example by Mose Zacuto in seventeenth-century Italy, and even by

222 Modern literature in the Near and Middle East

Matityahu Shoham in the Warsaw of the 1920s and 1930s, were not performance plays (although Shoham would dearly have loved to have his plays produced on stage) (see Kartun-Blum 1969: 13). In the 'main, then, much of Hebrew drama was condemned to a theatrical vacuum written first in the absence of a spoken language and later against the background of a limited vernacular. In view of this limitation, it is not surprising that if we look at the record of dramatic productions since Statehood, only about one in five productions was of a native play in the early years (see tables in Kohansky 1974). Native Israeli drama was composed in the main by non-specialist playwrights. For example, Shamir adapted his early novel *hu halakh basadot* for the Cameri production in 1948. But this *genre* did improve. The Israeli theatre became more autonomous, and by the 1970s, two major Israeli dramatists had emerged, the satirist H. Levin, whose *malkat haambatyah* (*Queen of the Bathtub*, 1970) had rocked the Israeli public, and Y. Sobol who, at about the same time, began to delve into Jewish history, not in order to resolve conflicts but to present options in dramatic terms.

In poetry, the same dialectical pattern noted above was again manifest. Whereas the first years of the State were marked by prosaic sparseness and understatement, there was a return in the late 1960s and 1970s to a more romantic expression. A poetess of a previous generation, Leah Goldberg (1911–71) produced perhaps her greatest volume on her awareness of approaching death, *sheerit hahayim* (*Remnant of Life*, 1971), invoking Bialik's own poem *aharey moti* which anticipates a song still unwritten after the poet's life is ended. This collection is a sublimation and acceptance of his life as a totality. Following on in an intense, lyrical self-inspection is Dahlia Ravikovitch (b. 1936) who searches for love and is aware of her own fragility. In the younger poetry there are experiments with form such as the collection *tzurot* (*Forms*, 1985) by Yona Wallach (1946–86). Lines are put into proximity of association rather than of logical sequence. Yair Hurvitz's language is even more difficult; grammar is sacrificed completely in an attempt to grasp the ecstasy of the moment. A return has been made to more exotic themes, fanciful notions, wondrous regions, experiments with sensation and perception of another world (see Yudkin 1974: 150–68). There has also been a renewed interest in mystical religiosity, as with Sadeh (discussed above as a prose writer) and the ecstatic Zelda.

Fiction has also gone through major re-orientations, although sometimes general tendencies only emerge. A predominant mood of recent Israeli fiction is nostalgia. The generation which grew up in Palestine/ Israel can now look back on the early days of settlement and match present reality with earlier and purer visions. The country has grown and

Israel 223

become heterogeneous. Colonies have become cities. Cities have become large, decadent and anonymous. The cutting edge of idealism has been blunted. Yet any kind of sustained recollection might look like nostalgia (see Yudkin 1986). David Shahar (b. 1926) has been writing since the 1950s, but in 1969 he inaugurated a *roman fleuve* with the first volume of an ongoing novel, the fifth part of which was *yom harefaim* (*Day of the Ghosts*, 1986). This work follows the careers of connected families in Jerusalem, from the narrator's own childhood and first memories in 1936. Like Proust, Shahar attempts to construct an edifice made up of the primary element of time, past, present and future. Unlike Proust, however, the narrator is largely absent as he takes up stories of different individuals at various points. In fact, a more permanent focus than the narrator is the place, Jerusalem, to which *Ningal* (vol. 4 in the series) concludes with a doxology. Yitzhak Ben-Ner (b. 1937) adopts a directly confessional tone in his novels and stories which are presented emotionally by the highly-charged narrator seeking release through a distant land.[11] The stories of Y. Knaz (b. 1937) are set in the recent past, the time of the author's own child-hood. He recalls his youth and background, so that they comprise an autobiographical sketch.

One of the most remarkable of all recent Israeli novelists is Yaakov Shabtai (1934–81) who only managed to write two novels, the second of which, *sof davar* (*Past Perfect*, 1984), was edited by his widow and published posthumously. The first, *zikhron dvarim* (*Past Continuous*, 1977), follows the life of three friends in one unbroken narrative sequence without paragraphs, over a period of nine months marked by two deaths, that of the father of one of the friends, Goldmann, and then the suicide of Goldmann himself. The decay observed in the Tel-Aviv environment is matched by the decay in the three lives, recounted comically but with a tragic awareness. The second novel is monochromatically bleak, concentrating on one character, on his despair, decline and death, followed ambiguously by a surrealistic reconstruction of life after death. It is divided into four parts, with significant movements of tone and treatment.

Confrontation with major themes is combined with formal experimentalism by David Grosman (b. 1954). The two novels, *hiyukh hagdi* ('Smile of the Lamb', 1982) and *ayen erekh ahavah* ('See under Love', 1986), deal respectively with Jewish–Arab tension and the Holo-caust. The first uses A. B. Yehoshua's technique (itself borrowed from Faulkner) of telling the story through the participants' monologues, which take the plot forward with each statement. The unexpected *dénouement* probes the attitudes and interrelationships of the protagonists and is itself a study of power and domination. Continuing this investigation, the later novel opens with a statement of aspirations to viewing the Holocaust

224 *Modern literature in the Near and Middle East*

afresh.[12] He can do this by seeing it as if for the first time, through the eyes of a child, who reads all he can about what happened, picks up his parents' comments and eventually meets the 'grandfather', the story-teller from over 'there'. The other parts of the novel jettison this stance, moving first to the Polish writer Bruno Schulz and a monologue of the sea, then to the grotesque and parodic, and finally, to the encyclopaedic, from which the novel takes its title. The layers of the past come together in the present and in different versions of that reality. The 'grandfather' is spoken of by the child as a 'prophet of the past'. And he is indeed a teller of tales that would otherwise be forgotten.

Drama, poetry and fiction in Israel are produced in abundance in a variety of modes. We have seen that literary history does not move in a straight line which rejects the past in a funnelling of evolutionary purpose. On the contrary, in this instance there is an ongoing dialectic, with themes and techniques dropped at one moment to be taken up again later. And so with moods and attitudes. Fashions of yesteryear return. Reconstruction of the past puts the writer and reader in that past.

NOTES

1 B. Kurzweil (1958) sees modern Hebrew literature as definable in terms of its secularity. The issues raised are discussed in Yudkin, (1974: 1–14).
2 This term is used in a variety of ways. It was first propounded in a journal, *Réalisme*, founded by Duranty in 1856. Style was to be subservient to representation of Nature. I am using the term in its general sense of approximation to life. In the 1860s, a new term was developed, *naturalisme*, but this word also gave rise to confusion and disagreement.
3 Some of the issues raised by Mendeli's use of language are discussed in Yudkin, (1982: 13–15)
4 See the iterative imagery in the verse of H.N. Bialik (1865–1934), e.g. in the early poem 'al saf bet hamidrash' (1894).
5 See R. Kritz's (1978) attempt at a definition. His title hypothesizes the generation fighting for independence 'as lending the literature its specific character'.
6 Zohar Shavit (1982) tries to establish a model for the 'literary life' of the Land of Israel, which, on her criteria, only crystallized there after the First World War, with an active and consistent publishing centre and durable periodicals.
7 For an account of the growth of the *yishuv* and its demography see Lucas (1973: 109). The Jewish population grew from 55,000 in 1918 'to an estimated 475,000 ... at the end of 1939'.
8 His first novel was *hu halakh basedot* (Tel-Aviv, 1947).
9 For a generous representation and characterization of Israeli poetry see Bargard and Chyet (1986).
10 So called because many of these writers belonged to this command corps, later to be incorporated into the Israeli Defence Forces.

Israel 225

11 Title of a collection, *eretz rehoqah*, published in 1981.
12 This is sort of thematic 'defamiliarization' of the type that Victor Sklovsky characterized as specifically literary. The purpose of art is to impart the sensation of things as they are perceived and not as they are known. The technique of art is to make objects 'unfamiliar', to make forms difficult. 'Art is a way of experiencing the artfulness of an object; the object is not important'. See Lemon and Reis (1965: 12)

Bibliography

'Abbasi, Muhammad, 1958, *Tarikh-i Matbu'at va Adabiyat-i Iran dar Dawrah-yi Mashrutiyat*, 2 vols. Tehran.

'Abbud, Marun, 1950, *Saqr Lubnan*, Beirut.

'Abdul-Hai, Muhammad, 1976, 'A Bibliography of Arabic Translations of English and American Poetry 1830–1970', *Journal of Arabic Literature*, VII , 120–50.

'Afifi, Hafiz, 1938, *'Ala Hamish al-Siyasa*, Cairo, Dar al-Kutub al-Misriyya.

'Arif, Abu'l-Qasim, 1948, *Kulliyat-i Divan-i Mirza Abulqasim 'Arif Qazvini*, Tehran, Saif-i Azad.

'Awad, Luwis, 1972, 'Maskh al-Ka'inat', *al-Ahram*, 24 Nov. 7

'Abduh, Ibrahim, 1942. *Tar'ikh al-waqa'i' al-misriyya, 1828–1942*, Cairo.

— 1949, *Ta'rikh al-tiba'a wa'l-sahafa khilal al-hamla al-faransiyya*, Cairo.

Abrahamian, E., 1982, *Iran between two Revolutions*, Princeton.

Abramson, G., 1979, *Hebrew Drama*, London.

Abramson, G. and Parfitt, T. V. (eds), 1985, *The Great Transition, The Recovery of the Lost Centres of Modern Hebrew Literature*, New York.

Ahmad, F., 1969, *The Young Turks*, Oxford.

— 1977, *The Turkish Experiment in Democracy 1950–75*, Colorado; Westview Press.

Ajami, F., 1981, *The Arab Predicament, Arab Political Thought and Practice Since 1967*, Cambridge: C.U.P.

Akhundzadah, Fath-'Ali, 1970, *Tamsilat*, trans. by Muhammad Ja'far Qarajahdaghi, Tehran.

Akünal, Dundar, 1980, 'İlk Sefiller Çevirisi Üzerine', *Milliyet Sanat Dergisi*, Eylül 1980: 110–11.

Al-i Ahmad, Jalal, 1952, 'Hidayat-i Buf-i Kur', *Ilmu Zindigi*, vol.1, no.1.

— 1978, *Dar Khidmat va Khiyanat-i Rushan-fikran*, Tehran, Ravaq.

Alangu, Tahir, (ed.), 1962, *Ömer Seyfettin' in Toplu Eserleri*, Istanbul.

Alavi, Bozorg, 1964, *Geschichte und Entwicklung der modernen persischer Literatur*, Berlin.

Allen, R. 1982, *The Arabic Novel: An Historical and Critical Introduction*, University of Manchester.

al-'Amri, Muhammad al-Mahdi, 1951, *Tarikh al-Tarjama wa Harakat al Thaqafa fi 'Asr Muhammad 'Ali*, Cairo.

— 1980, *al-Qissa al-Tunisiyya al-Qasira min khilal Majalla al-Fikr*, Tunis: Dar Bu-Salama.

Aryanpur, Yahya, 1961, *Az Saba ta Nima*. 2 vols., Tehran.

Auden, W. H., n.d. *The Collected Poetry of W. H. Auden*, New York: Random House.

Bibliography 227

Avery, P., 1965, *Modern Iran*, London.

Babinger, F. 1919, *Stambuler Buchwesen im 18 Jahrhundert*, Leipzig.

Badawi, M. M., 1969, *An Anthology of Modern Arabic Verse*, Beirut: O.U.P.

— 1973, (trans.), *The Saint's Lamp* [Yahya Haqqi], Leiden.

— 1975, *A Critical Introduction to Modern Arabic Poetry*, Cambridge: C.U.P.

— 1982, 'Modern Arabic Poetry: the Search for Modernity', *The Literary Review Supplement: the Arab Cultural Scene*, London: Namara Press, 47–50.

— 1987, *Modern Arabic Drama in Egypt*, Cambridge: C.U.P.

— 1988, *Early Arabic Drama*, Cambridge: C.U.P.

Bahar, Muhammad Taqi, 1337, *Sabk-shinasi*, vol. III (2nd ed.), Tehran.

— 1942 (poet-laureate), *Tarikh-i Mukhtasar-i Ahzab-i Siyasi-yi Iran*, Tehran.

— 1956, 1957 (poet-laureate), *Divan*, 2 vols. Tehran, Amir Kabir.

Bakhash, S., 1978, *Iran: Monarchy, Bureaucracy and Reform under the Qajars, 1858–1896*, London.

Ballas, Shimon, 1985, 'Itlala 'ala Manhaj Muhammad 'Uthman Jalal fi-'l-Tarjama', *al-Karmil*, 6, 7–36.

Bamiya, 'A'ida Adib, 1982, *Tatawwur al-Adab al-Qasasi al-Jaza'iri 1925–1967* (Arabic translation by Muhammad Saqr, Algiers: Diwan al-Matbu'at al-Jami'iyya)

Banani, Amin, 1961, *The Modernisation of Iran, 1921–1941*, Stanford.

Barash, A. (ed.) 1930, *Mivhar ha-Shirah ha-Ivrit ha-Hadashah*, 'An Anthology of Modern Hebrew Poetry', Jerusalem.

Bargard, W. and Chyet, S. (eds.), 1986, *Israeli Poetry*, Bloomington.

Batatu, H., 1979, 1982, *The Old Social Classes and the Revolutionary Movements of Iraq*, Princeton University Press.

Bedreddin, Hasan Rifat Mehmed, 1876, (trans.) *Othello* [J.F. Ducis' adaptation], *Temaşa*, Istanbul.

Belhaj, Nacer Abdelkader, 1981, *Quelques aspects du roman tunisien*, Tunis: Maison Tunisienne de L'Edition.

Bennigsen, A. and Lemercier-Quelquejay, Ch., 1964, *La Presse et le mouvement national chez les Musulmans de Russie avant 1920*, Paris.

Berkes, N., 1964, *The Development of Secularism in Turkey*, Montreal.

Bey, Âlî, 1871 (trans.), *Hikaye-i Hikemiye-i Mikromega* [Voltaire, *Micromégas*], Istanbul.

Bey, Mohammed El-Nagary, 1903, 1905, *Dictionnaire Français–Arabe*, 2 vols., Alexandria: Imprimerie Mizrahi

Bianchi, T. X. 1843, *Catalogue général des livres arabes, persans et turcs imprimés à Boulac en Égypte*, Paris.

Bin 'Ashur, Muhammad al-Fadil, 1972, *al-Haraka al-Adabiyya wa'l-Fikriyya fi Tunis*, Tunis: al-Dar al-Tunisiyya li'l Nashr.

Bin Shaykh, 'Abd al-Qadir, 1970, *Nasibi min al- Ufuq*, Tunis.

Black, C. E., 1967, *The Dynamics of Modernization*, New York.

Blaubstein, Rachel, 1972, *Shirat Rahel*, (23rd ed.), Tel-Aviv.

Bombaci, Alessio, 1968, *Histoire de la littérature turque.*

Browne, E. G., 1928, *A Literary History of Persia, IV Modern Times*, Cambridge.

— 1983 rpt., *The Press and Poetry in Modern Persia, IV Modern Times*, Cambridge. First published 1914.

Brugman, J., 1984, *An Introduction to the History of Modern Arabic Literature in Egypt*, Leiden: Brill.

Bullata, Issa J. (ed. & tr.), 1983, *Modern Arab Poets*, London: Heinemann.

228 Bibliography

Cachia, P. J., 1956, *Taha Husayn*, Luzac, London.

Cevdet, Dr. Abdullah, 1908a, (trans.), *Hamlet* [W. Shakespeare] Mısır: Kütüphane-i İçtihad.

— 1908b (trans.), *Jül Sezar* [W. Shakespeare, *Julius Caesar*] Mısır: Kütüphane-i İçtihad.

— 1909 (trans.), *Macbcth* [W. Shakespeare] Mısır: Kütüphane-i İçtihad.

— 1909–10 (trans.), *Romeo ve Juliet* [W. Shakespeare] Şehbal: Istanbul.

— 1912 (trans.), *Kral Lear*. [W. Shakespeare, *King Lear*] Istanbul.

Cheikho, L., 1900, 'Ta'rikh fann al-tiba'a' in *Mashriq* 3.

Cobban, H., 1984, *The Palestinian Liberation Organisation: People, Power and Politics*, Cambridge: C.U.P.

Coon, C. 1952, *Caravan*, London.

Cottam, R. W., 1979, *Nationalism in Iran: Updated through 1978, Pittsburgh:* Pittsburgh University Press.

— 1982, *Nationalism in Iran*, Pittsburgh, Pittsburgh University Press.

Dariyush, Parviz, 1962, 'Aday-i Dain beh Sadeq Hidayat', *Kayhan-i Mah*, September

Dast-i Ghaib, Abdul'ali, 1975, *Naqd-i Asar-i Sadeq Hidayat*, Tehran.

Davison, R. H., 1963, *Reform in the Ottoman Empire, 1856–1876*, Princeton.

Dawlat-Abadi, Yahya, 1950, *Hayat-i Yahya*, Tehran.

deLange, N., 1976, (trans.), *Touch the Water, Touch the Wind* [Amos Oz], Fontana.

Eisenstadt, S. N., 1966, *Modernization: Protest and Change*, Englewood Cliffs: New Jersey.

— 1973, *Tradition, Change and Modernity*, New York.

Emin, Ahmed, 1914, 'The Development of Modern Turkey as Measured by its Press,' in *Studies in History, Economics and Public Law*, No. 142 vol. 59 1–142, New York: Columbia University.

Enginün, İnci, 1979, *Tanzimat Devrinde Shakespeare Tercümeleri ve Tesiri*, Istanbul: İ.Ü. Edebiyat Fakültesi Yayınları.

Ercilasun, Bilge, 1981, *Servet-i Fünunda Edebi Tenkid*, Ankara: Kültür Bakanlığı Yayınları.

Even-Zohar, Itamar, 1978a, 'The Position of Translated Literature within the Literary Polysystem', *Papers in Historical Poetics*, Tel Aviv, Porter Institute for Poetics and Semiotics.

— 1978b, 'The Position of Translated Literature within the Literary Polysystem, in J. S. Holmes, J. Lambert and R. van den Broeck (eds.) *Literature and Translation: New Perspectives in Literary Studies*, Leuven.

— 1979, 'Polysystem Theories': *Poetics Today*, 1, Autumn, 287–310.

Evin, Ahmet O., 1983, *Origins and Development of the Turkish Novel*, Minneapolis: Bibliotheca Islamica.

Farruki, Sayyed Mehdi, 1967, *Khatirat-i Siyasi-yi Farrukh*, vol.1, Tehran.

Findley, Carter V., 1980, *Bureaucratic Reform in the Ottoman Empire*, Princeton.

Fraşeri, Naim, 1887 (trans.) *İlyada* [Homer, *Iliad*]., Karabet ve Kasbar Matbaası.

Furruki, Yazdi Muhammad, 1953, *Divan*, ed. H. Makki, Tehran.

Ghali, Mirit, 1953, *The Policy of Tomorrow*, Washington DC: American Council of Learned Societies.

Gibb, H. A. R., 1928–30, 'Studies in Contemporary Arabic Literature', *Bulletin of the School of Oriental Studies*, V. Pt. 3, 1–2.

Gibb, H. A. R. and Bowen ,H., 1950–7, *Islamic Society and the West*, (2 vols.) London.

Bibliography 229

Goldberg, Leah, 1970, 'Massa Lelo Shem' in *Yalkut Shirim*, Tel Aviv.

Greenberg, U. Z., 1924, *Eymah gdolah veyareah*

— 1939, *Jerusalem*, (trans.) by C. A. Cowen, New York.

Gregorian, V., 1969, *The Emergence of Modern Afghanistan*, Stanford.

Ha-Am, Ahad, 1950, *Kol Kitvei Ahad Ha-Am*, (2nd ed.) Tel-Aviv.

Hafez, Sabri, 1979, *The Rise and Development of the Egyptian Short Story, 1881–1970*, University of London PhD thesis.

— 1982, 'The State of the Contemporary Arabic Novel: Some Reflections', *The Literary Review Supplement: the Arab Cultural Scene*, London: Namara Press, 17–23.

Haikal, Muhammad Husain, 1951, *Mudhakkirat fi 'l-Siyasa al-Misriyya* (Arabic), Vol. I , Cairo: Maktabat al-Nahda al-Misriyya.

— 1953, Vol. II, Cairo: Matba‘a Misr.

al-Hakim, Tawfiq, 1974, *Hayati*, Beirut.

Halliday, F., and Alavi, H., 1988, *State and Ideology in the Middle East and Pakistan*, London: Macmillan.

Halman,Talât Sait, 1969, *Selected Poems of Fazıl Hüsnü Dağlarca*, Pittsburgh.

— 1982, *Contemporary Turkish Literature*, East Brunswick.

Halpern, M., 1965, *The Politics of Social Change in the Middle East and North Africa*, Princeton: Princeton University Press.

Hartmann, M., 1899, *The Arabic Press of Egypt*, London.

Hermans, Theo, 1985, 'Translation Studies and a New Paradigm', *The Manipulation of Literature: Studies in Literary Translation*, ed. Theo Hermans, London: Croom Helm.

Heyworth-Dunne, J., 1940, 'Printing and translation under Muhammad Ali', *Journal of the Royal Asiatic Society*, July.

Hidayat, Sadiq with 'Alavi, Buzurg and Partaw, Shirazpur, 1931, *Aniran*, Tehran.

Hikmet, Nâzim, 1963, *Jokond ile Si-Ya-U*, Ankara.

Hillmann, Michael, 1976, (ed.) *Major Voices in Contemporary Persian Literature*, Literature East and West, Vol. XX.

— 1982, *Iranian Society, An Anthology of Writings by Jalal Al-i Ahmad*, Lexington: Mazda.

— 1985. 'Sociology of The Iranian Writer', *Iranian Studies*, Spring – Autumn.

Hilmi, Selânikli, 1900 (trans.), *İlyas yahud şair-i şehir Omiros* [Homer, *Iliad*], Istanbul, Şirket-i Mürettibiye Matbaası.

Hoe, R., 1902, *A Short History of the Printing Press*, New York.

Holt, P. M., 1966, *Egypt and the Fertile Crescent, 1516–1922*, London.

Hourani, A., 1962, *Arabic Thought in the Liberal Age, 1798–1939*, London.

Husayn, Taha, 1920, *Suhuf Mukhtara min al-Shi‘r al-Tamthili ‘inda 'l Yunan*, Cairo: Hilal.

— 1937, *Hadith al-Arbi‘a'*, Cairo, al-Matba‘a 'l-Tijariyya 'l-Kubra.

Iraj, Jalal al-Mamalik, *Kulliyat-i Divan*, ed. K. Iraj, Tehran, Muzaffari, n.d.

Isaac, R. J., 1976, *Israel Divided: Ideological Politics in the Jewish State*, Baltimore: Johns Hopkins University Press.

Isaacs, G. A., 1931, *The Story of the Newspaper Printing Press*, London.

'Ishqi, Muhammad Reza, *Kulliyat*, ed. A. Salimi, Tehran, n.d.

Iskandari, Iraj, 1986, 'Hizb-i Tudeh va Ittahad-i Shawravi', *Fasli dar Gul-i Surkh*, New Series, no.3, Autumn.

Issawi, C., 1982, *An Economic History of the Near and Middle East and North Africa*, London.

230 Bibliography

al-Jabri, Muhammad Salih, 1978, *Dirasat fi'l-Adab al-Tunisi*, Tunis, al-Dar al-'Arabiyya li'l-Kitab.

al-Jayyusi, S. K., 1976, *Trends and Movements in Modern Arabic Poetry*, Leiden: Brill.

Jerrold, B. (ed.), 1979, *Egypt under Ismail Pasha*, London.

Johnson-Davies, Denys (tr.) 1967, *Modern Arabic Short Stories*, London, O.U.P.

— 1987, *Arabic Short Stories*, London, Quartet Books.

Jones, Robert, 1986, 'Arabic Publications of the Medici Oriental Press, 1584–1614,' paper presented to the BRISMES/MESA International Conference, July 9.

Jones-Brydges, H. 1834, *His Majesty's Mission to Persia*, London.

Kamshad, Hasan, 1966, *Modern Persian Prose Literature*, Cambridge: C.U.P.

Kannun, 'Abdullah n.d.,, *Ahadith fi'l-Adab al-Maghribi'l-Hadith* Cairo: Dar al-Ra'id li'l-Tiba'a.

Kartun-Blum, R., 1969, *From Tyre to Jerusalem*, Berkeley and Los Angeles.

Kasab, Teodor, 1871 (trans.), *Monte Kristo* [A. Dumas Père, *Le Comte de Monte Cristo*], Istanbul: Ahmed Midhat Matbaası.

Kasravi, Sayyed Ahmad, 1967, *Tarikh-i Mashrutah-yi Iran*, Tehran, Amir Kabir.

Kassem, Ceza and Hashem, Malek (eds), 1985, *Flights of Fancy*, Cairo, Elias Modern Publishing House.

Katira'i, Mahmud, 1970, *Kitab-i Sadeq Hidayat*, ed. M. Katira'i, Tehran, Ashrafi. (This book was banned from publication and has not been publicly available.)

Katouzian, Homa, 1977, 'Sadeq Hidayat's "The Man Who Killed His Passionate Self"', *Iranian Studies*.

— 1979, 'Nationalist Trends in Iran, 1921–1926', *I.J.M.E.S.*

— 1981a, *Khatirat-i Siyasi-yi Khalil Maleki*, Tehran: Ravaq.

— 1981b, *The Political Economy of Iran*, London: Macmillan.

— 1982, 'The Aridisolatic Society, A Model of Long-Term Social and Economic Development', *I.J.M.E.S.*

Kâmil, Paşa Yusuf, 1862 (trans.), *Terceme-i Telemak* [F. Fénelon, *Les Aventures de Télémaque*], Istanbul, Tabhane-i Âmire.

Keddie, N., 1962, 'Religion and Irreligion in Early Iranian Nationalism', *Comparative Studies in Society and History.*, Vol. 4, no. 3, 265–95.

— 1972, *Sayyed Jamal al-Din 'al-Afghani'*, Berkeley.

— 1981, *Roots of Revolution, An Interpretive History of Modern Iran*, Yale University Press.

Kemal, Yahya, 1963, *Kendi Gök Kubbemiz*, Istanbul.

Kerman, Zeynep, 1978, *1862–1910 Yılları Arasında Victor Hugo'dan Türkçe'ye Yapılan Tercümeler Üzerinde bir Araştırma*, Istanbul: İ. Ü. Edebiyat Fakültesi Yayınları.

Khameh'i, Anvar, 1982, *Panjah Nafar va Seh Nafar*, Tehran, Intisharat-i Hafteh.

— 1983, *Fursat-i Buzurg-i az Dast Rafteh*, Tehran, Intisharat-i Hafteh.

— 1984, *Az Inshiab ta Kudita*, Tehran, Intisharat-i Hafteh.

Khanlary, Parviz, 1947, 'Nasr-i Farsi Dar Dowreh-yi Akhir', *The First Congress of Iranian Writers*, Tehran.

al-Kharrat, E., 1984, ''Ala Sabil al-Taqdim', *al-Karmal* (14), Nicosia, Cyprus, 5–14.

Khemiri, Taher and Kampffmeyer, Georg, (2nd ed.) 1975, *Leaders in Contemporary Arabic Literature*, Pt. 1, (Leipzig, 1930), translating from *al-Ghirbal*, 127.

Bibliography 231

Khvajeh-Nuri, 1942, 1943, *Bazigaran-i Asr-i Tala'i*, Tehran.

Kilpatrick, H., 1974, *The Modern Egyptian Novel*, London: Ithaca Press.

Kitabevi, Ahmet Halit, 1943, (trans.), *The Shirt of Fire* [Halide Edip, *Ateşten Gömlek*], Istanbul.

Kitabevi, Remzi, 1945, (trans.), *The Stranger* [Yakup Kadri], Istanbul.

Klausner, I., 1950, *Historiah shel ha-sifrut ha-'ivrit ha hadashah*, Jerusalem.

Kohansky, M., 1974, *hateatron haivri*, Jerusalem.

Kritz, R., 1978, *hasiporet shelidor hamaavak leatzmaut*, Tel Aviv, vol. 1.

Kudret, Cevdet, 1979 (1965), *Türk Edebiyatında Hikâye ve Roman*, I, Istanbul, Varlık Yayınları.

Kurzweil, B., 1958, *sifruteynu hahadashah – hemshekh o mahapekhah*, Jerusalem.

Kut, A. Turgut, 1985, 'Ermeni Harfli Türkçe Telif ve Tercüme Romanlar: I-Victor Hugo'nun Mağadurîn Hikâyesinin Basılmış Nüshası' in the proceedings of *Beşinci Milletler Arası Türkoloji Kongresi*, Istanbul, 23–28 Eylül 1985.

Lambert, José and van Gorp, Hendrik, 1985, 'On Describing Translations', *Manipulation of Literature: Studies in Literary Translation*, ed. Theo Hermans, London: Croom Helm.

Lemon, L. T. and Reis, M. J., (eds.), 1965, *Russian Formalist Criticism*, Nebraska.

Levy, M. J., 1966, *Modernization and the Structure of Societies*, Princeton.

Lewis, B. 1962, *The Emergence of Modern Turkey*, London: O.U.P.

— 1964, *The Middle East and the West*, Bloomington: Indiana U.P.

— 1973, *Islam in History*, London: Alcove Press.

Lhimdani, Hamid, 1985, *al-Riwaya al-Maghribiyya wa Ru'ya al-Waqi' al-Ijtima'i* Casablanca, Dar al-Thaqafa.

Lucas, N., 1973 (1974), *The Modern History of Israel*, London: Weidenfeld and Nicholson, 109.

Machalski, F, 1965, *La Littérature de l'Iran contemporain*, Warsaw.

al-Madani, 'Izz al Din, 1967–71, *al-Insan al-Sifr*, Tunis.

— 1972, *al-Adab al Tajribi*, Tunis.

al-Madini, Ahmed, 1975, *al-Qissa al-Tunisiyya: Nash'atuha wa Ruwwaduha*, Tunis: Dar b. 'Abdallah.

— 1982, *Fann al-Qissa al-Qasira bi'l-Maghrib: al-Nash'a, al-Tatawwur, wa'l-Ittijahat*, Beirut: Dar al-'Awda.

— 1985 Fi'l-Adab al-Maghribi 'l-Mu'asir, Casablanca: Dar al-Nashr al-Maghribiyya.

Makki, Husain, 1946, *Tarikh-i Bist Saleh-yi Iran*, 3 vols., Tehran.

Maleki, Khalil, 1953, 'Yadi Az Sadiq Hidayat', *Niruy-i Sevvum*, 6 April (unsigned).

Mardin, S., 1962, *The Genesis of Young Ottoman Thought*, Princeton.

Marshall, J. E., 1928, *The Egyptian Enigma, 1890–1928*, London.

Marsigli, L. F., 1732, *L'Etat militaire de l'empire ottoman*, La Haye and Amsterdam.

Mayer, A. E., 1978, 'Abbas Hilmi II: The Khedive and Egypt's Struggle for Independence,' 2 vols., Ph.D., Michigan.

McMurtrie, D. C., 1943, *The Book*, New York.

Megged, A., 1962, *Fortunes of a Fool*, transl. by A. Hodes, London.

Meisels, Samuel, 1922, *Deutsche Klassiker im Ghetto*, Vienna.

Mellini, P., 1977, *Sir Eldon Gorst*, Stanford.

Menemencioğlu, Nermin (ed.), 1978, 'Modern Turkish Poetry 1850–1975', *The Penguin Book of Turkish Verse*, Penguin.

Midhat, Ahmed and Tevfik, Ebuzziya, 1877 (trans.), *Üç Yüzlü Bir Karı* [P. de Kock, *La Fille aux trois jupons*], Istanbul, Mihran Matbaası.

232 Bibliography

— 1879 (trans.), *La Dam o Kamelya* [A. Dumas Fils, *La Dame aux Camélias*], Istanbul.

— 1881 (trans.), *Derebeyleri* [V. Hugo, *Les Burgraves*], Istanbul, Mahmudbey Matbaası.

— 1886 (trans.), *Hüsrevname* [Xenophon, *Cyropaedia*], Istanbul.

— 1891 (trans.), *Udolf Hisarı* [A. Radcliffe, *The Mysteries of Udolpho*] , Istanbul.

Mintz, R. F., 1966, *Modern Hebrew Poetry*, Los Angeles.

Miron, D. 1962, *arba panim basifrut haivrit bat yamenu*, Jerusalem and Tel Aviv.

Mirza, Iraj, n.d., *Kulliyat-i Divan-i Iraj Mirza*, Tehran.

Moosa, Matti I., 1970 'Early 19th century Printing and Translation, ' *Islamic Quarterly*, Oct–Dec. XIV, 4, 207–9.

— 1983, *The Origins of Modern Arabic Fiction*, Washington DC, Three Continents Press.

Moreh, S., 1976, *Modern Arabic Poetry 1800–1970*, Leiden: Brill.

Mumby, F., 1949, *Publishing and Booksellers*, Oxford.

Musaddiq, Muhammad, 1986, *Khatirat va Ta'allumat-i Duktur Muhammad Musaddiq*, Tehran.

Mustawfi, 'Abdullah, 1945, *Sharh-i Zindigani-i Man*, vol. 4, Tehran.

Münif, Paşa, 1859 (trans.), *Muhaverat-ı Hikemiye*. ['Philosophical Dialogues' from Fénelon, Fontenelle and Voltaire], Istanbul, Ceridehane Matbaası.

— 1862 (trans.), *Mağdurîn Hikâyesi* [V. Hugo, *Les Misérables*] Istanbul, *Ruznâme-i Ceride-i Havadis*, Nos. 480–503.

Najm, Muhammad Yusuf, 1961, *al-Qissa fi-'l-Adab al-'Arabi'l-Hadith*, Beirut.

Nashat, G., 1982, *The Origins of Modern Reform in Iran, 1870–80*, Urbana, Illinois.

Nazim al-Islam, Kermani, 1983, *Tarikh-i Bidari-yi Iraniyan*, 2 vols., ed. A. Sa'idi-Sirjani, Tehran: Agah-Nuvin.

Ostle, R. C. (ed.), 1975, *Studies in Modern Arabic Literature*, Warminster, Aris and Phillips.

Owen, R. 1981, *The Near and Middle East in the World Economy, 1800–1914*, London.

Özön, Mustafa Nihat, 1941, *Son Asır Türk Edebiyatı Tarihi*, Istanbul, Maarif Matbaası.

— 1946, 'Batı Dillerinden Şiir Tercümeleri,' *Tercüme*, 6, 16 Mart.

— 1966, 'Türk Tiyatrosuna Toplu Bir Bakış', *Türk Dili*, No. 178, Temmuz 1966: 656–73.

— 1985 (1936), *Türkçede Roman*. (Baskıya Hazırlayan: Alpay Kabacalı), Istanbul: İletişim Yayınları.

Paker, Saliha, 1986, 'Translated European Literature in the Late Ottoman Literary Polysystem', *New Comparison*, 1 (Summer 1986), Paris.

Parry, V. J. and Yapp, M. E. (eds.), 1975, *War, Technology and Society in the Near and Middle East*, London.

Patterson, D., 1961, *The Foundation of Modern Hebrew Literature*, London.

— 1964a, *Abraham Mapu*, London.

— 1964b, *The Hebrew Novel in Czarist Russia*, Edinburgh.

Paxton, E. H., 1981, *al-Ayyam*, I, by Taha Husayn, tr. as *An Egyptian Childhood*, London, Heinemann.

Pérès, Henri, 1937, 'Le Roman, le Conte et la Nouvelle dans la Littérature Arabe Moderne, *Annales de l'Institut d'Études Orientales*, tome III, 1937, 266–337.

Polk, W. R. and Chambers, R. L. (eds.) 1968 *The Beginnings of Modernization in the Near and Middle East*, Chicago.

Bibliography 233

Rabinowitz, A. S., 1887, *Al ha-Pereq*, Warsaw.

Raffat, Donne, 1985, *The Prison Papers of Bozorg 'Alavi*, Syracuse: Syracuse University Press.

Raji', 'Abdullah, 1987, *al-Qasida al-Maghribiyya al-Mu'asira: Binya al-Shahada wa'l-Istishhad*, Casablanca: Manshurat 'Uyun.

Rakibi, 'Abdullah, 1968, *al-Qissa al-Qasira fi'l-Adab al-Jaza'iri al-Mu'asir*, Cairo: Dar al-Kitab al-'Arabi li'l-Tiba'a wa'l-Nashr.

Ramitsh, Yusuf, 1980, *Usrat al-Muwaylihi wa Atharuha fi'l-Adab al-'Arabi*, Cairo: Ma'arif.

Ramsaur, E., 1957, *The Young Turks*, Princeton.

Recaizade, Ekrem, 1872 (trans.) *Atala yahud Amerika Vahşileri* [Chateaubriand, *Atala*], Istanbul: Terakki Matbaası.

— 1874 (trans.), *Meprizon Tercümesi (Mahbeslerim)* [S. Pellico, *Le mei prigioni*], Istanbul: Matabaa-i Tasvir-i Efkâr.

Robinson, Richard D., 1963, *The First Turkish Republic*, Cambridge: Harvard University Press.

Rudolph, S. H., 1967, *The Modernity of Tradition*, Chicago.

Rypka, Jan, 1968, *History of Iranian Literature*, Dordrecht.

Sabry, M., 1924, *La genèse de l'esprit national égyptien, 1863–1882*, Paris.

Sa'dallah, Abu'l-Qasim, 1966, *Dirasat fi'l-Adab al-Jaza'iri al-Hadith*, Beirut: Dar al-Adab.

Saedi, Gholamhosain, 1985, 'Sociology of the Iranian Writer', *Iranian Studies*, Spring–Autumn.

— 1986, 'Buzurq-i 'Alavi, Zindeh-yi Bidar', *Alifba*, Autumn (posthumous).

Salibi, K. S., 1955, *The Modern History of Lebanon*, London.

Sâmi, Semsettin, 1879 (trans.), *Sefiller* [V. Hugo, *Les Misérables*], Istanbul, Mihran Matbaasi.

— 1885 (trans.), *Robenson* [D. Defoe, *Robinson Crusoe*], Istanbul.

Sâmi Şemsettin and Bedreddin, Hasan, 1934 (trans.), *Sefiller*, Istanbul, Cihan Kütüphanesi.

Schinasi, M., 1979, *Afghanistan at the Beginning of the Twentieth Century*, Naples.

Schölch, A., 1981, *Egypt for the Egyptians*, London.

Sevük, Ismail Habib, 1944, *Tanzimattanberi*, I, Istanbul, Remzi Kitabevi.

Seyfettin, Ömer, 1918, *İlyad/Iliade* [Homer, Iliad], *Yeni Mecmua*, nos. 45–57.

— 1970, *Bütün Eserleri*, Ankara, IV, 96–125. al-Shabbi, Abu'l-Qasim, 1966, *Aghani al-Hayat*, Tunis.

Shaked, G., 1983, *hasiporet haivrit, 1880–1980*, Vol. 2, Tel Aviv.

Shavit, Zohar, 1982, *hahayim hasifrutiyim beeretz y israel, 1910–1913*, Tel Aviv.

Shaw, S. J. and E. K., 1977, *History of the Ottoman Empire and Modern Turkey*, Cambridge.

Shaw, S. J. 1971, *Between Old and New*, Cambridge, Mass.

al-Shayyal, Jamal al-Din, 1950, *Tarikh al-Tarjama fi Misr fi 'Ahd al-Hamla al-Faransiyya*, Cairo: Dar al-Fikr al-'Arabi.

— 1951, *Tarikh al-Tarjama wa Harakat al Thaqafa fi 'Asr Muhammad 'Ali*, Cairo.

Shimoni, D., 1962 *Sefer ha-Idilyot*, Israel.

Shukri, 'Abd al-Rahman, 1960, *Diwan*, Alexandria.

Siyavuşgil, Sabri Esat, 1953, *L'Âme turque à travers les nouvelles*, Istanbul.

Somekh, S., 1973, *The Changing Rhythm*, Leiden: Brill.

Somekh, Sasson, 1981, 'The Emergence of Two Sets of Stylistic Norms in the Early Literary Translation into Modern Arabic Prose', *Poetics Today*, 2, No. 4: 193–200.

234 Bibliography

al-Sulami, Ibrahim, 1974, *al-Shi'r al-Watani al-Maghribi fi 'Asr al-Himaya 1912–1956,* Casablanca: Dar al-Thaqafi.

al-Sulh, 'Imad, 1980, *Ahmad Faris al-Shidyaq: Atharuh wa 'Asruh,* Beirut: al-Nahar.

Szyliowicz, J. S., 1973, *Education and Modernization in the Near and Middle East,* Ithaca.

Sıddık, Emin, 1870 (trans.), *Pol ve Virjini* [B. de Saint-Pierre, *Paul et Virginie*].

Şinasi, İbrahim, 1859 (trans.), *Tercüme-i Manzume (Fransız Lisanından Nazmen Tercüme Eylediğim Bazı Eş'ar)* [Translations of Verse from Gilbert, La Fontaine, Lamartine, Racine], Istanbul, Presse d'Orient.

Sırrı, Hasan, 1884 (trans.), *Venedik Taciri* [W. Shakespeare, *The Merchant of Venice*], Istanbul.

— 1887, (trans.), *Sehv-i Mudhik* [W. Shakespeare, *The Comedy of Errors*], Konstantiniyye.

Swanson, G. W., 1975, 'War, technology and society in the Ottoman Empire from the reign of Abdulhamid II to 1913: Mahmud Sevket and the German Mission' in V. J. Parry and M. E. Yapp (eds.) *War, Technology and Society in the Near and Middle East,* London.

Tajir, Jak [c.1945] *Harakat al-Tarjama bi Misr khilal al Qarn al-Tasi' 'Ashar,* Cairo: Ma'arif.

Taner, Haldun, 1983, *Bütün Hikâyeleri,* Ankara, IV, 133–46.

Tanpınar, Ahmet Hamdi, 1982 (1956), *19. Asır Turk Edibiyat Tarihi,* Istanbul, Çağlayan Kitabevi.

Tansel, Fevziye Abdullah, 1946, 'Garp Dillerinden Manzum Tercüme' *Tercüme,* 6, 16 Mart 1946: 464–75.

Tibawi, A. L., 1966, *American Interests in Syria, 1800–1901,* London.

— 1969, *A Modern History of Syria,* London.

Tignor, R. 1966, *Modernization and British Colonial Rule in Egypt, 1882–1914,* Princeton.

Toury, Gideon, 1980, *In Search of a Theory of Translation.* Tel-Aviv.

— 1985, 'A Rationale for Descriptive Translation', *Manipulation of Literature: Studies in Literary Translation.* Ed. Theo Hermans, London: Croom Helm.

Ubicini, L. 1853, *Lettres sur la Turquie,* 2 vols. Paris,

UNESCO 1966, *History of Mankind, Vol. VI, The Twentieth Century,* 2 vols., UNESCO.

Uşaklıgil, Halid Ziya, 1969, *Kırk Yıl,* Istanbul, İnkılap ve Aka Kitabevleri.

Uyguner, Muzaffer, 1967, *Orhan Veli Kanık,* Istanbul.

Vambery, A., 1906, *Western Culture in Eastern Lands,* New York.

Van Dyck, E. A., 1896, *Iktifa al-qunu',* Cairo.

Van Nieuwenhuijze, C.A.O., 1965, *Social Stratification and the Middle East,* Leiden.

Vatikiotis, P. J., 1969, *The Modern History of Egypt,* London.

Vefik Paşa, Ahmed, 1871 (trans.), *Hikaye-i Feylesofiyye-i Mikromega* [Voltaire, *Micromégas*], Istanbul.

— 1881 (trans.), *Terceme-i Telemak* [F.Fénelon, *Les Aventures de Télémaque*], Ahter Matbaası.

— 1933, *Molière – Ahmed Vefik Paşa Külliyatı. I-IV,* Istanbul: Kanaat Kütüphanesi.

Veli, Orhan, 1973, *Bütün Şiirleri,* Istanbul.

Von Grunebaum, G. E. (ed.), 1973, *Arabic Poetry, Theory and Development,* Wiesbaden.

Ward, R. E. and Rustow, D. R. (eds.) 1964, *Political Modernization in Japan and Turkey,* Princeton.

Bibliography 235

Waterbury, J., 1983, *The Egypt of Nasser and Sadat*, Princeton, Princeton University Press.

Welch, A. and Cachia, P. (eds.), 1979, *The Assumptions and Aspirations of Egyptian Modernists in Islam: Past Influence and Present Challenge*, Edinburgh University Press.

Williams, Raymond, 1961, *The Long Revolution*, London: Chatto and Windus.

Wizara al-Shu'un al-Thaqafiyya, 1985, *Mukhtarat min al-Adab al-Tunisi al-Mu'asir*, Tunis, al-Dar al-Tunisiyya li'l Nashr, Vols. I and II.

Yalkut Shirim, 1970, 'A Pack of Poems', Tel-Aviv.

Yapp, M.E., 1987, *The Making of the Modern Near East, 1792–1923*, London .

Yardeni, G. (ed.), 1967, *Sal Ha-'Anavim*, Jerusalem.

Yudkin, L. I, 1971, *Isaac Lamdan: A Study in Twentieth Century Hebrew Poetry*, London.

— 1974, *Escape into Siege: A Survey of Israeli Literature Today*, London.

— 1982, *Jewish Writing and Identity in the Twentieth Century*, London.

— 1984, *1948 and After: Aspects of Israeli Fiction*.

— 1985, 'The Pain of Transition' in G. Abramson and T. Parfitt (eds.), *The Great Transition*, New York.

— 1986, 'Looking back with Longing in Hebrew Fiction', *World Literature Today*, Oklahoma, Spring.

— 1986–7, 'On Moses Mendelssohn', *Jewish Quarterly*, Winter.

Zahlawi, Habib, 1949, 'Kitaban wa Katiban,' *al-Risala*, 28 March, XVII, 821, 379–81.

Zaydan, Jurji, 1900, 'Kuttab Urubba wa Kuttab al-Sharq' *al-Hilal*, VIII, 8, 15 Jan, 230.

Index

al-'Aal, Mahmud 'Awad 'Abd 190
Abasıyanık, Sait Faik 97
'Abbas Hilmi II 12, 13
'Abbas Mirza 8
'Abbasi, Muhammad 131
'Abbud, Marun 36
'Abd al-Halim, Prince 12
'Abd ül-Hamid II 7, 11, 28
'Abdalla, 'Abd al-Halim 182
'Abdulla, Yahya al-Tahir 191
'Abduh, Muhammad 37, 39, 196
'Abdul-Hai, Muhammad 38
al-Abnudi, 'Abd al-Rahman 188
Abramowitsch, Shalom Ya'akov, see
Mendele
Abramson, Glenda 63, 70
absolutism 79, 86, 132, 151, 185–6
Acts of the Apostles, tr. 39
adaptation, age of (1850-1914) 1–75
Adunis ('Ali Ahmad Sa'id) 188:
Qasa'id Ula 183
al-Afghani, Jamal al-Din 12, 197
Africa, North 115, 168–9, 193–212
Ağaoğlu, Adalet 178
Agnon, S.Y. 74, 120, 214, 215–16
Agop Efendi 26
Ahali group 87
Akhavan-i Salis, Mehdi 143, 149–50, 155
Akhundzadah, Mirza Fath-'Ali 49,
55–7, 61, 156
Akünal, Dundar 22
Al-i Ahmad, Jalal 143, 147–48, 153,
155, 156: *Az Ranji Keh Mibarim*
147, 155; *Bach-che-yi Mardum*
147–8; *Basij-i Mellat* 147; *Did u
Bazdid* 147; *Seh-tar* 147

Alangu, Tahir 90
'Alavi, Buzurg 136, 143, 144–5, 151;
Chamidan 137; *Chishmhayash* 145;
Div, Div 137; *Gileh Mard* 145, 155;
Nameh-ha 145; *Panjah-u-seh Nafar*
144; *Varaq-Pareh-ha-yi Zindan*
144–5, 154–5
'Alawis 83, 161, 166
Algeria 168, 194, 208–12
Ali, Sabahattin; Kagni 96
'Ali Yusuf, Shaykh 12, 106
'al-Alim, Mahmud Amin 184
aliyah, third (1919–24) 216, 217, 219
'Allam, 'Abbas 41
'Allu, Muhammad Ibrahim Abu 207
American Presbyterian Mission,
Lebanon 36
Amichai 217
Amiri, Adib al-Mamalik 59
Anacreon 75
Anatolia 5, 80, 94–5
Anday, Melih Cevdet 172, 176
Anglican Church Missionary Society,
Malta 36
Anglo-Persian Agreement (1919) 133
Anis, 'Abd al'Azim 184
Apaydın, Talip 177
Apollo poets 108
Appelfeld, A. 221
'Aql, Sa'id 184
al-'Aqqad, 'Abbas Mahmud 38, 107,
110
Arab world 33–44, 104–15
Arab–Israeli war (1967) 115, 161, 166
Arab–Israeli war (1973) 161, 166
'Arabi, Ibn 187, 192

Arabic language 35, 39, 184–5, 189, 201, 204
Arabic literature 104–15, 180–92, 193–212
Arabization 37, 40–1
Aramaic 65, 126, 214
'Arif, Abu'l-Qasim 133, 136
Arif, Ahmed 176: *Hasretinden Prangalar Eskittim* 175
Armenian script 31–2
Armenians 8, 12, 25–6, 80
articles (al-maqala), Tunisian 201
Aruz (syllabic verse) 20, 28
Aryanism 139, 152
Aryanpur, Yahya 47–48, 50, 51, 52–3, 55, 59, 62, 157
Asiatic mode of production 178
Aslan, Ibrahim: *Buhairat al-Masa'* 191
Association of Algerian Ulama 208
Aswat 189
Atatürk, Kemal (Mustafa Kemal) 12, 80, 81, 82, 86, 88, 95, 163
Atay, Cahit 179
Atay, Oğuz: *Oyunlarla Yasayanlar* 179; *Tutunamayanlar* 178
Auden, W.H. 170
Averroes 43
Avicenna 43
'Awad, Lewis 180: *Mozzakerat Taleb Ba'asa* 184: *Plutoland and Other Poems* 188
Ayhan, Ece 172, 172–3: *Devlet ve Tabiat* 174–5: *Kınar Hanımın Denizleri* 174: 'Master's Work' 175
al-'Ayyadi, Samir 204
Azari Turkish 49, 55–6
Azerbaijan 3, 136, 163

Babiâlî Tercüme Odası (Translation Chamber) 19
Bacher (or Bacherach), Simon 69–70
Badawi, M. M. 42, 107, 112
Badi, Hasan-i: *Dastan-i Bastan* 53
Bahar, Muhammad Taqi 131, 133, 148–9, 155, 156: *Karnameh-yi Zindan* 139
al-Bahrawi, Sayyid 184
Baihaqi: *Tarikh* 130
al-Bakkar, Tawfiq 201
Ballas, Shimon 40, 42

Barash, A. 120
al-Barudi, Mahmud Sami 106
al-Bashir 181, 186
Basil 12
Baykurt, Fakir 177
al-Bayyati, 'Abd al-Wahhab 188
Bedreddin, Hasan 23, 27
Behramoğlu, Ataol 176, 177
Behruz, Zabih 136
Ben Yehudah, Eliezer 67
Ben-Ner, Yitzhak 223
Bentham, Jeremy 38
Berfe, Süreyya 175, 176
Berk, İlhan 176
Berkowitz, M. 69
Berköz, Egemen 176
Bey, Âlî 26
Bey, Mohammed El-Nagary 42
Bialik, Chaim Nachman 65, 74, 117, 122, 125, 215, 219: *Aharey moti* 222; *al saf bet hamidrash* 224
Bianchi, T. X. 8
Bible, translations of 36, 39, 64
Bidi, Muhammad 207
Bikkurei ha-'Ittim 68
Bilium 67
Bin Shaykh, 'Abd al-Qadir: *Nasibi min al-Ufuq* 203
Binnani, Muhammad 205
Blaubstein, Rachel 123
booksellers 11
Boudhiba, Idris: *Huna Yabar 'im al-Rafd* 210
bourgeoisie, Egyptian 104
Bourguiba, Habib 168
Brainin, R. 69
Braudes, Reuben Asher 72, 116
Brenner, Y.H. 73, 117, 120, 127, 216, 217
Brill, Joseph 69
Britain 80, 81, 133, 162
British influence 5, 13, 37, 71
Browne, E.G. 9, 12, 15, 45, 47, 48, 55, 56, 58, 131
Brugman, J. 33
Bulaq press, Cairo 8
Bunyan, John, *Pilgrim's Progress* 71
Burak, Sevim 178: *Sahibinin Sesi* 179
al-Bustani, Butrus 36
al-Bustani, Sulayman 38

238 *Index*

Byron, Lord George Gordon 38:
  Hebrew Melodies 69

Cachia, Pierre 33–44
Çağan, Sermet: *Ayak Bacak Fabrikası*
  179
Camp David Agreements 161, 166, 186
Canaanism 217
Cansever, Edip 172: 'The Gravitational
  Carnation' 174
Çapan, Cevat 170–8
Cemiyet-i İlmiye Osmaniye (Ottoman
  Scientific Society) 19
censorship 11–12, 27, 28, 29, 30, 163
Ceride-i Havadis 19, 22
Cervantes, Miguel de 24
Cevdet, Abdullah 28
Cevdet, Melih 101
Chateaubriand, François René 48:
  Atala 22
Chiang Kai-Shek 133
Christians 5, 6, 35, 36; *see also* Syrian
  Christians
Chubak, Sadiq 147, 148, 153, 156:
  'Adl 148; *Antari Keh Lutish
  Murdeh Bud* 148; Khaimeh Shab
  Bazi 148
Churchill, William 19–20
Çilingirian, Kirkor 31
Confederation of Reformist Workers'
  Union, Turkey 171
Coptic factions 12
criticism, literary: Arab 183–4; French
  194; Moroccan 206–7; Turkish 30
Cromer, Evelyn Baring, 1st Earl of 12
Cumalı, Necati 176, 177
Cumberland, Richard, *The Jew* 69

Dağlarca, Fazıl Hüsnü 102–3, 172–3,
  176: *Çakırın Destanı* 102–3;
  Sehitlerle Ölüler 103; *Toprak Ana*
  103; *Üç Şehitler Destanı* 103
Dar al-Funun 7, 11, 46, 47, 54
dar al-'ulum 104
al-Dar al-Tunisiyya li'l-Nashr 200
Darwin, Charles: *Origin of Species* 14
Darwish, Mahmud 188
Dastgirdi, Vahid 133
Daudet, A. 29
Dawlatabadi, Yahya 59

de-Lange, N. 121
Defoe, Daniel: *Robinson Crusoe* 36,
  47, 71
Dehkhuda, 'Ali-Akbar 131
Demirel administration, Turkey 171
Democrat Party, Turkey 171
Demolins, Edmond, *À quoi tient la
  supériorité de Anglo-Saxons?* 13, 38
Destour Socialist Party, Tunisia 169,
  204
al-Dib, Badr 181, 186
Dickens, Charles 74
Dilmen, Güngör 179
Disraeli, Benjamin: *David Alroy* 69
Divan poetry 18, 21, 100
Diwan school 38
Diyojen 22–3
Doyle, Sir Arthur Conan: Sherlock
  Holmes novels 47
drama: Arabic, 37, 112–3; Iranian 54–7;
  Israeli 220–2; and modernization 15;
  Turkish 25–9, 56, 178–9
Druzes 83
al-Du'aji, 'Ali: *Jawla hawla Hanat al-
  Bahr al-Mutawassit* 202
Dubois, Jacques 194
Ducis, Jean François 27
Dumas fils, Alexandre; *La Dame aux
  Camélias* 24
Dumas père, Alexandre 43, 47, 53: *Le
  Comte de Monte Cristo* 22
Dunqal, Amal 188
Durbaş, Refik 176
Duruel, Nursel 178

economics 4, 84–5
Edip, Halide: *Ateşten Gömlek* 91–4
education 6–7, 84–5, 104
education, military 10–11
Egypt 5, 12, 13, 80–1, 86, 88, 104, 114,
  161, 162, 165–7, 180–3, 185–6:
  Bonaparte's expedition to (1798) 33;
  Israeli peace treaty 161, 166, 186
Egyptian University 104
Egyptianization 40–1
Ekrem, Recaizade 23
Eliot, George (Mary Ann Evans):
  Daniel Deronda 69
élites: Arab 33, 34, 84, 85; Ottoman 14,
  80, 81

Eloğlu, Metin: *Düdüklü Tencere* 172
Emin, Ahmed 8, 10
Encümen-i Daniş (Academy) 19
Enginün, İnci 26, 27, 28
English Romantics 38
Eray, Nazlı 178
Erbil, Leyla 178
Ercilasun, Bilge 30
Eretz Yisrael 66, 117–25
Escarpit, Robert 194
Esendal, Memduh Şevket 97
essay, and modernization 15
Europe, Eastern, Jews of 65–6, 117, 213–14
European Community, Turkey membership proposed 163, 171
Europeanism 88, 136, 151, 154
Even-Zohar, Itamar 17–18, 22, 24, 28, 30
Evin, Ahmet 25
Evren, General 171

F.L.N., *see* National Liberation Front
Fahmi, Ibrahim 192
al-Fajr 112
Farahani, Qa'im Maqam 60
Farhang 48
Farman, Gha'ib Tu'ma: *Hasid al-Raha* 182
Farrukhi Yazdi 132, 134, 137
al-Farsi, Mustafa 203
Fathi, Ibrahim 184
Fawzi, Husayn 180
Fénelon: *Les Aventures de Télémaque* 21, 36, 47, 52
Fertile Crescent 161, 167
Fikret, Tevfik 28
Firdawsi: *Shanamah* 49, 58
Fontenelle, Bernard 21
France, 13, 81, 162
Frankl, Ludwig August; *Rachel* 69
Fraşeri, Naim 29
freemasonry 36
French, Maghribi literature in 194–5
French influence 18, 33, 36, 79, 168
Friedrich, Berta 72
Friends of the People, The 176
Furughi, Mirza Muhammad Husayn Zaka' al-Mulk 48
Füruzan 178

Fusul 181
Future, The 176

Galatasaray 7
Gallery 68, 181, 186
Gandhi, Mohandas Karamchand 133
Ganjinah-i Funun 48
Garmadi, Salih 204
al-Gawad, Khayri 'Abd 192
Gedikpaşa Tiyatroyi Osmanî 26, 27
Genlis, Madame S. F. de 69
genres, and ideology 99, 194, 198–200
Germany, 13, 29, 63–4, 133, 213
Gessner, Salomon 68
Ghallab, 'Abd al-Karim 207
Ghamuqat, Isma'il; *al-Shams Tushriq 'ala'-Jami'* 211
Ghanim, Fathi 181
al-Ghazali 43
al-Ghitani, Gamal 191–2
Ghurab, Amin Yusuf 182
Gibb, H. A. R. 40
Gilbert, Nicholas-Joseph-Laurent 20
Gilgamesh, Epic of 75
Goethe, Johann Wolfgang von 75: *Faust* 70
Goldberg, Leah 123: *Sheerit hahayim* 222
Goldmann, Lucien 194
Gordon, S. L. 69
Gordon, Y. L. (Yalag) 69
Gorgi, Nabil Na'um 192
Gorst, Sir Eldon 12
Gottlober, A. B. 69
Greek influence 8, 13, 33
Greenberg, U. Z. 123, 215, 216: *Le-Margelotayikh Yerishalayim* 120
Gronich, W. 71
Grosman, David: *Ayen erekh ahavah* 223; *Hiyukh hagdi* 223–4
Gubair, 'Abdu 191, 192
Güntekin, Reşat Nuri 97

Ha-Am, Ahad 65, 74, 117: 'Truth from *Eretz Yisrael'* 119
Ha-Maggid 66
Ha-Meassef 63, 68, 70, 213
Habibi, Emile 192
Habl al-Matin 10
Haddad, Qasim 188

240 *Index*

Hadiqat al-Akhbar 37
Hafez, Sabri 184
Hagganah 125–9
Haidar, Haidar 190, 191
al-Haj, Unsi 188
Hakayiku' l-Vekayi 22
al-Hakim, Tawfiq 40–1, 43–4, 110:
  Awdat al-Ruh 113: *People of the*
  Cave 112; *Shahrazad* 112; *The*
  Unwelcome Guest 112–13;
  Ughniyat al-Mawt 113; *Yawmiyyat*
  Na ib fi' Aryaf 113
Haller, Albrecht von 68
Halman, Talât 96, 97, 102–3
Hâmid, Abdülhak 27, 28
Hamidi, Mehdi: *Sal-ha-yi Siyah* 149
Hamrawi, al-Madani 205
Hamzawi, Muhammad Rashad 202,
  204
Haqqi, Yahya 111, 113, 185, *The*
  Saint's Lamp 112
Harbiye 7
al-Harradi, Muhammad 207
Hasan, King of Morocco 169
Hasan, Muhammad 48
Haskalah (Jewish enlightenment)
  63–72
Hawi, Khalil 188
Haykal, Muhammad Husayn 104–6:
  Zaynab 104, 105–6, 110, 111
Hebrew, modern literature 13, 63–75,
  116–29; *see also* Israeli literature
Hebrew language 64, 65 67–68,
  127–28, 214
Hertzberg, Joseph 71
Herzl, Theodor: *Das Neue Ghetto* 69;
  Der Judenstaat 69
Heyworth-Dunne, J. 35
Hidayat, Sadiq 54, 136, 143–4, 151,
  153: *Akharin Labkhand* 138;
  Alaviyeh Khanum 140–1; *Dash*
  Akul 140; *Farda* 144; *Haji Aqa* 143,
  155; *Isfahan Nisf-i Jahan* 139;
  Maziyar 138; *Mihan-parast (The*
  Patriot) 141, 143; *Muhallil* 140;
  Murdeh-Khurha 140; *Parvin*
  Dukhtar-i Sassan 138; *Payam-i*
  Kafka 144; *Sag-i Vilgard* 143;
  Sayeh-yi Mughul 137; *Talab-i-*
  Amurzish 139; *Turaneh-ha-yi*

Khayyam 139; *The Blind Owl* 141;
  Tup-i Murvari 144, 155
Higab, Sayyid 189
Hijazi, Muhammad 141–2, 152, 153:
  Ayinah 141; *Homa* 141; *Shirin-Kula*
  142; *Ziba* 141
Hikmet, Nâzım 100–1, 175, 176:
  Benerci niçin kendini öldürdü 101
Hilmi, Selanikli 29
Hirsch Chajes of Zolkiew, Rabbi Zevi
  70
Hitler, Adolf 133
Hoga, S. 71
Homer: *Iliad,* translations of 29, 38, 75;
  Odyssey 75
Hugo, Victor: *L'Âne* 71, *Les Burgraves*
  24; Les Misérables 22, 43
Hurvitz, Yair 221
Husaini, Ashraf al-Din (Qazvini) 131
Husayn, Taha 39, 44, 107, 110, 180,
  184: *al-Ayyam* 181; *al-Mu*
  'adhdhabun fi' l-Ard 181
Hüseyin, Hasan 176

I'timadzadah 156
Ibrahim, Gamil 'Atiyya 192
Ibrahim, Hafiz 43, 106
Ibrahim, Sun 'alla 192
Ibtihaj 155
Ida 'a 75, 189
ideology; genres and 198–200; in
  Maghribi literature 193–8; of
  modernity 197–8; and polarization
  161–9
Idris, Suhail; *al-Hayy al-Latini* 182
Idris, Yusif; *Arkhas Layali* 182
İlhan, Attila 176
Imru'l-Qays 107
İnönü, İsmet 88, 170–1
İnşa style 21
iqtibas 40–1
Iran 48
Iran 5, 6, 7, 10, 11, 14, 45–62, 80, 81,
  82, 86, 88, 130–57, 161,
  164–5;Constitutional Revolution
  (1908) 13, 17, 28, 46, 130, 131–2
Iran-i Naw 12
Iraq 5, 87, 88, 106, 161, 167, 181, 186
Isfahani, Mirza Habib 47, 55
Ishaq, Adib 12, 37

Index 241

'Ishqi, Muhammad Reza 133, 136
Iskandar, Amir 184
Islam 79, 82, 136,151, 154
Islamic fundamentalism 162, 181, 186
Isma'il, Khedive 5, 12, 13, 104, 106
Israel, State of 89, 115, 161, 162,
    166–8, 217–21
Israeli literature 213–25
Istiqlal party 205

Jahine, Salah 185
Jakobson, R. O. 17
Jalili, Jahangir 152; *Az Daftar-i
    Khatirat* 142; *Man Ham Giryeh
    Kardeh-am* 142
jam at al-madrasat al-haditha (The
    New School) 111
Jamalzadah 53, 54, 61, 134–5, 153,
    154, 155, 156: *Dar al-Majanin* 145;
    Dusti-yi Khaleh Khirseh 135; *Farsi
    Shekar Ast* 135; *Qultashan Divan*
    145–7; *Rah-ab Nameh* 146–7;
    Rajul-i Siyasi 135; *Sahray-i
    Mahshar* 146; *Yaki Bud va Yaki
    Nabud* 46, 135
Jami, 'Abd al-Rahman 130, 139
Janat, Mukhtar 202
al-Jarida 10, 105
al-Jawa'ib 39
al-Jawahiri, Muhammad Mahdi 106
Jerrold, B. 12
Jews of the Pale, *see* Russia
Jones, Robert 36
Jones-Brydges, H. 10
Jordan 161, 166, 167
Josza, Pierre 194
Judaism 68–70, 167
Jum'ah, Muhammad Lutfi 112

Kabir, Amir 60
Kadri, Yakup 94–6, 103: *Nur Baba* 95;
    Yaban 94, 95–6
al-Kafrawi, Sa 'id 192
Kahana-Carmon, A. 221
Kalevala 75
Kamil, Adil: *Millim al-Akbar* 113
Kamil, Anwar 180
Kamil, Mahmud 182
Kâmil Paşa, Yusuf: *Terceme-i Telemak*
    21

Kampffmeyer, Georg 42
Kamshad, Hasan 51, 52, 53, 62, 145
Kaniuk, Y.: *Hayored lemaalah* 220
Kansu, Ceyhun Atuf 176
Karakoç, Sezai 175
Karni, Y. 217
Karru, Abu'l-Qasim 208
Kartun-Blum, R. 222
Kasab, Teodor 26
Kasravi, Sayyed Ahmad 155
Katouzian, Homa 131–57
Kaufmann, General 10
Kaveh 133
al-Kawakibi 12
Kayacan, Feyyaz 174
Keddie, N. 12, 143
Kemal, Namık 20, 25, 28: *Intibah* 25;
    Vatan-yahut-Silistre 27
Kemal, Orhan 177
Kemal, Yahya: *Açık Deniz* 100
Kemal, Yaşar 177–8
Kemal (Kamil), Mustafa, *see* Atatürk,
    Kemal
Kerman, Zeynep 22, 23
al-Khal, Yusif 184, 187: *al-Hurriya*
    183: *Herodia* 183
Khalifa, Sahar 192
Khameh'i, Anvar 149
Khanlary, Parvis 156: *'Uqab* 149
al-Kharrat, Edwar 180–92: *Hitan
    'Aliya* 186; *Ramah and the Dragon*
    192; *The Other Time* 192
Khashaba, Sami 184
Khemiri, Taher 42
Khomeini, Ayatollah 165
Khrayyif, al-Bashir 202
Khudair, Muhammad 192
Khurasan 5
Khuri, Ilyas 191
al-Khuri, Idris 207
Khusravi, Muhammad Baqir: *Shams u
    Tughra* 53
Kibbutz ideology 124, 125–9, 168
Kilpatrick, Hilary 114
Kirmani, Mirza Aqa Khan 57–8, 61,
    156: *Salarnamah* 49, 57–8
Kirmani, San'ati-zadah; *Dam-gustaran
    ya Intiqam-Khakan-i Mazdak* 54
Kitabevi, Ahmet Halit 91
Kitabevi, Remzi 95

242 Index

Kitchener of Khartoum, Horatio
  Herbert, 1st Earl 12
Kiyanuri, Nur al-Din 154
Klausner, I. 73–4
Kleist, Ewald Christian von 71
Klopstock, Friedrich Gottlieb: *Der Tod
  Adams* 69
Knaz, Y. 223
Kock, Paul de 24
Kohansky, M. 222
Köhler, Erich 189
Kubickova, Vera 46
Kudret, Cevdet 19, 21
Külebi, Cahit 176
Kür, Fınar 178
Kurds 80, 83, 162, 163, 167
Kurzweil, B. 224
Kut, A. Turgut 22

La Fontaine, Jean de 20, 36, 37, 42, 59
Lahuti, Abu al-Qasim 59, 131, 133, 136
Lamartine, Alphonse 20, 38
Lamdan, I. Y. 124: *Masada* 216
Lamsaddi, 'Abd al-Salam 201
Lanson, Gustave 194
Laroui, 'Abdallah 207
Lashin, Mahmud Tahir 111, 181: *Eve
  without Adam* 111–12
Le Bon, Gustave 38
Lebanon 36, 161, 167, 186
Leenhardt, Jacques 194
Lemon, L. T. 216
Lenin, V. I. 137
Lesage, Alain-René; *Gil Blas* 47
Lessing, Gotthold Ephraim 71: *Die
  Juden* 69, 70; *Nathan der Weise*
  69–70
Letaif-i Rivayat 25
Letteris, M.: *Ayyalet ha-Shanar* 69;
  Geza Yishai 70
Levant 81, 87, 114, 181
Levin, H.; *Malkat haambatyah* 222
Levin, Judah 69
Lewis, Bernard 18
Lewis, Geoffrey 90–103, 176
Lewner, J. 71
libraries, public and private 11
Libya 161
literacy levels (1850–1914) 4–5, 66
literary theory 193–8

lithography 8, 62
Litinsky, Menham 69
Longfellow, Henry Wadsworth 75
Luncz, A. M. 66
Luzzatto, Ephraim 63

al-Ma'arri: *Risalat al-Ghufran* 52
Mabruk, Muhammad 190
Machalaski, F. 59
al-Madani, 'Izz al-Din: *al-Adab al-
  Tajribi* 203; *al-Insan al-Sifr* 203
al-Madini, Ahmed 193–212
Mağdurîn Hikâyesi 22
Maghrib (or *Maghreb*) 168–9,
  193–212; *see also* Africa, North;
  Algeria; Libya; Morocco; Tunisia
al-Maghut, Muhammad 188
Mahfuz, Naguib 113–14, 182, 184,
  192: *al-Qahura al-Jadida* 113;
  Khan al-Khalili 113; *Zuqaq al-
  Midaqqı* 13–14
al-Majalla al-Jadida 180
Majlis 7–8
Makal, Mahmut, *Bizim Köy* 97, 177
al-Makhzangi, Muhammad 192
al-Mala'ika, Nazik 188
Maleki, Khalil 147, 149
Malkum Khan, Mirza 56
al-Manfaluti, Mustafa Lutfi 40, 41, 42,
  182
manuscript copying 8
Mao-Tse Tung 133
Mapu, Abraham 67, 116, 127; *Ahavat
  Tziyyon* 65, 66, 71–2, 119, 213;
  maqama 104
Maraghah-i Hajj Zayn al- 'Abidin 131;
  Siyahat-namah-i Ibrahim Beg 51–2
Marsigli, L. F. 8
Marxism 143, 155, 181
Mas'ud, Muhammad: *Ashraf-i
  Makhluqat* 142; *Bahar-i 'Umr* 147;
  Dar Talash-i Ma'ash 142; *Guha'i
  keh dar Jahannam Miruyand* 147;
  Mard-i Imruz 147; *Tafrihat-i Shab*
  142
Mashriq 169, 180–92, 197; *see also*
  Egypt; Middle East; Sudan
maskilim 66–7, 68, 71, 212
masnavi verse 59
Matar, Muhammad 'Afifi 189

Index 243

al-Matwi, al-'Arusi 202
Maupassant, G. de 27
Mayer, A. E. 12
al-Mazini, Ibrahim 107, 110
Mecmua-i Fünûn 19, 21
Meddah story 25
Medici Oriental Press, Arabic version of Gospels 36
Megged, Aaron: *Fortunes of a Fool* 128–9; *Hevda and I* 128; *The Living on the Dead* 128, 219
Meisami, Julie 45–62
Meisels, Samuel 72
Mendele Mokher Seforim (Mendeli Mocher Sforim) 65, 72–3, 74, 117, 126, 214: *Be-Emek ha-Bakha* 72; *Ha-Avot ve-ha-Banim* 72; *Limedu Hetev* 72; *Sefer ha-Kabtzanim* 72; *Toledot ha-Teva* 71
Mendelssohn, Moses 64, 70, 213: *Biur* 64
Mendès, David Franco 70
Menemencioğlu, Nermin 172–3, 176; *Penguin Book of Turkish Verse* 171–2
Meriç, Nezihe 178
Mert, Özkan 176
Mesopotamia 81
Metastasio, Petro 68
Midhat, Ahmed 20, 23–4, 25, 27, 29: *Felâtun Bey ile Rakım Efendi* 25; *Hasan Mellah* 25; *Hüseyin Fellah* 25; *Letaif-i Rivayat* 24
Militant, The 176
Millî Edebiyatçilar 90
Milton, John: *Paradise Lost* 69
Mina, Hanna 192: *al-Masabih al-Zurq* 182
Mintz, R. F. 125
Minuvi (Mujtaba) 138
Miron, D. 217
Mirza, Iraj 59
Mirza, Muhammad Tahir 47
missionaries, as patrons 12
modernity, ideology of 134, 196, 193–8
modernization: in Arabic literature 180, 195–5; definition 3–4; and literature (1850–1914) 3–16
Molière, translation of 20, 25, 26, 30, 37, 40, 47, 55, 75

Montepin, Xavier de 24
Montesquieu, translations from 20, 43
Moosa, Matti I. 35, 36
Moreh, S. 36
Morier, Sir John; *Hajji Baba* 47, 51
Morocco 168–9, 186, 204–8
Muhammad 'Ali 5, 33, 34, 35, 80
Mujahidin 210
Mukhtarat min al-Adab al-Tunisi 'i-Mu 'asir 200
al-Mulk, 'Ali Khan Nazim 62
Mülkiye 7
Mumeyyiz 22
Munif, 'Abd al-Rahman 192
Münif, Paşa 19, 20, 22, 30, 31: *Muhaverat-ı Hikemiye* 21
Muqaddam, Muhammad 136
Murad Bey 12
Musa, Salama 179
Musaddiq, Muhammad 133, 152
Musayif, Muhammad 208
Muslim Brothers 167
Muslims 5, 6, 14, 36, 84, 181
Mustagab, Muhammad 192
al-Muwaylihi, Muhammad: *Hadith 'Isa b. Hisham* 52, 104

Naci (Naaci), Muallim 20, 28
al-Nadim, Abdallah 110: *al-Watan wa'l-Arab* 112
Nadir, Mehmed 28
Nadirpur, Nadir 143, 149
nahda 34, 35
Najm, Muhammad Yusuf 36
al-Naqqash, Marun: *al-Bakhil* 37
al-Naqqash, Salim 37
Nash'at Badr: *Holm Leilat Ta'ab* 184; *Messa' el Kheir ya Ged'an* 184
Nasir al-Din Shah 48, 55, 62
Nasri, Shaykh Musa: *'Ishq u Saltanat* 53
Nasser (al-Nasir), Jamal 'Abd 133, 164, 165, 180, 181, 182, 184–6, 185–6
National Liberation Front (F.L.N.) 209–10, 211–12
nationalism; Arab 87, 165–6, 180, 204, 205, 209–12; *see also* Pan-Arabism; romantic 77–157, in Iran (1914–41) 132–42
al-Newwab, Muzzaffar 184–5

244 *Index*

Necatigil, Behçet 176
Nemet-Nejat, Murat 175
Nesin, Aziz 97
newspapers 8, 9–10
al-Niffari 187
Nima Yushij 46, 60, 134, 149, 150, 155–6: *Afsanah* 46
novels: Arabic 37, 39, 104, 113, 189–92, 199, 200, 201; Hebrew 65, 72, 213–14; historical Persian 131; Iranian 51–4; Israeli 222–4; and modernization 15; Moroccan 207; Turkish 'village' 176–7
Nu'ayama, Mikha' il 42
Nushin, 'Abdulhasain 143

Oakshott, Michael 3
Oflazoğlu, Turan 179
Omar Ibn Abrahim el Khayyam 139
oral literature 6
Orientalization 52
orta oyunu (Turkish farce) 26
Ostle, R. C. 104–15
Ottoman Empire 4–5, 6–7, 8–11, 13, 33, 79, 80, 81
Oz, Amos: *Mikhael sheli* 221; *Touch the Water, Touch the Wind* 222
Özakin, Aysel 178
Özel, İsmet 176
Özer, Kemal 175
Özön, Mustafa Nihat, 19, 20, 21, 22, 23, 24, 25, 27

Pahlavi state 132–4, 142, 143, 164, 165; *see also* Reza Shah
Paker, Saliha 17–32
Palestine 64, 65–6, 67–8, 83–4, 87, 88–9, 117–25, 166, 186, 215–17
Palestine Liberation Organization (PLO) 167
Palmach 126, 218–19
Pan-Arabism 83, 161–2, 185, 186
Parfitt, Tudor 63–75, 117
Partaw, Shin (Shirazpur) 37–8: *Aniran* 136–8
Parvin I'tisami 139–40
patronage (1850–1914) 11–13
Patterson, David 65, 72, 116–29
Paxton, E. H. 44
Pellico, Silvio: *Mes Prisons* 22

Pérès, Henri 37
periodicals 9–10: Egyptian 'little' magazines 180–1; Iranian 48–9
Persia 80
Persian language 135
Persian literature, modern 45–62, 130–5
Persian Revolution (1905–9) 9, 130, 150–1
plagiarism, Arabic 41–2
Plato: *Symposium* 75
poetry: Arabic 38, 106–10, 188–9; Hebrew 124–6; Iranian 57–60, 148–50; Israeli 219, 222; and modernization 13; Persian 130, 131, 134; Turkish 26, 100–3, 172–7
polarization, ideology and 161–9
political parties 12, 163
politics: (1914–50) 79–89; traditional and modern societies 3–4
'polysystem' theory 17–18, 24
Pool, David 161–9
Posner, Simhah 71
printing presses 8, 62
prose, Persian 130, 131, 134–5
prose poetry *(Shi'r-i mansur)*, Iranian 57
Proust, Marcel 223
Psalms, in Arabic 36
publishing 7–11
Pur-Davud, Isma'il 131

al-Qa'id, Yusif 192
Qa'ani 46
Qabbani, Nizar 108
Qajar, Abd al-Husayn Mirza 49
Qajar Persia 46, 79, 81
Qarajahdaghi, Mirza Ja'far 55–6
qasida 106
Qasim, 'Abd al-Hakim 192
al-Qasim, Samih 188
Qazvini, Mirza Muhammad 131, 134
Qazvini, *see* Husaini, Ashraf al-Din
Qohelet musar 213

Raab, Esther 215–16, 217
Rabi', Mubarak 207
Rabi'ah bint Ka'ab 139
al-Rabi'i, 'Abd al-Majid 192
Rabinowitz, A. S. 119

Racine, Jean 20, 37, 70: *Athalie* 70
Radcliffe, Ann: *The Mysteries of Udolpho* 24
Reffalowich, Shmuel 66: *Toledot Adam ve Hava* 69
Regab, Muhammad Hafez 190
Rahib, Zakhur 35, 36
Rakibi, 'Abdallah 208, 209
Ramzi, Ibrahim 112
Rashid Ali al-Gaylani 88
Ravikovitch, Dahlia 222
Rayya, Yusif Abu 192
Réalisme 224
Reis, M.J. 216
Rekowski, Abraham 69
religious communities, as patrons 12
Republican People's Party, Turkey 170, 177
"Revolutionary Young Poets", Turkey 176
Reza Khan (later Shah) 46, 80, 132, 133, 164
Reza Shah Pahlavi 52, 81–2, 86, 88, 142, 164
Reza Shah Pahlavi, Mohammad (son) 164
Rıfat, Manastırli 27
Rifat, Oktay 101, 172, 176, 177
Risha, 'Umar Abu 110
al-Risuni, Khadir 205
riwaya 39
Riyad, Mahmud 12
Robinson, Richard D. 171
romantic nationalism, *see* nationalism
Rossi, Ernesto 28
Rousseau, Jean Jacques 105, 106
rumaniyyat 39
Rumsey, M. 71
al-Rusafi, Ma'ruf 106
Russia 5, 10, 64–5, 124, 132, 133; *see also* Soviet Union
Russian influence 13, 31, 49, 56, 60, 80
Ruznâme-i Ceride-i Havadis 22, 25
Rypka, Jan 46

Sa'di: *Gulistan* 130
Sa'id, Ahmed Khayri 111
Sa'id, 'Ali Ahmad, *see* Adunis
al-Sa'adani, Mahmud: *al-Sam'a al-Sawda'* 183

Sabra writers 125–9, 218–19
Sabri, 'Uthman: *Bei Sirri* 185; *Rehla fi'l* 184
Sabry, M. 12
al-Sabur, Salah'Abd 188: *al-Nas fi Biladi* 182–3
Sadat, Anwar 166, 186
Sadeh, P. 221: *Hahayim Kemashal* 220
Safavid period 130
al-Sahhar, 'Abd al-Hamid Guda 182
Saint Pierre, Bernardin de 48: *Harmonie de la Nature* 70; *Paul et Virginie* 22, 40
Sait Faik Abasıyanık: *İki Kişiye Bir Hikâye* 97
Sal-nama A. H. 1313 48
Salafiyya ideology 197, 205
Salama, al-Bashir b. 200
Salih, al-Hadi b. 203
Salih, al-Madani b. 203
Salih, al-Tayyib: *Bandar Shah* 192
Salomon, Yoel Moshe 66
al-Saltana, Muhammad Hasan Khan Sani'al-Dawla I'timad 47
Salvini, Alessandro 28
Sâmi, Şemsettin 23, 25, 30: *Taaşşuk-i Talat ve Fitnat* 25
Sanu 'a, James 12
Sarmad, Sadiq 156
Sassanid Iranians 151
Savak 164, 165
Sayın, Hidayet 179
al-Sayyab, Badr Shakir 188 'Ode to the Rain' 182
Sayyed Zia 132, 133
al-Sayyid, Ahmad Lutfi 105
Schiller, Johann Christoph Friedrich von 29, 59
Schölch, A. 12
Schulman, Kalman 71
Schulz, Bruno 223
Scott, Sir Walter 37, 53
'Second New Movement', Turkey 172–5
Sehabeddin, Cenab 28
Servet-i Fünûn period 17, 28, 29–30, 31
Sevük, Ismail Habib 19, 24, 25, 26, 28
Seyfettin, Ömer 29, 90–1: *Fon Sadriştayn' ın Karısı* 90–1; *Fon Sadriştayn' in Oğlu* 90–1; *İlk Düşen Ak* 90

246 *Index*

Sh'ir 188
Shabaka, Ilyas Abu 110
al-Shabbi, Abu'l-Qasim 107–9, 110
Shabtai, Yaakov: *Sof davar* 223;
  Zikhron dvarim 223
Shadi, Ahmad Zaki Abu 108
Shadli, Faraj 202
al-Shafi'i, 'Abd al-Majid: *Qissa min
  Samim al-Waqi'* 209
Shahar, David: *Ningal* 223; *Yom
  harefaim* 223
Shaked, G. 217
Shakespeare, William; translations of
  27–9, 59, 70, 75
Shamir, Moshe 218–19: *Hagvul* 220;
  Hu halakh basadot 222
Shamlu, Ahmad 143, 149–50, 155;
  Pariya 150
al-Sharqawi, 'Abd al-Rahman 185: *al-
  Ard* 182
Shavit, Zohar 216, 224
Shaw, S. J. 9
Shawqi, Ahmad 38, 107, 108
al-Shayyal, Jamal al-Din 35
Shevket, Mahmud 12–13
Shi'i Islam 162, 163, 164
al-Shidyaq, Faris (later Ahmad Faris)
  36, 38–9
Shimi, 'Abd al-Jabbar 207
Shimoni, D.: *Yovel ha-Eglonim* 122–3,
  124
Shirazi, Jahangir Khan 131
Shlonsky, A. 124, 215
Shoham, Matityahu 221
short stories: Arabic 110–12, 196, 199;
  Iranian 54; Moroccan 206; Tunisian
  201–4; Turkish 90–100
Shukri, 'Abd al-Rahman: *Confessions*
  109–10
al-Siba'i, Muhammad 38
al-Siba'i, Yusif 182
Sidqi, Muhammad 183
Silbermann, Eliezer 66
Şinasi, İbrahim 20, 28, 30: *Sair
  Evlenmesi* 19, 25; *Tercüme-i
  Manzume* 20–1
Sırrı, Hasan 27
Sklovsky, Victor 225
Smilansky, M. 217
Smolenskin, Peretz 72, 116

Sobol, Y. 222
social criticism 77–157
socialist-realism 180–5
societies: traditional and modern 4;
  transformation of 84–5
sociology of literature 194
Sophocles 75
Soviet Union 142–3, 154
Soysal, Sevgi 178
Spencer, E. 43
Sperling, Isaas Wolf 71
Spiro; *English–Arabic Dictionary of
  the Colloquial Arabic of Egypt* 39
Stalin, Joseph 133, 215
state: authoritarian repressive regimes
  161; European model 79; literature
  and Algerian 210–12; models of
  development 4–5; as patron 11–12;
  publishing 10–11
Stern, M.E. 69
'Strange' movement 172
stream of consciousness 73, 214
Sudan 162, 186
Sue, Eugène 24, 71–2, 74
Suez (1956) 112, 161, 165
al-Sulh, 'Imad 39
Sunni Muslims 163, 167
Süreya, Cemal 172, 173: *Papirus* 173;
  Uvercinka 173
Swanson, G.W. 13
Swift, Jonathan; *Gulliver's Travels* 47
Syria 5, 13, 83, 166, 167
Syrian Christians 14, 35, 36
systems theory 17

ta'rib 40–1
ta'ziyah religious drama 55
Tabari, Ihsan 144, 155
Tabrizi, Mirza Aqa 56
Taha, 'Ali Mahmud 108
Tahir, Baha'; *al-Khutuba* 191
Tahir, Kemal 177, 178; *Esir Şehrin
  İnsanlar. Esir Şehrin Mahpusu
  Yorgun Savaşçi* 178
al-Tahtawi, Rifa'a Rafi' 35, 36, 37, 62
Tajir, Jak 35, 38
al-Takarli, Fu'ad 192
Takiyah-i Dawlat 62
Taliboff, 'Abd al-Rahim 49, 132
Tamer, Ülkü 172

Tamir, Zakariya 192
tamsir 40–1
Tancred 69
Taner, Haldun; *Sonsuza Kalmak* 98–101
al-Tankit wa'l-Tabkit 111
Tanpınar, Ahmet Hamdi 19, 20, 21, 23, 24, 25, 178
Huzur 178
Tansel, Fevziye Abdullah 20, 28
Tanzimat 17, 18–25
Taqiov, Hajji Zayn al-'Abdin 12
Taqizadah, Sayyed Hasan 131, 133
Tarbiyat 48
Tarbiyat, Muhammad Ali 49, 54
Tasvir-i Efkâr 20
al-Tatawwur 179
Tavallali, Firaidun 143, 149, 155
Tawfiq, Khedive 112
Taymur, Mahmud 111, 180
Taymur, Muhammad 111, 112
al-Tazi, Muhammad 'Izz al-Din 206
Tchernikhovski, Saul 65, 75, 117
Tekin, Latife 178
Temasa (Rifet and Bedreddin) 27
Terakki 22
Tercüman-i Ahvâl 20, 25
Tercüman-i Hakikat 20, 23
Terrail, Ponson de; *Memoirs of Mademoiselle Montpensier* 47, 48, 50
Tevfik, Ebuzziya 24, 27
threatre: Ottoman 26; travelling companies 25; *see also* drama
Third Force Party 147, 149
Thomas, Dylan 102
Thousand and One Nights 49
Tibawi, A.L. 8
Tolstoy, Leo 29: *Anna Karenina* 43
translation: age of (1850–1914) 1–75; bureaux 10
Triki, Tayyib 202
Tripolitanian Republic 80
Tripp, Charles 79–89
Tschernichowsky, *see* Tchernikovski
Tudeh (later Iran Communist) Party 143, 145, 149, 150, 152, 154: (1948) split 147, 149, 155
al-Tunisi, Bairam: *El-Sayyed we Merato fi Bareez* 184

Tunisia 107, 161, 168–9, 200–4
Turkestan 10
Turkey 17–32, 81, 82, 86, 88, 90–103, 162–3, 170–9: Memorandum (1971), 171, 176; military coup (1960) 160, 163, 171, 175; military coup (1980) 161, 163, 171
Turkish Republic 80
Turkish Workers' party 171
Turks, outside Turkey 5, 136, 165

'Uf, Abd al-Rahman Abu 184
'ulema 12
Umma party 12, 106
United Arab Republic 166
United Nations, Turkey in 170
urbanization 14, 84, 114, 223
USA 8, 164, 165, 166
Uşaklıgil, Halid Ziya: *Nâkil* 29
USSR, *see* Soviet Union
al-Ustadh 110
'Uthman Jalal, Muhammad 37–8, 40, 42, 44: *al-Shaykh Matluf* 40
Uyar, Tomris 178
Uyar, Turgut 172: 'Triad of Sea-Blues Reduced to One' 173–4
Uyguner, Muzaffer 101

Vallejo, Cesar 173
Vambery, A. 10
van Dyck, E. A. 9
Vefik, Paşa, Ahmed 20, 21–2, 23, 26, 30
Veli, Orhan 101–2, 172: *Cevap* 102; *Eskiler Alıyorum* 102; *Garip* 101; *Vatan için* 102
Verdi, Giuseppe 28
Verne, Jules 28, 47, 48, 49, 71
violence 87, 89, 161, 169, 180
Voltaire, François Marie Arouet de 21, 22
Von Grunebaum, G.E. 107

Wadi' l-Nil 37
Wafd 81, 86, 88
Wallach, Yona: *Tzurot* 222
al-Wardani, Mahmud 191
Wattar, Tahar: *al-Laz* 212; *al-Zilzal* 212
Welch, A. 34

248 *Index*

Westernization 18, 33–4, 178, 197–200
Williams, Raymond 172
women: portrayal in literature 107–9;
    position of 14, 41, 112, 209;
    Turkish writers 178
World War I 79–87, 90
World War II 88–9

Xenophon; *Cyropaedia* 24

Ya'avetz, Ze'ev 66
Yalag, *see* Gordon, Y.L.
Yalkut Reim 125
Yapp, Malcolm 3–16
Yardeni, G. 66
al-Yaziji, Nasif 36
Yehoshua, A.B. 221, 223–4: 'Facing
    the Forests' 221; *Gerushim
    meuharim* 221; *Hameahev* 221
Yiddish 65, 72–3, 119, 213–14
yishuv 87, 168, 214, 215, 216, 224
Yizhar, S. 215–16, 217–18: *In sipurey
    mishor* 218; *Yemey tziglag* 218
Young, Edward 71
Young Ottomans 13
Young Turks 13
Yücel, Can 176

Yudkin, Leon I. 213–25
Yunan, Ramsis 180
Yunis, Muhsin 192
Yusuf, Magid 189
Yusuf, Sa'di 188

Zaccone, Pierre; *La Vengeance* 37
Zacuto, Mose 222
Zaghlul, Fathi 38, 43
Zahlawi, Habib 40
Zamoscz, David; *Ro'ot Midyan o
    Yaldut Moshe* 69
Zangwill, Israel: *Ghetto Tragedies* 69
Zaydan, Jurji 34, 49: *'Adhra' Quraysh*
    53
Zaytouna mosque-university 107
Zelda 222
Zevaco, Michel 26
Zifzaf, Muhammad 207
Zima, Pierre 194
Zionism 69, 83, 87, 118, 162, 167
Ziya, Halid, *see* Uşaklıgil
Ziya Paşa 28
Zola, E. 24, 29
Zoroastrian faith 135, 136
Ztily, Muhammad: *Huna Tahtariq al-
    Akwakh* 211

PGMO 07/04/2018